The Theory of the Naked Truth of Allah, Muhammad, and the Quran

The "Satanic Verses" written by Salman Rushdie is a childish prank as a 'blasphemy', compared to "The Theory of the Naked Truth of Allah, Muhammad, and the Quran", authored by Wequar Azeem. But it is a serious reading for any student of Islam."

Thanks
Fayyaz Sheikh, M.D. M.S.L.
President, Thinkers Forum USA

The Theory of the Naked Truth of Allah, Muhammad, and the Quran

WEQUAR AZEEM

ARPress
ILLUMINATING IDEAS.
EMPOWERING VOICES.

ARPress
45 Dan Road Suite 5
Canton MA 02021

Hotline: 1(888) 821-0229
Fax: 1(508) 545-7580

Ordering Information:

Quantity sales. Special discounts are available on quantity purchases by corporations, associations, and others. For details, contact the publisher at the address above.

Printed in the United States of America.

ISBN-13:   Softcover   979-8-88853-757-2
             eBook   979-8-88853-758-9
             Hardcover   979-8-89262-600-2

Library of Congress Control Number: 2023915688

TABLE OF CONTENTS

CHAPTER 1
Preamble

The following notes are essential to be read in the beginning, as a preamble, for understanding the discourse with clarity. Keeping these notes in mind will ensure candid understanding of this exposé and what makes this "Theory" both credible and probable.

Note 1.

This note deals with the question 'Why do we see that a Muslim's parents and forefathers are also Muslim for the past many generations? Likewise, a Jew's parents and forefathers have been Jewish for the past three millennia, and so is the case with Hindus, Christians, and Zoroastrians. There is a bio natural cause behind this phenomenon, which is described below.

Biological and cognitive features of the human species, as Altricial mammals.

There is a significant distinction between humans and most other mammals. Humans are **Altricial** mammals, quite different in significant aspects, from the rest of the animal population on Earth which consists mostly of **Precocial** mammals.

The word 'Altricial' means "Incapable of moving around on its own as a newborn for a fairly long period". Human mammals are so named because of the condition at birth of the principal organs like the brain, liver, eyesight, and few other internal body parts.

The brain of a human baby at birth is not fully formed and therefore a new-born has no cognitive ability. Few other mammals like Owls, Kangaroos, Cats and Dogs also happen to be Altricial, as exceptions.

The vast majority of Precocial mammals are mobile and substantially independent of any need for adult supervision, within hours or days following birth. Precocial mammals like horses, cows, etc. are pure, perfect, and complete creatures with all organs of the body completely formed and fully functional. Mentally too, the Precocial mammals are almost completely autonomous, at birth. The new-born Precocial mammals, to a large extent, take care of themselves. They only need to be breast-fed for the first few weeks or months, and need to be nominally supervised by the mother, or both parents, for a brief period after birth.

In the case of human babies (Altricial mammals), since several organs are not fully formed, they are utterly limited in what they can do. They cannot find food, or feed themselves or protect themselves from predators. They need to be protected, fed, and trained for life preserving skills by elders who train them, and raise them, **for many years after birth**.

Beside the still growing cognitive ability in the brain, the liver of a human at birth, is equipped only to digest the breast milk of a lactating female, who is almost always the infant's biological mother. Likewise, the infant has no hand-eye coordination. The only motor skills of a human baby are limited to twitching his/her mouth or pout lips seeking the nipple to suck on it for drawing milk from mother's breasts. Ref: "A Manual of the MAMMALIA", by Douglas A. Kelt & James L. Patton, sold by Amazon.

The infant cries when it has hunger pain, or when any other irritant is in touch with its skin and causes discomfort. Baby's weeping and yelling draws the attention of the baby's mother or other elders who check and find out what is bothering the infant and provide relief and comfort to the baby. The baby soon learns that the cries result in someone bringing comfort. Soon after, the baby uses crying to draw the attention of elders. Above all, the elders teach them the first language, called vernacular or 'mother tongue', for communicating with fellow humans. Human baby's brain is like a blank computer waiting to be programmed. Infant's thinking and 'thought-process' is not autonomous. A human baby cannot choose his/her actions and is unaware of his/her options. However, Nature has provided human infants and toddlers with an uncanny ability to keenly observe the actions of elders around him/her and absorb, acquire, and assimilate those traits in the programming of their own traits. Whatever conduct they observe in those elders, they acquire it, own it, and absorb it like a thirsty sponge. Soon, the babies, toddlers, and children, watch and learn the life-skills from the conduct of elders who are raising them.

Babies and children learn the difference between truth and lies, refined manners, callous behavior, neatness and clumsiness, kindness, and cruel treatment, and so on and so forth. They pick up all the traits of lying or being truthful, cheating or being fair and honest, dirty, clumsy, or neat, depending on what they observe in the conduct and character of elders who raise them. Nature makes them adopt those traits abidingly in their own behavior when they grow up and enter adulthood.

On the contrary, the new-born Precocial mammals are independent, mentally autonomous, and take care of themselves in most respects, to a large extent.

As a result, one often sees the human toddlers and young children being lectured by parents to be truthful, polite, and kind to others, not to indulge in back-biting, and to be well-mannered and polite etc. However, the pontification and advice fall on deaf ears. They stick to what they had observed and acquired from their parents in their formative years of infancy and childhood, or from whoever raised them during the first 10-15 years of their life. If the parents lied, talked ill of others behind others' backs, and behaved rudely with some people; the children observed and acquired the same traits in their own behavior.

Children's palates and taste buds also develop over the initial 10-15 years of growth and record the taste and texture of the food they were fed in infancy and early childhood. They prefer that taste over most other foods which they come across in later years. The taste of foods eaten from early childhood gets stamped on the juvenile taste buds. Those tastes are fondly referred to as "Mothers' cooking"

The elders, while raising the new-born, till the age of first 10-15 years, unknowingly impart their own good/bad manners and behavioral pattern in general, and pass on their own religious and sectarian identification features to that child. This action is like branding the identification marks/numbers on the cattle with red hot iron. The identifying features include national identity, culture, traditions, social norms, religion, and caste etc. Unbeknown to themselves, the human adults program the children's brain, through their own manifest action and conversations with others, during the process of raising them, establishing a code of conduct in the personality of those children, which they will adhere to in future, as adults. This kind of virtual imprinting of a child's brain gets done as a slow and gradual process during the formative period of the first 10-15 years, when the child's cognitive ability is getting shaped and is not yet autonomous. Thus, the foundation of individual and collective psyche among humans gets shaped and installed by the actions, treatments and integrity or lack thereof, in speech and conduct, of those who raised the child while he/she was still dependent on elders for making fundamental choices impacting their entire adult life.

During infancy and early childhood an infant & toddler of Altricial mammal keeps observing and absorbing the conduct, and all kinds of behavior of the elders who raise that child, **without asking any critical questions, because that child's own thinking is not yet autonomous.**

Once the child grows up approaching teen-age, his/her basic character, conduct, religious convictions and thought process are already carved in stone. When they reach mental autonomy, children start critically checking, analyzing, and questioning every new concept placed before them. **However, the concepts and convictions firmly engraved on their brains during the first 10-15 years remain shielded from scrutiny and portend minimal likelihood of change.** Little wonder that the Muslims world over, who procreate comparatively a lot more than others, for reasons like polygamy etc., boast of being approximately 1.8 billion out of a total of 7.8 billion in world population. The point that they did not consciously choose to become Muslims by examining the rationale and reasoning, or by comparing the precepts of different religions, completely escapes them. They had observed in their childhood that their elders were Muslims, and hence they too are Muslims. The children of today will be parents of tomorrow continuing the same natural tradition. Hence the system perpetuates. This is food for thought for those who take pride in religious advocacy.

All Muslims, barring a rare convert here and there, are Muslims by birth. They could have been a person of Jewish, Zoroastrian, Pagan, Buddhist, Hindu or Christian Faith, or of no Faith at all, depending upon the household they were born into. This is true for the followers of all other religions too. Most adults remain unaware of the finer details of their own Faith, and whose efforts established it in their heart and soul. Likewise, no individuals or communities, including their parents and several generations of their ancestors, had any part in any decision-making process, such as seriously comparing all known options of faiths and creeds, to pick and choose the specific religion they would have liked to be raised in.

A person's professed Faith in all cases, barring minimally few exceptions, is an accident of birth. This is true because all humans at birth are Altricial mammals, dependent on elders who raise them, for acquiring what faith, caste, culture, and traditions they will claim to belong with pride, as grownups, unlike many other mammals and primates which are precocial and do not need parental guidance in most cases, even for learning the survival technique. The secret of perpetuating any religion is to work on the new-born and usurp their right of choosing or rejecting a faith, a culture, a value-system, or code of conduct, long before they grow up and become mentally autonomous to pick and choose such fundamental options in life. Being an altricial mammal facilitates that.

This note in the preamble gives an ample idea of limitations of the human psyche, and why and how they react to various experiences in adult life.

Note 2.

History of the Arabic Script.

The second important fact to understand upfront, for clearly understanding the discoveries which led to this 'Theory', is the history of the Arabic language, particularly the Arabic script. Knowing this fact in depth is necessary to examine the contents of the Quran and realize exactly what analytical part it plays in the postulation of this theory.

Arabic was the combined name of over two dozen dialects of an oral lingo which had no script or alphabets until the 5th century A.D. Developing a script, to represent all those oral dialects uniformly in writing, duly organized and equipped with grammar and syntax, was initiated by the prominent members of the society in major Arabian cities like Damascus, Baghdad and Cairo.

The nomads and sedentary tribes of desert-dwellers were overwhelmingly illiterate. A few who were considered literate, knew how to read and perhaps write simple texts in the Syriac, Hebrew or Greek language.

It took a 4 and a half century long evolutionary process, from the 5th to the 9th century to develop a literary, standardized, and uniform script of Arabic language equipped with grammar, syntax and alternate vowels. That fully literary version was called "Al-Fus'ha" Arabic (Highly refined and literary). The Quran today has its text in the 'Al-Fus'ha' version of Arabic, but only since the 9th century A.D. when the fully literary version came to fruition. The original revelations which Muhammad announced in his native dialect between 610-632 C.E. had to be rephrased, paraphrased and transliterated to be made suitable for writing in Al-Fus'ha Arabic. Therefore, strictly speaking, the Quran in Al-Fus'ha Arabic, does not contain most of the original words of Allah, supposedly brought by ArchAngel Gabriel.

Knowing and fully understanding the thoroughly investigated history of Arabic script, and the slow and gradual timeline of its development, in a four century long evolutionary process of transforming the dialectal lingo, into the Al-Fusha version, is an absolute prerequisite. This is necessary for critically analyzing the theory presented in this book. *The evolutionary process commenced two centuries before Muhammad was born. It continued for nearly two more centuries after Muhammad's death in 632 C.E., until it accomplished a sound literary level of a wholesome language duly equipped with all the essential elements.*

Muhammad had claimed that Allah had sent the revelations to him through ArchAngel Gabriel in the native dialect spoken by Muhammad. Muhammad announced each revelation, as is, in his oral native version in Qureshi dialect. Readers must remember that the evolutionary changes in the script reached the final literary 'Al-Fus'ha' version in approximately 160 years after Muhammad had passed away. **In other words, what Muslims read today in the Quran is NOT exactly what Muhammad had announced in his oral/dialectal lingo.**

The Muslim tradition appears for the first time in written form in the 9th century, nearly 2 centuries after Muhammad's stated death in 632 A.D. Until then, there was a complete absence of written history in the Arabic language in the Arabian Peninsula, simply because Arabic till then, was not a fully developed written language. No mention was found of Muhammad, Quran, or Islam, as the name of the new religion, in sources directly linked to Muhammad or his companions, neither in the lifetime of Muhammad, nor up to a couple of centuries after his death. What appeared in written text in Arabic script, for the first time, was in the ninth century. That was entirely drawn from, or extracted from, the oral tradition which was dubious and devoid of factuality to satisfy the standard of accuracy required for historicity. Ref: Muhammad ibn Jarir ibn Yazid al-Tabari (838-923) "Muruj adh-dhahab wa ma'adin al-jawahir"

Here's the detail of several century long evolutionary process of Arabic script (whole of 5th, 6th, 7th, 8th and part of 9th century), starting from the status of oral lingo with no script at all, before 5th century, to →pictorial inscriptions, to →phonetic symbols called phonemes (Similar-looking in essence, to shorthand signs of stenography) during the 6th, 7th and part of 8th century, to →early forms of confusing and indistinct alphabets of Semitic origin with no vowels, (borrowed from Nabateans) during the latter part of the 8th century, to→ Finally, a completely developed and comparatively more wholesome number of alphabets, making each alphabet distinct from other alphabets, by middle of the 9th century. Ref: "Arabic Script: Styles, Variants" by Gabriele Mandel, Google Books, originally published 20001.

The Arabic lingo, as stated before, consisted of many different dialects of strictly oral communication, some of those dialects were not even mutually intelligible. The word 'Arab' in that oral communication meant a 'hospitable desert dweller'. Hence 'Arabi' ('Arabic' in English) was the collective name for all those dialects spoken by desert dwellers of different regions of the Arabian Peninsula. The community leaders in several prominent and urban areas like Damascus, Baghdad and Cairo etc. of the pre-literate era, were desirous of developing their spoken lingo into a fully developed language, duly equipped with a uniform script for writing like their advanced neighbors such as Jews, Christians and Zoroastrians who had literary languages like, Hebrew, Greek, Aramaic and medieval Persian etc., duly equipped with linguistic rules (grammar), punctuations and syntax. Arabs pursued the undertaking of having Arabs' own script, to bring about uniformity of a fully   developed literary language, to progress from pre-literal stage to a proud literary stage. Some leading Arabs, as a first step, borrowed a set of phonetic symbols, for use as alphabets called 'Abjad', from the Nabateans who lived in the northwestern region of the Peninsula, modern day Jordan.

The total number of the borrowed phonetic symbols, later called 'Huroof' ' (Plural for Harf), were only 14. Most Harf of those Huroof represented several different sounds and caused confusion between the writer and reader. But the long drawn evolutionary process of adding signs to those huroof to distinguish which sound they represented, took a total of more than four centuries to reach their intended goal. Here is how they began.

Arabic alphabet or phonemes (total 14), borrowed from Nabateans, called ABJAD letters, were used in the 5th, 6th and 7th century, as shown in Table 1.

ي و ه م ف ع ط ص س ر د ح ب ا

4 2 2 2 2 2 2 3 3

The number written under each phoneme indicates the number of different sounds they represented. Those with no number underneath, represented just one distinct sound.

This caused considerable confusion. Often the writer would have one sound in mind, while the reader would take it as a different sound represented by that same alphabet, and thus get a different word. The problem was solved, a very long time later, by increasing the number of phonemes to represent each sound separately by a distinct new alphabet. That feature was achieved by using dots and diacritical marks on the letters. Also added a few signs used as alternates for vowels (not alphabets) called zer, zabar, pesh, shadda, hamza and mudd, completed in the 9th century.

The Arabic alphabets, after enhancement (total increased from 14 to 28) in the 9th century, are shown in Table 2.

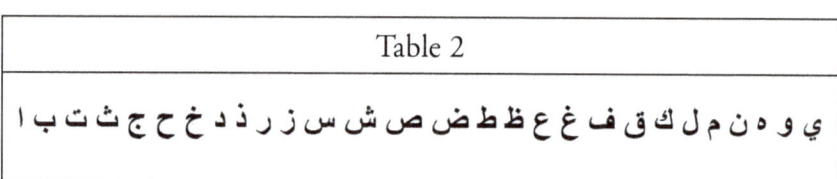

Table 2
ا ب ت ث ج ح خ د ذ ر ز س ش ص ض ط ظ ع غ ف ق ك ل م ن ه و ي

Here's a very informative blog on this aspect:

"The Inception of Dotting and Diacritics in Arabic"
إِبْنُ الْيَمَن A blog by Ibn Alyemen

"During the early days of Islam, Arabic scripts had neither dots nor diacritics. As illustrated in Table 1. A word without these typographic features had multiple meanings. Figuring out what was the writer's intended meaning, depended primarily on Arabs' intuition, memory, and the context. By the time of the fourth Caliphate Imam Ali ibn Abi Talib, large influxes of non-Arabs had embraced Islam. Due to the linguistic differences between their native languages and Arabic, mispronunciation became prevalent. It was Deemed hideous.

After dotting and diacritics	Prior to dotting and diacritics
بَيْتٌ ، بِنْتٌ ، نَبْتٌ ثَبَتَ ، يَبِتُّ ، يَنِبُ	ٮٮٮ
ثَابَ ، تَابَ ، بَاتَ بَابْ ، نَابَ ، نَابْ	ٮاٮ
بَحْرٌ ، يَحِرُّ ، يَجِرُّ نَخَزَ ، نَحْرٌ ، يَخِرُّ	ٮحر

Consequently, it was pressing that the rules and regulations be established to repair errors in articulation to rid of ambiguity and improve comprehensibility of speech in reading written Arabic texts, reciting the Quran, or in daily oral communication. Diacritical marks, namely fat'hah, Dam'mah, kasrah, and sukoon, were introduced which had slightly different shapes than is the case today. As well as dots above or below certain letters had to be employed to lessen resorting to intuition and context in deciphering what similar letters stood for.

The introduction of diacritics was known as شَكْل shakl, the verbal noun of the verb شَكَلَ shakala 'to tie'. In modern Arabic, it is always referred to as تَشْكِيْل tashkeel, the verbal noun of the verb شَكَّلَ shakkala 'to assign diacritics/to shape in a in a particular way.' Put simply, shakl meant tying letters with diacritics (i.e., short vowels) so that they are pronounced in a certain way.

Dotting was known as إِعْجَام 'jaam, the verbal noun of عَجَمَ 'ajama 'to get rid of the ambiguity of letters via dotting.' For instance, the shapes of ن, ت, ث, ب, and ي are nearly the same, especially word-initially and -medially; so are those of ح, ج, and خ. Essentially, what differentiates them from each other is the presence or absence of dots as well as the position of the dots, as illustrated in Table 2.

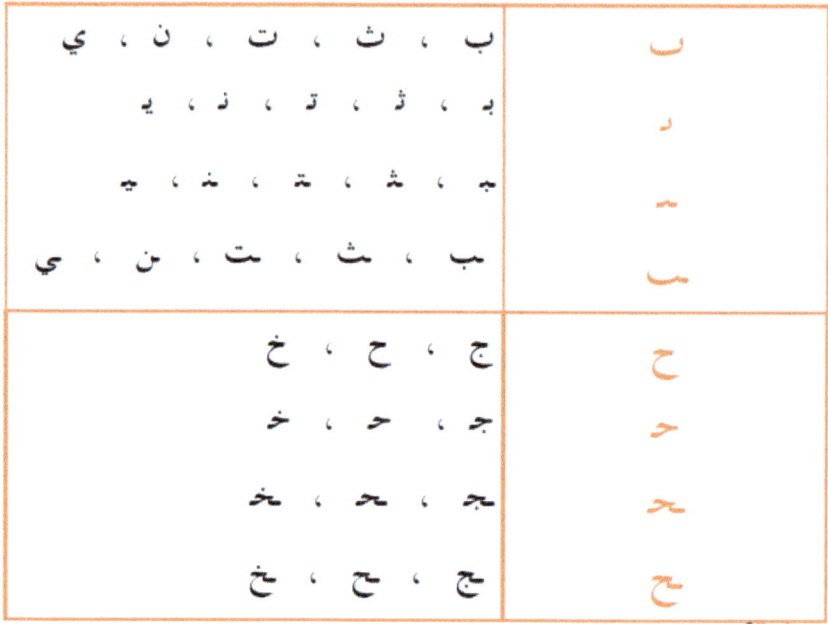

As you probably know, there are other letters that have the same shape. The only way to differentiate between them is through the usage of dots. These are ق ف ، غ ع ، ظ ط ، ش س ، ز ر ض ص and د ذ. Just imagine how knotty it had been for native speakers to guess what a word containing two undotted letters ق + ط mean, let alone non-natives. It can be قَطّ 'cat', فَظّ 'rude', or قَظّ 'To annoy'.

History of shakl

Prior to employing it with Arabic, shakl was used with other languages, namely Syriac and Hebrew. When the Syriacs embraced Christianity in the fourth century AD, they had to translate the Bible into their language, and to ensure accuracy in reading it, they had to use dotting, specifically they used big dots above and below some letters.

In Hebrew, it is reported that the Jews, in the fifth and sixth century AD, initially used certain letters above or below others as a means of restricting pronunciation. Owing to its impracticality (i.e., increasing the number of letters in each word), this system was supplanted by another, that is the usage of dots above and below the letters.

As to Arabic, since Arabic script is derived from Nabataean Aramaic scripts which had no dots or diacritics, there is a strong likelihood that the Arabs mimicked the Syriacs, or the Jews given that some Muslims spoke Syriac and Hebrew since the time of the Prophet.

Development of dotting and diacritics

Abul Aswad al-Du'ali, a companion of the fourth Caliph, is said to be the first person to introduce diacritics based on the movement of his lips as he was reciting the Quran. For spreading the lips, al-Duali suggested a dot above the letter, a dot below the letter for lowering the lower lip, and a dot right on the letter for rounding the lips. These dots represent fatha, kasrah, and Dammah of today, respectively.

Later, disciples of Abul proposed three distinct shapes for dotting: a small empty circle, a small, shaded circle, and a small rectangle. Also, they came up with a symbol for the shaddah, that is an arc placed on or below the letter. For a letter with shaddah and fatHah, an arc with its head upward, like this ‿, is placed on the letter; an arc like this ⌒ below the letter indicates shaddah with kasrah; and one like this ⌒ on the letter indicates shaddah with Dammah.

While there was consistency in using dots and shapes in all Muslim regions at the time, coloring of these symbols varied from one area to another. In Iraq, red color was used; in Madinah, red was used for dots and yellow for shapes. In Maghreb, they copied the Madinah system, yet in the nearby al-Andalus they used four different colors, namely black, red, yellow, and green.

Abulaswad's method continued to be in use throughout the Umayyad era. During the Abbasid Caliphate, to ease the job of copyists and transcribers, it was proposed that the coloring of the Quran be ceased. Owing to certain similarity in the dotting and the diacritical system, a new method had to be improvised. This was resolved by al-Khaliil ben Ahmed, a leading Arabic linguist of the time.

Al-Khaliil proposed that diacritical marks be in shapes of letters. Therefore, Dammah was represented by a small waw و to be placed on the letter; fatHah was represented by a small tilted alif placed on the letter; and kasrah was denoted by a small yaa' ـِ under the letter, which eventually lost its dots and became a small tilted alif placed under the letter. These are the diacritical marks that we use today.

Al-Khaliil also proposed a small zero-like symbol called sukoon to indicate the absence of a vowel with the letter. For shaddah, he employed a small shiin ـّ, which is taken from the word شَدَّة (i.e., the first letter). It was practical to strip of the dots of ـّ, so it eventually become ـّ as we see it today. He also used small Saad ـص for wasl and small 'ayn ع for qaT', both are still being used in Quranic writings.

As for lettering, the Kufic form of calligraphy was the most popular during both the Umayyad and Abbasid eras. A post will be dedicated to Arabic Calligraphy at some point". (End of blog).

Note 3.

There is an annoying and irritating repetition of a couple of points in several chapters which will irk the serious readers. The author sincerely apologizes for it. However, the inclusion of those repetitions is not an accidental mistake; they have been inserted to serve a purpose.

The casual readers may just ignore them in the beginning. The repetitions bring back to focus the foundational bricks in the edifice of this theory, thus reminding and emphasizing by repeating some facts and features, how and why the postulation of this theory emerged as a natural progression.

Now that background information is out of the way, we can proceed with issues related to the exposé and postulation of this theory.

CHAPTER 2

My Theory

The time-tested proverb, stated below, is universally accepted.

"If it walks like a duck, swims like a duck, and quacks like a duck, it is definitely a duck."

The 'Theory' described in this book, concerning Muhammad, his character and life-long conduct, and what appeared to be his real objective, is an ideal illustration of the proverb cited above.

***The core concept of 'The Theory' is that* Muhammad, in retrospect, was just an illiterate but ambitious tribesman from the Arabian desert who wished to raise a large unified army under his command, to invade, conquer, occupy, and rule the entire Arabian Peninsula, as the sole Master of its destiny.**

The 'Theory' postulated by the author, and presented in this book, will hopefully stand in a clear light once the fundamentals of human perceptions and how they evolved, is refreshed in a reader's mind.

A peek in the distant past of Natural history helps in understanding the way humans think and behave. The long journey of human genetic evolution spanning six million years, led to some great apes and bonobos gradually evolving to become human species called Homo Sapiens. In the journey forward of that evolutionary process, the newly evolved humans became cognitively capable of developing languages to talk to each other. More capabilities like lying, conspiring, analyzing, planning, and executing their thoughts to arrive at intended results, followed soon after. The result of cognitive evolution enables humans to differentiate between one's own emotions as good and bad, which is quite a significant step towards separating humans from wild beasts. Several other significant cognitive abilities which developed in humans are foresight, far-sightedness, phronesis and legerity, and above all, a capacity to convince millions to follow the leader.

Telling a white lie and convincing masses to treat it as gospel truth, takes a lot of talent, intelligence, and manipulative skill. A very limited number of humans acquired those uncommon capabilities. The few humans endowed with it, did reach the peak of leadership.

Soon after developing languages, humans played with another mysterious feature of brains, called imaginations. They imagined and created in their minds some abstract objects, and contrived vague but elaborate descriptions of those imagined phenomena. The imagined phenomena were presented by several different ideologues in different eras as invisible and inaudible realities. Some of those imagined realities were called 'gods' and goddesses. The ideologues made up names for the imagined gods and goddesses and assigned infinite albeit imagined powers to them. That happened more than 10 to 12 thousand years ago.

Cultures developed out of necessity for a peaceful co-existence in a given geography. A huge milestone was achieved, when humans led by demagogues made a collective decision with mutual consent to adopt and practice rules of acceptable behavior to achieve and ensure mutual peace and harmony. That was the beginning of culture and civilization, and the process of establishing norms and traditions. The institution of monogamy, or the concept of a couple's cohabitation approved, acknowledged, and respected by the community at large, later called marriage, was born around the time agriculture was invented i.e., about 12000 years ago.

I theorize, particularly in this aspect, that gods/goddesses with superhuman powers were conceived by the wise men, to control and discipline the physically stronger humans who oppressed the old and weak persons with sheer physical

strength. *This was a clever idea to reign in the troublemakers and discipline them by instilling infinite fear of invisible and inaudible gods/goddesses who had limitless power and could be approached through prayers, for help in punishing the cruel and dishonest people.*

The institution of marriage and procreation of children of each couple led to formation of the basic unit of human society, in the oldest cultures of the world which are no longer in existence. However, a few, not so old cultures and communities, can be traced to the archeological digs in Mesopotamia, as well as the excavations of Indus civilization in the Indus basin in Pakistan. About the same twelve thousand years ago, some of those rare leaders presented and preached various imagined gods in their communities. Those demagogues shaped the perception of common humans within their physical reach. The demagogues convincingly spread their newly conceived beliefs about gods/goddesses to common folks. Those gods, and a plethora of various irrational beliefs, evolved over time and became organized religions within a few centuries. The religions, one must remember, were clearly based on the imagined realities relating to the obscure, invisible, inaudible and abstract phenomena. The beliefs gained perpetuity by actions of parents and elders who raise and train and look after the new-born. The elders, among other important teachings and training imparted to children they braised (babies, toddlers, and those in single digit age), their own beliefs and convictions, mostly unbeknown to themselves, simply as a process of 'parenting'. This refers to Note 1 in the Preamble. relating to human behavior as Altricial mammals.

The demagoguery initiated more than 10 thousand years ago, proved very enduring and has perdured so far for several millennia. As a result of cognitive evolution, some clever humans, especially the inherently exploitative ones, learned to bluff, con, defraud and manipulate the simpler and naive majority, in many ways. Mankind, since the cognitive revolution, has thus remained somewhat divided between con-artists and their conned victims. In the current era too, the population of the conmen runs into millions and those conned by them are in billions. Large-scale frauds, scams, con jobs, and many other such dark labels come in various shapes and forms.

A class of dignified-looking and authoritative scammers is busy at the stock exchanges, Wall-street, MNC's, mainstream media, trade-unions, and NGOs. Yet another category is in casinos, racecourses, institutional lotteries, number-games, and drug cartels. Conmen in the sphere of religious faiths are found selling their wares in religious seminaries and places of worship like churches, mosques, temples, synagogues, pagodas, and monasteries of various denominations, as clergymen. Their faith-based down-stream varieties are peers, faqirs, dervishes, Sufis, fortune-tellers, sunt, swami, rishi, maharishi, soothsayers, and occult men like shamans. Most of the population, though, consists of firm believers in imaginary gods/goddesses. A tiny minority of conmen labeled as religious clerics, exploit religious beliefs of common believers for their own selfish goals of power, prominence, influence, and material gain. However, the sophisticated and distinguished looking conmen are in national politics, geopolitics, bureaucracies, corporate functionaries of MNCs, and in the UNO including its subsidiary organizations like WHO WTO etc. Brevity permitted a mention of only prominent categories, while countless more con artists are active in everyday life. The modus operandi of scammers varies but the core mission of defrauding simpler humans, particularly in matters relating to foggy abstractions of religions and invisible gods, remains the same. Scientific advances have taken most worldly functions to sophisticated levels. The con-artists too, have enjoyed the progress likewise.

The primary sources of scholarship leading to postulation of this theory, which is sure to be labeled "Blasphemous", are the verses of Quran and several 'Mustanad' (verified as authentic)

Ahadith ('Traditions', Muhammad's sayings and deeds, orally narrated by his companions in pre-literate era). The primary sources also include the earliest written texts of Islamic history, collected, and recorded in writing, a couple of centuries after the passing away of Muhammad, based on the oral traditions. I expect the readers will use their dialectical power to examine and evaluate this theory.

The extensive secondary sources include, in addition to works by Sunni and Shia Muslims, writings by Christian Arabs, and other non-Muslims from the Middle East and Asia. A few works by modern Western scholars have also been consulted and considered very seriously. I like to acknowledge my gratitude to the following investigative historians and research scholars who have contributed invaluable findings for the truth seekers of today.

Rev. Sell, Patricia Croner, Ibn e Warraq (born and raised as a Muslim), Robert Spencer, Henry B. Wright, Jay Smith, Dan Taylor, Ryan Mauro, Miroslav, Pr. Maurice, Prof. Friedman, Prof. Roy Casagranda, Tom Holland, Mat Davies, Steve Ray, Dan Gibson, Prof. Gerald Hawting, Montgomery Watt, and John Wans Brough. This book reveals the bare facts of history, relating to Allah, Muhammad and the Quran, after shedding the fictional addenda, and hagiography. This work is primarily offered to those who seek it in earnest for a critical analysis of this theory before accepting or rejecting it.

'The Theory' is intended neither to promote, nor denigrate any organized religion. It has been inspired by an authentic moral engagement to let the world know what the **FACTS** are relating to Allah, Muhammad, and the Quran. It is simply a documentation of findings of academic research, based on deep analysis of the Quranic contents, a large collection of audio-visual research documentaries, and analyses of excavated historical facts in the interest of historicity – period!

This theory is not an endorsement of other Monotheistic religions either, because those too offer no empirical proof of their authenticity

Facts of history, if left unguarded, are very fragile, and unstable in their survival, or their lasting power. They need delicate, precise, and very careful handling. ***One can destroy a fact or make it a non-fact by adding a tiny bit of fiction to it, or, by taking away a tiny bit of fact from it. Let's not forget also that the Present has a tremendous capacity to alter the Past any which way, to suit its purpose.*** Muslim historians have done it countless times while writing history of religion and religious characters. The most rampant technique adopted has been the shoehorning of facts into ideological constructs. An infinite amount of proverbial photoshopping has been done and sugar coating applied by many generations of Muslim scholars and clergy to decorate Allah, Muhammad, and the Quran during the last fourteen centuries. My endeavor is to offer the theory based on the untouched Truth, the whole Truth, and nothing but the Truth!

The shocking nature of the disclosures detailed in this book will certainly be regarded as lese majesty and whip up a storm of deadly reaction from the evangelical Mujahideen, the Islamofacists. Fear and apprehension for my life and my loved ones was compelling me to pen this exposé under a pseudonym. However, in the end, my resolve prevailed, and I decided boldly to put my name to it.

Enjoy the truth revealed in this book while you can. Who knows when another person will wager his dear life to tell all? The facts revealed here are the logical assumptions deduced from the Quranic verses. Those verses and other excavated historical facts, form the dominant argument and rationale for postulating this theory. I made sure to cite the relevant verse in each case, as undeniable evidence supporting the theory.

Having said that, I insist that **my theory is just a Theory – not a Claim.** It must not be construed as a claim. Muslim scholars will waste no time in accusing me that the Quranic verses have been cherry picked by me to support the theory. I have not cherry picked the verses; in fact, the verses quoted by me stand out and make their purpose-based existence glare back at you. However, it is a historical fact that the Muslim clerics never failed to cherry pick Quranic verses during the last fourteen centuries, quite frequently and unabashedly, to support their narrative, with total disregard to the original context of the verses quoted by them. Whenever they fail to find a usable Quranic verse to support their argument, they do not hesitate to cook up a Hadith, sometimes on the spur of the moment. All one needs, to see it happen in front of your own eyes, is to watch the sermons of Tahir al Qadri, or Tariq Jameel, Engr Mirza Muhammads Ali, and several others of their ilk in Pakistan, on YouTube. The listeners of their sermons are already primed, since their childhood, to be completely convinced and charmed, without bothering to check the reliability of the chronological string of narrators of the Hadith quoted by the sermon giver. For all you know, it may be a Hadeeth freshly minted by the overzealous pontificator, for winning laurels from the audience.

Predominant sources for this 'Theory' are many Quranic verses, and refuting this theory would mean questioning those verses of Quran. The only way to reject the theory is to prove that the verses quoted in support of the theory have been concocted by the author just to validate this theory.

Muhammad conceived a well-planned strategy for achieving that goal and carried out a brilliant execution of that plan. His plan was to begin by uniting as many in-fighting Arabian tribes as possible, under his leadership, to raise a large and unified army. Owing to blood feuds and mutual hostilities spanning generations, unifying the feuding tribes was a tall order. That plan required Muhammad to be in a prominent and very influential position to achieve his goal of uniting the tribes. He needed people to be convinced of his extraordinary position and personality, and believe in him with total devotion and loyalty. Starting a new cult and gradually enlarging its core concept into a full-fledged Deen (Religion), built around the central theme of infinite submission and total obedience to him, seemed like a brilliant idea. The core essence of the proposed deen (Religion) laid emphasis on total obedience and infinite submission of the followers to its leader Muhammad and Muhammad's newly introduced God Almighty 'Allah'. Hence Muhammad's new deen was in fact a major link in the long chain of steps to reach his goal i.e., becoming a singular ruler of the entire Arabian Peninsula. As far as Muhammad's mission was concerned, the toughest part was the character building and social reformation of the 'Jahiliya' tribes to conduct themselves in a moral and civilized manner for promoting unity among former blood-thirsty enemies, and melding them into a lasting brotherly relationship, after burying all the hatchets and erasing all causes of enmity. Acquiring this unity among warring tribes was a precondition for raising a large, unified army.

Thus, the two major stages of Muhammad's life-long mission were:

1. Claiming to have been divinely ordained by God Almighty 'Allah' as His last holy Prophet and Messenger, to present and preach a new deen, **with a view to having the people follow him with devotional loyalty, without ever questioning his orders.**

2. Introducing and enforcing 'Social Reforms' to inculcate strong and lasting unity among the tribes, who had a history of hostility for generations as blood-thirsty enemies.

The end objective of Muhammad was, as emphasized before, to become the singular ruler of the Arabian Peninsula. Synthesizing a new deen, and reformation of feuding tribes were merely the 'planned' steps for reaching that goal.

Antecedents of Muhammad

Muhammad was a young orphan boy, belonging to a tribe named al-Quresh in the city of Makkah, in a region of Arabian Peninsula called Hejaz. Makkah was a city in Hejaz, famous for the renowned Pagan shrine Kaaba in it, from time immemorial. Muhammad was very poor, totally illiterate, with no influence or prominence of any kind. In hindsight though, Muhammad seems to have been extremely intelligent, lightning quick in thinking and understanding the situation at hand, and phenomenally observant and cognizant of elements affecting circumstances around him.

He started working in the trading caravans, for his uncle Abi Talib who was also his guardian, at the tender age of 12, initially employed as a menial caretaker of camels laden with his uncle's commercial merchandise. Muhammad's practical experience and assignments began very modestly as a menial camel attendant. However, being a genius with a 20:20 foresight, and also being an observant extraordinaire, he became upwardly mobile on the fast track, and rose to meteoric heights very soon. He ascended to upper management positions in a short time, soon becoming a highly successful business manager and a phenomenally reputed deal maker among the trade circles of Arabia. Muhammad's career in the trading caravans took him to many places in the Middle East and brought him in contact with a wide variety of people of different faiths, traditions, and mind-sets. Muhammad came across those people while they participated in the trading caravans as traders bartering goods with each other at various trading locations, and stored the details of their beliefs, culture, customs, and traditions in his sharp memory.

During his travels, while gaining a practical education in the school of hard knocks in the business world, he developed an almost dreamy and fantastical ambition. Looking back, that ambition initially appears to have been, indoctrinating some simple desert dwellers. Muhammad convinced and persuaded the successfully indoctrinated ones to conduct surprise raids on vulnerable tribes and other caravans, for looting and robbing, like a gang of bandits, with the object of overpowering them, taking away their valuables, cattle, precious belongings, and other assets, and enforcing upon them his own laws and policies.

That practice of pouncing and grabbing others' assets was nothing unusual in the traditional tribal life of desert dwellers since many centuries in the past.

That dream of ruling over the Arabian Peninsula, required Muhammad to be very persuasive and convincing, with tremendous leadership qualities. He made a consistent effort to develop the art of communicating with people of varied backgrounds and diverse convictions. Muhammad came up with a unique, out-of-the-box solution to build his personal position and image, or say an outstanding personal brand. He decided to claim the prophethood of the God of Jews, Christians and Zoroastrians, the main three mono-theist faiths.

Muhammad at age 40, announced in Makkah in 610 A.D. that Allah was the 'One & Only' God Almighty, the creator of 'Creation' itself, a transcendent entity who brought the entire Universe into existence merely by willing it. Muhammad also claimed that Allah had divinely, (albeit not verifiably), ordained Muhammad as the last Prophet and Allah's Regent on Earth. A Pagan god named Allah was well known as a significant deity of idol-worshippers of Makkah since past many centuries i.e., before Muhammad poached that name for his God Almighty in his new deen. Muhammad also claimed that 'Allah' bestowed upon him (again not verifiably), the honorifics **"Khatam un nabiyeen"** [distinguished like a bejeweled ring among prophets] and **"Rahmat ul lill Alameen"** [(Allah's) holiest blessing for the entire Universe].

After convincing a significant number of Bedouin Arabs that he had been divinely ordained as a holy Prophet by the Almighty God Allah, he became the Spokesperson of the 'One & Only' God, ordering the Arabs to do whatever he wanted, by announcing those orders as the divinely received instructions from the monotheist God Allah Himself. Coming up with religious rituals, edicts, and forms of worship to build the infra-structure of his new Deen, he figured, he could do a carefully planned copy-pasting of chosen edicts, rituals, forms of worship and religious rules from various pre-existing religions, like Judaism, Christianity, Zoroastrianism, Paganism and the Sabaean Faith. The process of copy-pasting the poached components was conducted slowly and gradually over the next 22 lunar years. The whole process would of course be carried out under the awesome pretext that God Almighty Allah sent those religious components, for compliance by the Arabs of Hejaz, through Mohammad as the latest Prophet and Regent of Allah.

Thus, the theory postulates that:

Muhammad was a self-proclaimed prophet, NOT a divinely ordained Messenger of any verifiable God Almighty. The above opening lines are enough to antagonize the professional clerics and religious scholars of Muslims of all denominations. Those individuals will be up in arms, because their interests are tied to the continuity of Islam continually decorated and photoshopped by them.

Common Muslims too, have remained conned and duped for the last 60 to 70 generations, due to cleverly planned and purposeful maneuvering of one individual named Muhammad bin Abdullah. Common Muslims are programmed to be averse to reading a book of this kind. Very few of them will be curious, or adventurous enough, to go on reading till they make some significant discoveries and wise up. All one needs is a bit of common sense and a rational thought process to make sense of this book.

This theory proposes that Muhammad chose the name 'Allah' for a precise reason. Historically, Allah had been the name of a significant deity of idol-worshiping Pagans since many centuries before Islam. 'Allah' as the name for Muhammad's Almighty God was chosen, most likely because it sounded similar to Eloh, the Jewish pronoun for their God Yahweh. This was a significantly meaningful part of Muhammad's plan to convert the Jews before converting followers of all other religions, to Muhammad's Deen. It explains how Muhammad characterized and upgraded Allah, after poaching it from Pagans, into 'One & Only' Almighty, Omnipotent, Omnipresent and Omniscient, Creator & Master of the Universe; same description as the God of Jews YHWH (Pronounced as 'Yahweh). Muhammad claimed that his Allah created the first Man and Prophet 'Adam', followed by Abraham, Moses, and a long list of numerous prophets from Abraham's progeny, ending with Jesus. Muhammad announced that Allah had honored him to be Allah's most glorified Prophet, and His 'Regent' on Earth. He used that regency (self-allocated of course), to manipulate the simple desert-dwellers, into helping him achieve his unannounced objective of becoming the sole ruler of the Arabian Peninsula.

As an orphan, penniless and completely illiterate, with no power, prominence, or influence, it was nothing but a sheer fantasy and seemingly impossible dream for Muhammad. This book describes in detail the tenacity and grim persistence of Muhammad in chasing that dream, step by step, to make it a vibrant reality, a lasting and world changing event before he died. The reader will be blown away by the inexorability of Muhammad, a penniless and illiterate person, turned into a demi-god, more like a humanoid God, to a current population of 1.8 billion Muslims. Until very recently. I had toyed with the idea of using 'Veritas' (Latin for pure uncorrupted Truth) as the title for this book but decided to replace it with "The Naked Truth" which is easily and commonly understood.

The reader will embark upon an arduous journey, trekking over an unforgiving terrain while critically analyzing the basic components of Islam i.e., Allah, Muhammad, and the Quran. What you read here is shockingly contrary to what Muslims are taught, at home, at madrasa (Religious seminary), in school textbooks, and firmly believe. Here you will find exactly what the objective analysis and fact-finding has determined.

'Allah and Allah's orders' were Muhammad's most effective tools. He used his crafts with remarkable success. Having no wealth, or a position of significance, or power of any other kind, Muhammad's only short-cut access to power and prominence was, claiming to be the prophet of the God of Jews, Christians, and Zoroastrians. Interestingly, being named a prophet by God Almighty and accepted by the people, after initial resistance, depended on how charismatic, intelligent, persuasive, and manipulative Muhammad was. Apparently, education, power, wealth, or a VIP background in the community; was not a prerequisite for God to bestow prophethood to anyone as His Messenger and Spokesperson. Besides, past prophets too, had not produced a hard copy of their formal 'Letter of Appointment' as a Prophet', from Almighty God. That was not a requirement, in the perception of the illiterate desert-dwellers. The carefully planned prophethood would enable Muhammad to do whatever he needed to reach his goals, per the norms and extent of human intellect in that region and in that era. Muhammad thus assumed the much-needed status, commanding extreme respect and reverence, as 'a Prophet ordained by the Almighty God' without having to offer verifiable proof. All praise goes to the brilliance of Muhammad; his plan met with a dazzling success.

This theory states that Muhammad himself composed the so-called 'divine' revelations, as best as he could as an illiterate person, in his native patois. The reader must remember that till that point in history the Al-Fusha Arabic as we know it today, had not evolved hence not existed. The revelations were used quite frequently to keep the illiterate tribesmen impressed and charmed, from time to time, with his special status as the 'Best and Most Blessed Human Being' ever. To top it all, Muhammad claimed to have been appointed as the 'Regent' of Almighty Allah on Earth.

The native dialect of Muhammad's tribe was his one and only oral mode for communicating with other humans. The oral-dialectal lingo, however, was not fit to be written down in the nascent Arabic script of that time. Muhammad's pronouncements were suited and evidently meant to be memorized as an ode, in the long-held tradition of oral culture from the past many centuries of pre-literate era. Whenever people liked, they could recount their past and recall the deeds of their ancestors by reciting the ode relating to times gone-bye, in a sing-song manner, around a campfire in the cold nights of desert. The poets who created those odes were treated as historiographers and held in high esteem. That act of reciting the odes in a sing-song manner was called 'Quran', being the precise word in Arabic for 'recitation'. Muhammad's revelations, announced in his native dialect, due to its tonality and colloquial nature, could not be written down as is. It could be inscribed though, in phonetic symbols called phonemes, on parchments, papyrus, clay plates and wooden boards etc. It was similar in nature to the dictation symbols jotted down today in phonetic short-hand signs by professional stenographers. The 'revelations' announced by Muhammad, were evidently designed to shape, and mold the perception of Bedouins, and to make them comply with Muhammad's orders (Perceived by them to be Allah's orders) to help Muhammad achieve his goals.

Muhammad's mission proceeded towards fruition in a sequential process, spread over several phases, beginning with very difficult, painful and harsh ones, easing away gradually in carefully handled maneuvers. The first phase marked by troubles and tribulations, was to proselytize and convert as many Jews,

Christians, Zoroastrians, Sabaean and idolatrous Pagans as possible, to his new Deen in Mecca, to make them infinitely submissive and compliant with Allah's commands. Muhammad announced the revelations, every time he secretly and carefully composed them, claiming that he received each revelation from Allah through the invisible and inaudible Archangel Gabriel. This phase was followed by taking necessary steps to unite the infighting Bedouin tribes, mired in blood feuds for generations, by introducing and enforcing social reforms, presented as Allah's orders. The raising of a large army was dependent upon uniting the infighting tribes into one strong, mutually loving, caring and harmonious community, enjoying a lasting brotherly relationship. The grand army of the united tribes, under Muhammad's command, would then invade the dissident tribes, under the holy name of 'Jihad'; subdue them, occupy their land, capture their valuables and rule over them. Muhammad planned to collect annual Jizya (protection money) from the vanquished and colonized tribes spread all over the Arabian Peninsula. This aspect of the theory is based on a long list of 'divine' revelations, carefully worded by Muhammad for several very obvious reasons, such as the following examples:

1. To introduce and enforce social reforms, for creating unity, harmony,   and lasting brotherhood among the former infighting tribes, by stopping occurrence and frequent recurrence of a variety of causes of hostilities culminating in permanent bones of contention. Those hostilities were common and frequent events as an integral part of a culture of loot & plunder plaguing Bedouin tribes, for centuries since antiquity.

2. To convince the Jews, Zoroastrians, Sabaeans and Christians, also known as 'People of the book,' that the God Almighty of their religions, Ahura Mazda, YHWH, Tetragrammaton, El,

Elohim, Eloah, Elohai, El Shaddai, Jehovah and Tzevaot etc. are one and the same as Muhammad's God Almighty Allah.

3. That, obeying Muhammad is the same as obeying Allah.

4. And pleasing Muhammad is the same as pleasing Allah.

5. That Allah decides, who after dying, goes to Heaven, and who goes to Hell.

Muhammad announced that Allah bestowed that authority on Muhammad too, being the Regent of Allah on earth. Clearly, a master stroke of Muhammad's genius, propelling him into the highest position ever of reverence and holy glory, parallel to Allah. There are many more such instructions in the so-called 'divine 'revelations' prompting the converts to practically treat Muhammad as an anthropomorphic God on Earth, albeit without saying so, in so many words. Muslims frown at the idea of Muhammad being mentioned as an anthropomorphic god, but in real life, even in the 21st century, Muslims treat Muhammad, practically and worshipfully, as a humanoid God. For a practical observation, watch Muhammad being worshiped virtually as a God in human form in the gatherings of "Tehreek-e-Labbaik Ya Rasul Allah" founded by late Khadim Hussain Rizvi in Pakistan, now run by his son Saad Rizvi.

This book is not commercially motivated for self-enrichment. It has been brought to fruition by a persistent desire to reveal the truth. The overzealous spin doctors among Muslims, and hagiographers masquerading as historians, had buried the truth under countless layers of fabrication, concoction, and deliberate misappropriation of 'Truth', over the last fourteen centuries.

I have no intention of putting a price on the countless hours of research, and cross checking of the discovered facts, during the 4 long years dedicated wholly to probing, digging deeper, and cross checking the findings for veracity. This analytical documentation is offered entirely in the interest of historicity.

I have no intention of putting a profit generating price on the countless hours of research, for cross checking the discovered facts, during the last 4 long years, dedicated wholly to probing, digging deeper, and cross checking the findings for veracity. This analytical documentation is offered, at a retail price decided by the publisher, entirely in the interest of historicity.

Publishers who wish to publish its translation commercially, in any language, anywhere in the world, have my full permission and encouragement to do so.

The people who might be well-served by this theory, which I reiterate is based mainly on the critical analysis of the Quran and life-long conduct of Muhammad, live in Malaysia, India, Pakistan, Bangladesh, Turkey, Iran and the whole of Middle East and North Africa. Therefore translations, particularly in the languages of those countries, would make more sense than translations into Anglo-European languages . The Theory of "The Naked Truth" is my oeuvre, prompted by the fact that I am in the ninth decade of my life. The countdown of Nature is on for dropping the curtain on me; one way or the other, qué será, será!

Wequar Azeem

"The Lie said to the Truth, 'Let's take a bath together, the well water is very nice.' The Truth, still suspicious, tested the water and found out it really was nice. And so, they got naked and bathed. But suddenly, the Lie leapt out of the water and fled, wearing the clothes of the Truth. The Truth, furious, climbed out of the well to get her clothes back. But the World, upon seeing the naked Truth, looked away, with anger and contempt. Poor Truth returned to the well and disappeared, hiding her shame. Since then, the Lie runs around the world, dressed as the Truth, and society is very happy...Because the world has no desire to know the naked Truth." (Jean-Leon Gerome, 1896)

CHAPTER 3

Overview

Islam, the youngest among Abrahamic religions, is today the focal point of controversy, malicious propaganda, and terrible accusations on one hand, and desperate attempts to defend it, on the other hand, by Muslims in general and many 'politically correct' politicians of the world in particular. However, there being too many sects and sub-sects of Islam, the arguments for and against, are quite confusing and grossly misleading for most non-Muslims.

One of the objects of this book, though not a dominant one, is to help the reader determine what the original Deen (Religion) happened to be on the day its Prophet i.e., Muhammad bin Abdullah announced that the Deen was complete, and revelations had come to an end. There was just one Deen on that day, without any sects or sub-sects. The multitude of sects, negating each other, started developing soon after Muhammad died. The widely known major sects gave birth to countless sub-sects over the last fourteen centuries. It's a food for thought for Muslims who claim that Allah protects the contents of Quran (A blatantly false claim as disclosed in the chapter on Quran) but shows no control over creation of proverbial 72 sects, each claiming to be the true Islam and rejecting all others as false; not to mention the fabrication of thousands of Hadith (Muhammad's words and deeds) to support one sect and negate the other. In order to comprehend the original Deen of Muhammad (now called Islam) as it was on the day he died, one has to understand the meanings of basic terms and expressions of the religious codes on that day, because Muhammad's Deen is a religion that has quite extensive codification. **Eemaan, Kalima, Salaat, Saom, Zaka,**

Hajj and Jihad are a few examples of the subject heads. Each has a long trail of subsequent changes in their meanings, purpose and manifestations. The raison d'être behind its existence in the original Deen is also important and explains why they were made a major part of its codification. Last but not the least; the details of the reason why Muhammad's deen was named 'Islam', long after the death of Muhammad, and what it means.

In order to fully comprehend the basis of my theory, and understand the essential message of this book, one would need to critically analyze the genesis of Muhammad's Deen. So here is a brief summation:

The region of the Arab world called Hejaz was far from the intellectual and urban areas like Cairo in Egypt, Damascus in Syria, or Baghdad in Iraq. Hejaz, a vastly arid region, was home to several sedentary desert-dwelling tribes and a larger number of nomadic Bedouin tribes. The culture, social mores and traditions were the culmination of many centuries of evolution in terms of history and geography of the region. Those traditions and customs, native to the region, were entrenched deep in the psyche of the people, like a second nature.

Muhammad, though illiterate, had extraordinary intelligence and a critical eye for insightful observation of all the tribes around him. His observation and how he analyzed what he observed, helped him a great deal in his mission, as you will notice later in the book.

The intra-tribe complexity of culture, and the never-ending inter-tribe strife were the building blocks of his thought process. At the mature age of 40 he was ready to synthesize a whole new mega Community called Al-Momineen, superior and more powerful than all other tribes in Hejaz. Each male member of the new community would be called a 'Momin'(Plural Momineen), and female a 'Momina'(Plural Mominat). He took his time to carefully build his own personal image, or brand if you will, to start the new tribe with a high moral authority, unmatched and unheard of ever before. He did build himself up as the greatest ever protagonist in medieval times. He prescribed carefully thought-out rules and regulations to replace the centuries old customs, traditions, and social mores. However, one has to bear in mind that Muhammad himself was born and bred in one of the tribes of the region and naturally could not have the mind-set of someone totally unaffected by the native environment, as though he was born and raised in, say, Japan or Scandinavia or South Africa, to design and build the new community called Al-Momineen (now called Muslimeen). Being illiterate, and a native of the region, he could only use what was available, and within his reach. He chose the following components that were available to him to build the new deen with:

1. Bayt Al Maqdis i.e., the land where the 'Temple on the Mount' of Jews, in Jerusalem is situated, used as their main shrine for worship of YAHWEH, their God Almighty.

2. Kaaba in Makkah (revered by most tribes of Pagans whose idols of gods and goddesses were housed in it). It is interesting to note that there were at least three more Kaabas in different parts of Arabian Peninsula, specially the white one in Yemen called "Dhul Khalasa", which was later destroyed completely under Muhammad's orders. The Muslim historians never mention the existence of those Kaabas during Muhammad's lifetime. Ref. https://www.youtube.com/watch?v=BdLk39fnY

3. Allah (one of the top-tier gods of the Pagans).

4. Rituals of Hajj performed by Sabaeans and the idol-worshiper Pagans who comprised most of the population of Hejaz.

5. The dietary restrictions of Halal (Kosher) and Haram (Non-Kosher) foods of the Jews.

6. Circumcision of baby boys performed religiously by Jews.

7. Fasting, during the Arab calendar month of Ramadan. It was done in several different ways by people of Sabaean Faith, Christians, and Jews.

8. Daily prayers to worship God Almighty, offered by Jews, Sabaeans, Hanifs and Christians, each in their own distinct style.

Abu Zanad, an Arabic writer from Iraq who lived in the century following the founding of Islam, around 747 CE, wrote that at least one Mandaean community (Sabaeans)located in al-Jazira (modern day northern Iraq) observed fasting for little over a month spanning Ramadan plus a week after, before converting to Islam. The five daily prayers comprising wudu (Ablution) and a set of prescribed movements of the body by a worshiper, labeled as qiyam, ruku and sajdah were a practice of Sabaeans and Hanifs (Worshippers of ONE true God), who offered prayers seven times during the 24 hours of a day and night, long before the advent of Islam in Hijaz. One exception is Zakat, which was called zakut in judaical tradition, mandatory today in Islam, was not so in Muhammad's lifetime. It was introduced by the first caliph Abu Bakr.

This book is bound to draw the ire of almost all sects of Islam for pointing out that formation of Islam is a personal plan and brainchild of Muhammad bin Abdallah, (And NOT of Allah Himself). That Muhammad synthesized a new Faith only for the region of Hejaz. As far as Muhammad was concerned, the structure of Islam designed by him, was intended for the psyche of Hejaz dwellers. It could not appeal, or even make sense, to the people far beyond Hejaz who had different history and geography and hence different customs, traditions and a different thought process. Muslim clergy of all sects never tire of force-selling Islam as a universal religion, to all other people who were, and are, alien to the mind-set and traditions of illiterate desert dwellers of Hejaz.

At the end of the book, an unbiased reader will conclude that the Deen defined and propagated by Muhammad, and the circumstances which were prevalent surrounding its genesis are no longer in existence. What we have is a huge display of fakes and counterfeits. Each sect tirelessly acts pious and disdainfully sanctimonious towards other sects. You are invited to read and discover what the real Deen planned by Muhammad was, why it was relevant to Hejaz only when it was presented by Muhammad, and most importantly, why Muhammad created it.

Excavated Facts of Mecca

The main character, around whom the total investigation and disclosure of facts revolve is its central figure Muhammad bin Abdullah, a tribesman of Banu Hashim clan of Makkah. Makkah was and still is, the hometown of Kaaba, Muslims' holiest Shrine in the world since 623 C.E. When Muhammad announced his divine ordination as the last and most glorious prophet of Allah in 610 C.E., **the Qibla and the holiest shrine of Muhammad's *Deen* was Bait al Maqdis in Jerusalem** (Temple on the Mount). There is no proof or evidence that Kaaba has been built by 'First Man' Adam, or angels, or Abraham and Ismail, as claimed by Muhammad. Kaaba was not given as much importance in the first 12-13 years of the new Deen preached by Muhammad. It became the sanctum-sanctorum and most sacred shrine after the change of Qibla from Bait ul Maqdis to Kaaba in the year 3 A.H. The history of Kaaba, popularly believed by Muslims, was first announced by Muhammad, to serve a particular purpose; that purpose was to establish his lineage to Prophet Abraham, who invented 'Monotheism' and all prophets before Muhammad were Abraham's progeny and belonged to the region which is currently called Israel and Palestine. It was a common understanding of Arabs that Prophets are born only in the bloodline of Abraham. In order to validate his claim to prophethood, Muhammad needed first to establish that he too was a descendent of Prophet

Abraham. The details of how Muhammad established his lineage to Abraham is part of the history he manipulated through switching of Abraham's son Isaac with his elder son Ismail in the 'anecdote of sacrifice'. The details of that manipulation will become evident later in this book.

Majority of the open-minded and educated adults, including some emancipated and secularly inclined Muslims, know or suspect, or conclude analytically, that Muhammad's 'Deen' is not a divinely revealed religion, although so claimed by Muhammad. Common Muslims of the world, however, take it as gospel truth. Here's a little narrative on why Muhammad is theorized to be a self-proclaimed prophet, instead of a Divinely Ordained Messenger of Allah:

Consider this scenario: What would have most likely happened if Muhammad were a divinely ordained Messenger of an empirically proven God, instead of an unproven, imaginary Creator Allah?

1.   Muhammad would have been at least a learned man who could write down the revelations from Allah in a well-known and fully developed literary language and keep a date-wise record of all the holy revelations himself.

2.   Whenever Archangel Gabriel supposedly brought a message from Allah, that angel would have been visible and audible to all persons present around Muhammad, at the time.

3.   Revelations would not be sent in an oral/dialectal lingo, which was itself struggling to become a proper language with a proper script.

4. Had Gabriel been visible and heard by all persons present around Muhammad, whenever the Angel conveyed words of Allah to Muhammad, his ordainment as Messenger of God would need no further proof of being a true Messenger of the 'One & Only' God named Allah.

5.   The holy revelations would not contain countless messages aimed at building people's perception that Muhammad is the holiest, most glorious, and the very best human-being ever created in the entire mankind.

6.   Muhammad's proclaimed, 'revelations' would not need to include capital punishment for Apostasy or declare 'Shirk' (an unpardonable sin) or insist on 'Wahdaniyah' (Oneness of Allah). All those concepts would be redundant if people saw and heard - Gabriel whenever he brought revelations to Muhammad from Allah.

7.   All circumstances surrounding Muhammad, all actions of Muhammad, and all pronouncements of Muhammad, only prove the credibility of the theory that Muhammad proffered a recycled God Almighty named Allah, and grandstanded Allah to grandstand himself being Allah's Regent on Earth, best human being ever, and the most glorified Prophet of Allah.

8.   Muhammad composed and used the 'divine' revelations, claiming they were from Allah, to have people follow his instructions obediently, without questioning the validity or purpose, (The word 'Islam', which is a verb, linguistically, means complete 'obedience') and helps Muhammad accomplish his unannounced goals.

A new religion was put together by the cutting-edge innovation and creative genius of Muhammad. He synthesized a religion by poaching and copy-pasting core beliefs, rituals, edicts and forms of worship from several different pre-existing religions (Already being practiced in the 7th century Arabia, by idol-worshiping Polytheist Pagans, Jews, Zoroastrians, Sabaeans and Christians). Some of those religions claimed to possess holy scriptures brought by their prophets, from their God Almighty, as divine guidance for mankind. The details of the components poached, and whence each component was poached from, is presented in detail in The Theory of 'The Naked Truth'.

How and why Muhammad accomplished this remarkable feat is visible to the analytical eyes of history detectives and investigative historians, who are not blinded by irrational beliefs and convictions. When you scope it in the hindsight 20:20, their analyses get affirmed and endorsed by Muhammad's own life-long conduct and how he manipulated the perception of desert-dwellers by composing the so-called 'divine' revelations. This book is unveiling the very purpose of putting together a new Deen (now called 'Islam') in the towns named Makkah and Madinah in the Hejaz region in Arabian Peninsula, circa early 7th century A.D.

The precaution of being politically correct and ensuring diplomatic distancing from sensitive nerves, has been overlooked for a bold, and no-holds-barred exposé.

The Theory of 'The Naked Truth' is going to be a rude awakening for the intellectually conscious Muslims who remained duped and conned for a millennium and half. The great majority of compliant Muslims, whether illiterate or educated, undergo the reaffirmation and re-enforcement of the 'Belief' preached by Muhammad, 5 times a day, through the mandatory 5 daily prayers, throughout their entire life. Every sermon in religious ceremonies of Muslims, and in large congregational prayers, like Eid, Hajj, Umrah etc., serves the purpose of consolidating Muslims' perception about Allah, Muhammad, and the Quran. No wonder Muslims prefer to remain in denial and bask in the comfort of a doctored history, and a manipulated belief re-enforced and re-charged by Muslim clergy and hagiographers several times every day without fail. Muslim scholars put a spin upon spin on real history and add more decor to it in almost every new generation which comes of age, making Islam and its associated features and characters ornate beyond recognition.

Based on the personal conduct of Muhammad, some aspects of which are described below, the non-Muslims, particularly Christians and Jews, made very scathing remarks and toxic comments in Medina, without mincing their words, while **rejecting Muhammad as a counterfeit prophet and declaring his Deen a reprehensible fake.** They considered Muhammad's Deen was born in sin.

Muhammad claimed that Allah awarded the following special privileges to him, which are strictly forbidden for Momineen & Mominat (Muhammad's followers). Reminds one, of the proverb **"What is good for a goose, is not good for a gander"**

a.   Muhammad was entitled to marry any woman he liked, even if the woman was a lawfully wedded wife of the man she was living with.

b.   Muhammad had the privilege to marry any woman without witnesses, or a Vakil (Male guardian of the female, like her father or uncle, or a brother) to give the   females' hand in marriage to Muhammad.

c.   Muhammad was free to take any woman and as many women as he wanted as his wife, without seeking anyone's permission, including the permission of the wife to be.

1. **How Muhammad ordered or approved the cold-blooded killing of personal   enemies.** (A detailed "Murder Chart" in the section under 'Muhammad', describes who, when, and why a person was ordered killed by Muhammad).

2. **How Muhammad pursued his carnal desires by betrothing 16 women, most of them being young enough to pass for his daughters and granddaughters.**

3. **Sawda**, the so-called 'oldest' woman he married after the death of his first wife Khadija, was in fact nearly 9 years younger than Muhammad. (Muhammad was 50 and Sawda was 41 at marriage). Muslim scholars and historians blatantly report that Sawda was 80 when Muhammad married her.

4. After the passing away of his first wife Khadijah with whom Muhammad had remained faithful and strictly monogamous, ostensibly because of her wealth and influence in the society, Muhammad went on a wedding spree. In addition to 16 marriages, Muhammad enjoyed extra-marital sex with an unaccounted number of concubines, during his last 10 years of prophethood. A detailed chart captioned "Muhammad's Harem" gives details of names, ages, dates of betrothal. 'Muhammad's Harem' has remained the biggest moral blot on Muhammad's image. Muslim scholars leave no stone unturned while struggling and scrubbing at that blot for the last 14 centuries).

5. **Taking away the wife of his adopted son Zayd bin Haritha when Muhammad accidentally saw her naked and was overcome by lust.**

Muhammad had his adopted son Zayd divorce his wife so Muhammad could marry her. The scandal triggered a whisper campaign among his followers and detractors, damaging his image. He tackled that problem by coolly composing and announcing a 'divine' revelation from Allah, "Disallowing Adoption" in the new Deen, thereby removing the stigma of Zayd having been his adopted son, or his wife having been his daughter-in-law. With one stroke of genius, Muhammad put an end to the scandalous rumors, nullifying the very adoption of Zayd, his son for 15 years, through 'new orders of Allah'. He simultaneously put a lid on the rumors. (Details of this incident have been recounted under "The story of Zayd bin Haritha", at the end of 'Muhammad's Harem').

6. **A revenue stream was created for his personal enrichment by virtually "Selling Muhammad's Intercession with Allah".**

Muhammad sold his services to Momineen who wished to obtain forgiveness of the 'Sins of omission and commission', and wished to buy Allah's forgiveness and blessings, to get the much-coveted entry-pass for Paradise. He composed several 'divine' revelations and used them to coax his followers to pay in cash and/or kind to

Muhammad, to intercede with Allah on their behalf.(Details are provided, of several Aya, chapter & verse, goading the followers into seeking Muhammad's intercession with Allah, in return for material gifts, to buy Allah's blessings, forgiveness, and above all, to secure an entry into Paradise in the life-after-death). By the way, this Sunnah of Muhammad is used by the Aga Khan to grab material gain from his followers the Ismaili Imami Shias, commonly known as 'Agakhanis', for procuring Godly favors from Almighty Aga Khan.

7. Muhammad committed the blunder of reproducing some fictional stories he had heard from illiterate Jews and Christians, relating to earlier prophets of Judaism and Christianity, during his trading caravan travels, and presented them as 'divinely revealed information' from   Allah. Muhammad was under the mistaken impression that those stories he picked up from illiterate fellow journeymen like himself, were part of the canonized text of the Old & New Testament. Muhammad was unaware that those stories belonged to the fabricated folklore of Talmud and Christian Apocrypha, stuff mostly made up by Rabbis and Christian priests over several centuries in the past. As a result of this blunder by Muhammad, the Jewish Rabbis and Christian Priests understood right away that Muhammad's sources were the illiterate Jews and illiterate Christians who could not read Greek or Hebrew to be aware of the canonized Testaments. The Jewish and Christian clergy also figured out that the Pagan deity Allah was also redesigned and upgraded by Muhammad himself, and that the so-called 'divine' revelations too were composed by Muhammad himself, to serve and sustain his planned mission. Educated Muslims generally disregard logic, reason, rationality, and scientific discoveries when discussing religion. Any Muslim trying to break free from that bondage is considered a sinner, bound for eternal hellfire.

8. The mortal fear of hellfire was interjected by Muhammad himself, in addition to introducing a draconian religious law called "Irtidad '' (A religious crime committed by a Momin/Momina when he/she gives up belief and renounces Muhammad's Deen. This is called 'Apostasy' in English). Muhammad secured the perpetuity of his Deen (religion) by hanging a sword of decapitation over the head

of the Murtad (One who commits Irtidad) (Ref.: Hadith from Bukhari and Muslim). The ruling on apostasy was based primarily on three Hadiths in Sahih al-Bukhari.

First, the Companion Ibn 'Abbās reported that the Prophet صلى الله عليه وسلم said, "Whoever changes their religion, kill them." Ṣaḥīḥal-Bukhārī: kitāb al-jihād wa'l-siyar, bāb lā yuʿadhdhabu bi-ʿadhāb Allāh.Second, Muʿādh bin Jabal told another Companion, Abū Mūsā al-Ashʿarī, that executing the apostate was the ruling of God and His Messenger. Ṣaḥīḥ al-Bukhārī: kitāb istitābat al-murtaddīn wa'l-muʿānidīn wa qitālihim, bāb ḥukm al-murtadd wa'l-murtadda. And third, the Prophet said that a Muslim could only be executed for the crimes of murder, adultery, or apostasy. Ṣaḥīḥ al-Bukhārī: kitāb al-diyāt, bāb qawl Allāh taʿālā inna al-nafs bi'l-nafs...; Ṣaḥīḥ Muslim:kitāb al-qasāma wa'l-muḥāribīn..., bāb mā yubāḥu bihi dam al-muslim.A critical study of Hadith (Tradition) reveals that Ahadeeth are in fact a docudrama by various Sheikhs of Hadith, especially during Umayyad and Abbasid caliphates, engaged in one-upmanship with one-another. It is note-worthy that NO other religion has such a gruesome law imposing the death penalty for renouncing the religion.

The self-proclaimed 'Lovers of Muhammad' adopt a murderous attitude at disclosures of unsavory facts relating to Muhammad, simply because those disclosures expose the falsehood of the doctored history taught in Muslims' textbooks. This posture of jingoistic vigilantism against unwelcome disclosures, is encouraged and admired among Muslims as an act of piety and considered worthy of much reward from Allah. The more militant they appear -- the more God-fearing and Muhammad-loving they are held. Therefore, many Muslims, make a big, albeit fake fuss of angry reactions, for optics only. The worst part of this law is that it is misused to settle personal Scoresby accusing their personal enemies as Murtad and killing them by lynching. The murders are conveniently perceived to be jihad against a murtad. This happens frequently to dirt-poor non-Muslim victims in Pakistan. Muslim clergy, in their own interest, incite simple and ignorant believers to react as violently as possible on such disclosures. The past history of Muslims is replete with numerous incidents of exposure of truth by investigative writers, but not without inviting personal peril to the whistle blower; none of the exposures perhaps as bold and blunt as The Theory of 'The Naked Truth'.

The Theory of 'The Naked Truth' is not just iconoclastic. It is an exposé of Muhammad's hidden intention and secret ambition. Muhammad's conduct, in hindsight, conclusively exposes Muhammad's real intention. All care has been taken to exercise studiously neutral impartiality to present a seasoned perspective and analysis. However, any objective analysis of Muhammad's character and conduct as a 'Rasul', never fails to arouse an angry response from Muslims, denouncing it as advocacy authorship, Islamophobic and below-the-belt bashing of Muhammad, like a seasoned practice of dramaturgy. The one prominent reason for this behavior is the deep-seated bias among Muslims, from childhood, that the history detectives and investigative historians are disdainful critics and Islamophobes, who spread anti-Muslim propaganda just to malign Muslims and Islam's religious belief and practices. This attitude of Muslims is evidently pre-emptive and defensive in nature, to discourage any serious academic research, analysis and exposure of history surrounding Muhammad and his actions.

The exposé and analysis of disclosed facts pertain to the conduct and pronouncements of Muhammad, particularly through the skillful 'divine' revelations he presented, following his actions, and sometime preceding it. Readers will draw their own conclusion based on facts flayed open by the investigative historians. This book unveils hard facts buried under tons of fiction piled up during the last fourteen centuries by Muslim hagiographers who have been putting spin on spin, upon spin, during the last 14 centuries. Consequently, the details of the naked truth, and the propagated ornate history, are poles apart. All varieties of romanticism of spirituality, fancy mumbo jumbo of Sufism, telepathy, divine inspiration, and in-dream communications, are conspicuous by their absence in The Theory of 'The Naked Truth'. Normally though, these are essential, integral and inevitable parts of any Islamic religious discourse. The readers can conclude, on their own, what appears to be Muhammad's entrenched intention and purpose behind his fanciful claim that Almighty Allah made him the "Exalted Apostle in the 7th century C.E. Muhammad's own stated mission was to be a warner, Law giver and preacher of the 'Final Version' of Allah's one and only Deen (Religion). Muhammad claimed that the one and the same Deen of Allah was sent, duly updated with each new prophet, from Adam to Jesus, and finally with Muhammad himself as the last and most exalted among the Prophets of Allah. (Ref.: Quran 69-40, 4-174, 33-56, 21-107).

According to Muhammad, all declarations made by him were 'divine' revelations sent to him from Almighty Allah through the ArchAngel Gabriel. Interestingly, as stated earlier, Gabriel was neither visible nor audible to any human being except Muhammad himself, who claimed to see that angel, hear that angel conveying divine revelation from Allah to him, and converse with that angel. Interestingly, that technique has been copied by many fake Pirs/Fakirs/Amils in the present times; they claim to their simple vulnerable clients that they have captivated and enslaved some Jinn who is invisible and inaudible to common folks, but visible and audible to the said Pir/Faqir or Amil. The fake Pir claims that he extracts hidden information about who is behind the misery of any of Pir's clients who pays a hefty fee to the Pir/Amil, by assigning that job to their captive Jinn. A lot of simple and illiterate Muslim women fall for such chicanery of the Pir or Faqir and pay him in cash or kind for that fanciful service.

There was not a single eyewitness who saw Gabriel delivering messages from Allah to Muhammad, even once, during the piecemeal revelations spread over 22 long years. The only narrative about Gabriel's existence and his activities, is the statement of Muhammad himself', presented as a 'divine' revelation from Allah. (Ref.: Quran 2:97-103).

قُلْ مَنْ كَانَ عَدُوًّا لِّجِبْرِیْلَ فَاِنَّہٗ نَزَّلَہٗ عَلٰی قَلْبِکَ بِاِذْنِ اللہِ مُصَدِّقًا لِّمَا بَیْنَ یَدَیْہِ وَ ہُدًی وَّ بُشْرٰی لِلْمُؤْمِنِیْنَ ﴿۹۷﴾

There was no proof or empirical verification that Muhammad was receiving messages from the Creator of the Universe. It was Muhammad's clever idea to add utmost awe and reverence to whatever he passed around as 'Words of the Almighty Allah, the Creator of the Universe'. Readers will notice the frequent use of 'divine' revelations, every time Muhammad tried to get out of a jam, or, whenever Muhammad had to ensure that people listened to him, and dutifully complied with his instructions, under the pretext that Allah had commanded them to do so.

Arabs in the 7th century were evidently gullible enough to accept that Muhammad was a divine Messenger of the invisible Almighty Allah, on Muhammad's own say-so. Can anyone imagine that to be possible at all if Muhammad were to appear today and make that claim? The fact that Allah's own existence has remained unverified and empirically unproven, is beside the point. Had Gabriel been visible and audible to every person around Muhammad, each time Gabriel appeared miraculously out of nowhere, to deliver a divine message from Allah, and disappear 'poof' into thin air after delivery … This theory would have no reason to be postulated.

Countries with a majority of the Muslim population, almost always have a low level of literacy. However, all Muslims angrily and vociferously demonstrate in the streets when any faults or weaknesses are pointed out in Muhammad's character or conduct. It's an irony that people who have no knowledge of researched history, contrary to those who spent years in research and excavation of facts, find each other on opposite sides of controversy, which often turns ugly, bloody and gruesome. There is a biological reason for this behavior which has also been explained in the coming chapter of this book.

Every time Muhammad's name comes up in conversation, a throaty Darood for Muhammad by saying **"Sallallahu wa alihi wa Sallam'**, which means "May Allah honor him, and grant peace and blessings upon him" has to be recited as a devotional act of showing reverence for Muhammad. This Darood however, is not recited when mentioning any other prophet of Allah in a conversation. Failing to recite the Darood when Muhammad's name is uttered, as though it is a part of Muhammad's name, is sinful, disrespectful, and a form of blasphemy – virtually guarantees serious punishment and social condemnation!

The readers can conclude on their own why this Darood is assigned a mandatory status, and who is the sole beneficiary of its effect on Muslims' perception. The Theory of 'The Naked Truth' is sure to draw the ire of all Muslims, each Muslim having been subjected to relentless indoctrination throughout infancy and early childhood, followed by reminders of Salat and reinforcements five times a day. The feature of uploading a religious belief on a child's brain, during infancy and preschool age (like tattooing a child's cerebrum), has been discussed in detail in the next chapter. It is a universal practice of parents and other grownups who raise a child, in all religions. Consequently, later in life as adults, they possess neither the curiosity nor the will to question the beliefs tattooed on their brain in early childhood. The shocking exposure of Muhammad's reality adversely affects the down-stream franchisees of Muhammad's much touted spiritual legacy and Regency of Allah.

The most prominent among the franchisees is his son-in-law Ali ibn Abi-Talib, and Ali's progeny of 12 Imams (Muslims' sect of Twelvers), through Ali's wife Fatima (Muhammad's youngest daughter). These legatees consequently lose their raison d'être for being held in spiritual awe and reverence. The 12 Imams are virtually treated by Shias as Jesus is treated by Catholics – an anthropomorphic God. As a consequence of Muhammad being exposed to be a counterfeit and self-proclaimed prophet of Allah, those 12 Imams too, stand bereft of spiritual authority, because Muhammad, their only legator of holiness through bloodline, stands exposed as a counterfeit and self-proclaimed prophet. Like Muhammad, these 12 Imams have also been decorated and credited with volumes of miraculous acts over the centuries, in the identical style of Muhammad's generously fabricated Ahadith.

The first cousins of 12 Shia Imams are the founders of Zaidis, Dawoodi Bohras and Ismailis' sects of Shia Islam. The locus-standi of spirituality of these sects too, stands demolished in perception of serious readers, as a consequence of Muhammad's exposure as a common man, devoid of any divinity, spirituality, or claimed vice-regency of Almighty Allah.

In the 1830s, Aga Hassanaly Shah, the 46th Ismaili Imam was granted the honorary hereditary title of Aga Khan by the Shah of Persia. In 1843 the first Aga Khan left Persia for India, which already had a large Ismaili community. **The Aga Khan II, who died in Poona, India in August 1885 declared to his followers in the 19th century that he was the human manifestation of Almighty Allah, the Creator of the Universe, as well as, the Avtar of trimurti of Hinduism (Gods Brahma, Vishnu and Shiva).**

The Aga Khans, hereditary heads of Ismaili community, use the umbrella of Islam to hide among Muslims. The 'holy' pronouncements of Aga Khans are conveyed to his followers through secret "Farmans" (Royal or Godly Decrees or Commandments) strictly for the eyes & ears of their cult followers only, in the protected and secretive confines of their place of congregation called "Jamat Khana". Entry of non-Ismaili persons is strictly forbidden in all the 'Jamat Khanas' world-wide. This community, which currently comprises 15 million followers world-wide, was ordered by Aga Khan II to pay 12.5% of their income to him, as their worshipful offering to him, being their God. The clandestine way in which the cash collections of 12.5% of the whole community's income regularly reaches Aga Khan, is the oldest crime of money laundering and currency trafficking. The worshippers of the GOD Almighty Hazir Imam Aga Khan are one more compelling reason to hide my identity, because the worshippers of Ismaili Aga khan have a world-wide regiment of highly respected "Fidayeen" (The persons who are willing to sacrifice their life, in the tradition of Hasan bin Sabbah, the head of of "Assassins", several centuries ago), are the bodyguards of the ruling Aga Khan of time. They would exterminate any person/persons likely to bring bodily harm to Aga Khan, or to his godly image.

Ref.:26 episodes of 'God and Money: The Secret World of Aga Khan' - Introduction - YouTube

There is a formidable population of commercial exploiters of Faith among both the Sunni and Shia Muslims, bearing honorifics like Mulla, Maulvi, Maulana, Sheik, Mufti, Mohaddis, Qadhi, Mujtahid, Ayatollah. Besides, there are a whole lot of money-grabbing institutions --- completely devoid of good conscience, known as Mausoleum or shrines of Sufi Saints (Dargah, Mazar), 'Khanqahs'(Monasteries), Aastanas, Darbars --- the list goes on, who collect hundreds of millions in local currencies in cash, as worshipful offerings from simpleton Muslim believers, on a daily basis. The entire infra-structure of exploitation of faith of simple believers, is a sham founded on the raw ambition of one person fourteen centuries ago, who secretly pursued a completely secular ambition of becoming an oligarch and followed through by creating a religion and used its followers to accomplish his goal.

Muhammad claimed to have received the oral-dialectal revelations from Allah, through Archangel Gabriel. Those oral revelations were compiled and converted into literary Arabic two centuries later, in a book-form called "Quran". This book is treated by Muslims as Holy Scripture, 'divine' words of Allah. **We have now determined analytically that the Creator of 'revelations' was none other than Muhammad himself. Expressed in today's lexicon, Muhammad just used 'Allah' as his virtual 'pen-name'.** Muhammad designed the 'divine' revelations as a smokescreen, operating from behind it as its secret operative force

The two holiest shrines of Islam ("Sanctum Sanctorum") i.e., Kaaba in Makkah, and the Grand Mosque' Masjid-e-Nabvi' named after Muhammad, along with the tomb of Muhammad in the same premises in Madinah, now stand collectively stripped of any spirituality, reverence, or holiness, for serious students of history. The organization of 'Quranists', founded in 1977 in Egypt by learned scholars of Quran, and sheikhs of Al-Azhar, also consider Muhammad's grave as an insignificant heap of dirt for followers of 'Quranist' Islam.

Muhammad availed all possible opportunities to build his personal brand as the greatest ever icon, presenting himself in the persona of a Prophet of the Almighty God. He composed hundreds of messages in his native dialect of Arabic as 'words from Allah' to resolve problems as and when they arose over 22 long years of his ministry. The prophethood was an effective tool to aid and abet him in accomplishing his goals which can be identified as follows.

Uniting infighting tribes, mired in blood feuds.

Raising a unified army, after establishing solid unity.

Using that unified army under his command to conquer dissident tribes and become an autocrat Ruler of the Arabian Peninsula.

Satiating his humongous lust for young girls.

Exterminating personal opponents whenever necessary.

CHAPTER 4

Details Of Pre-Existing Religions In the 7th Century Arabia

How religions emerged and got promoted by different demagogues in different eras of the distant past, beginning as a conviction, then gradually evolving into an organized religion, has been mentioned in passing in the earlier segment of the book. Now is time to elaborate this aspect a little more, thereafter we can delve into the description of religions which prevailed in the Arabian Peninsula at the dawn of Islam in the early 7th century A.D.

The basic features of religion, any religion for that matter, are in fact irrational (eerie, mystical, spiritual, supernatural, and rationally inexplicable), evidently born out of fear of the unknown. Prof Yuval Noah Harari, Jewish by birth and an atheist by choice, is a professor of History and author of International Best Seller "Homo Sapiens' '. He coined the famous term "Imagined Reality" for basic components of all organized cultures and Faiths. That term "Imagined Reality" is self-explanatory and quite apt for explaining the state of mind of believers of organized religions. 'Imagined Reality' is applicable to many other beliefs outside the religious domain too. In a secular approach while discussing non-religious issues, e.g., corporate affairs, politics, geo-politics, the 'imagined realities' in secular affairs also are frequently referred to.

https://youtu.be/zen-m0rMp41

A presumptuous but highly probable explanation for the inception and growth of the imagined realities has been in circulation for a couple of millennia. Here are my analytical determinations on it.

In the early stages of evolution, human species had only one source of information for acquiring awareness. That basic source was the natural set of five organic senses of the human body i.e., sound, sight, touch, smell, taste. The brain (central cognitive organ) processes the input from those five senses (ears, eyes, nose, sense of touch, and tongue for tasting), and enables the person to identify and somewhat distinguish and differentiate between things, both for storing it in his information bank, and for exchanging it with other humans, for expanding their common sphere of awareness. No two individuals, ethnicities, nations, or regional communities, however large or small, are completely alike. Some individuals are comparatively more intelligent, perceptive, insightful, creative, and innovative; have fast comprehension, and above all, possess the uncommon quality of leadership, compared to the rest in the community. For understanding and referring to them in future, let's call those outstanding individuals the 'wise guys' of their community.

In hindsight, we discover that the organic means of awareness i.e., the five natural senses, act as dots, which were situated far apart with gaping holes in-between. Therefore, the initial extent of awareness to figure out the possibilities and probabilities relating to various questions e.g., purpose of presence of human beings on the planet, purpose of life, or reason for existence in the world, with the limited help of organic sensors, was nowhere near wholesome. The huge gaps between the dots needed to be filled with something to connect the dots. The 'wise-guys', mentioned before, filled the gaps with imagined realities to facilitate the understanding of the concepts presented by the 'Wise guys' in each community in their individual time frame. The concepts presented by the 'wise guys' were proportional to the extent and level of cognitive intelligence attained by the community in the ongoing process of cognitive evolution, (say in the ancient, primitive and medieval times). The 'wise-guys' provided support for the veracity of imagined realities with even more imagination. Prominent among such wise guys are:

1.   The founder of Zoroastrianism named Zarathustra Spitama, زرتشت in native Persian, Zoroaster in Greek, (C 523-550 B.C. E) in ancient Iran. The founder of Abrahamic Monotheism named Abraham (c. 1996 BC-1821 BC) and his progeny (Noah, Moses, Jacob, Joseph, Job, David etc.) most of them belonging, reportedly, to the region now called Palestine/Israel, and some to remote parts of the Arabian Peninsula.

2.   Ratnakkardah Valmiki, a.k.a Adi Kavi of India.

The harbinger poet in Sanskrit literature. The epic Ramayana, dated variously from the 5th century BCE to the first century BCE, is attributed to him, based on the attribution in the text itself. He is revered as the first poet, author of Ramayana, the first epic poem. Valmiki is the poet, scholar of the Indian sub-continent, anthologist of the mythological stories, compiled together in a book form as holy scripture of Sanatana Dharma (Hinduism).

3.   Judaism: Preached by Abraham, founder of Monotheism, followed by a long line of his progeny, most prominent being Moses.

4.   Biological parents of Jesus Christ.

Born c. 6–4 B.C.E, Bethlehem—died Circa 0-33, A.D. Jerusalem. Jesus was evidently told by his mother that Lord Almighty was his father. Jesus grew up to an age of approximately 30 years and preached for 2-3 years only. His ministry was curtailed short as he was accused of rebellious conduct against the Jewish Emperor and arrested. Jesus was given a sentence of 'death by crucifixion', around the age of 32-34. Few years later his disciples founded Christianity, the leading religion today on the planet Earth. Interestingly, Jesus Christ himself died young, never married, hence he was not a role model as a husband or father, or a warrior for that matter. One of his disciples St. Paul built him up as God, as well Son of God, and the Forgiver and eraser of all sins of his worshipers.

5.   Arab Paganism.

Polytheism (Idolatry) with obscure origin in antiquity.

6.   Abul Qasim Muhammad bin Abdullah of al-Quresh tribe. Founder of the latest monotheist Deen (Religion) in the Hejaz region of the vast waste land of Arabian Peninsula in the medieval time, about fourteen and a half centuries ago. Contrary to common belief, 'Muhammad' was quite a common name for boys in the Arabian Peninsula, from long before the birth of Muhammad bin Abdullah.

Population in Arabia in the 6th century A.D. consisted of nomadic and sedentary tribes of idolatrous Pagans, and a small segment of monotheist and tri-theist immigrants from the neighboring empires. A detailed account of religions practiced there has been given later in this book. Polytheism, Christianity, Judaism, and Iranian religions were already in practice in the Arabian Peninsula in the 6th and 7th century A.D. Arabs were aware of Hinduism too because some Hindu traders frequently came to the Peninsula to trade and barter the goods brought by boats from India. Other religions were represented to lesser degrees. The influence of the adjacent Roman, Aksumite and Sasanian Empires resulted in Christian communities in the northwest, northeast and south of Arabia. Christianity made a lesser impact, but secured some conversions, in the remainder of the peninsula. Apart from Nestorianism in the northeast and the Persian Gulf, the dominant form of Christianity was Monophysite. (Ref. Robin, Christian Julien, "South Arabia, Religions in Pre-Islamic", in McAuliffe 2005, pp. 8)

A quick glance at the list of religions, followed by a brief description of each, practiced by people in and around the region, would help readers in understanding the circumstances in which a new Faith (Later named Islam) was introduced by Muhammad bin Abdullah of Makkah. It will also explain how Islam was contrived and put together with the components poached from the pre-existing religions described later in this book.

The following two religions and one mythology were already 2500 years old and practiced by a minority in the Arabian Peninsula when Muhammad declared that he is the divinely ordained Messenger of the 'One & Only' Creator of the Universe.

1. Judaism: Followed mostly in the eastern Mediterranean coast. The native name of Judaism in Hebrew is יהודה, Yehuda, "Judah.

2. Zoroastrianism: Followed mostly in the Persian Empire. Zoroastrians call their faith "Mazdayasna".

3. Hinduism: It is an exonym of a mythology, followed almost entirely in the Indus valley and regions east of it in the Indian subcontinent. The native name of Hinduism in Sanskrit is 'Sanatana Dharma' which means the "Eternal way" In addition to the above 3, there were worshipers of the following 3 creeds in the Peninsula.

4. Sabaean Faith: It was an old religion, claimed by its followers to be much older than 3 mentioned before. It had a small and diminishing number of followers. There are only 70,000 now surviving in a remote part of Iraq.

5. Christianity: The youngest religion with second largest number of adherents in the Peninsula, after the majority population of idolatrous Pagans.

6. Arab Paganism: Most of the population in the Arabian Peninsula worshiped deities and their idols which included indigenous animistic-polytheistic beliefs. The above narrative is a bare introduction. A little detailed description of each of

these religions will follow shortly. With the advent of digital media and unstoppable social media, the print medium is undergoing obsolescence. The findings by history investigators are now minimally recorded in print. The new emerging record keeping system is primarily audio-visual in nature. The audio-visual lectures of the highly acclaimed researchers are available on the internet. The videos can be borrowed from prominent libraries, You-tube and prestigious universities of the USA and Europe. The video documentaries of those six religions, showing the basics of those faiths, have been attached at the end of the narrative of each Faith, as a reference for the readers. The descriptions of each are as under:

Judaism:

Judaism is an Abrahamic religion that has its foundation around 3800 years back in the regions of the Middle East, by the eastern coast of the Mediterranean Sea. Prophet Abraham is the first Prophet of Monotheism and the Patriarch of Judaism. Moses is one of the most important figures in Judaism who gave Jews their Holy scripture Torah, the religious Scripture of Judaism. The most important thing in Judaism is following the 613 mitzvot (Commandments) of the Law of Moses.

The followers of Judaism are called Jews. Hebrews, Jews and Israelites are all names of the same people. The name Israelite came from the name of Israel, which was a symbolic proper name of Jacob that extended to his descendants. It is from Hebrew Yisra'el "he that strives with God" as was mentioned as an incident in the book of Genesis. The word Jew came from the name of people who were from the ancient Kingdom of Judah, also in turn the name of one of the sons of Jacob (Judah). Ref: "A History of ISRAEL" from the Bronze Age through the Jewish Wars. Walter C. Kaiser Jr. and Paul D. Wegner. Amazon.

BELIEF:

Jews believe in one God. In the 1100s a Jewish philosopher Maimonides wrote the 13 Articles of Faith which summarized Jewish beliefs. These 13 Articles are: 1- God exists, 2- God is one and unique, 3- God is incorporeal, 4- God is eternal, 5- Prayer is to God only, 6- The prophets spoke truth, 7- Moses was the greatest of the prophets, 8- The Written and Oral Torah were given to Moses, 9- There will be no other Torah, 10- God knows the thoughts and deeds of men, 11- God will reward the good and punish the wicked, 12- The Messiah will come, 13- The dead will be resurrected. These 13 precepts of belief existed in vague and unseparated features, during the time of Muhammad.

Jews believe that God will send a Messiah to save them. The word Messiah (Hebrew Mashiah) means "the anointed one." The Messiah will be a human born as a direct descendant of King David through Judah and Solomon. He will be preceded by Elijah, who will announce his arrival, and there will be an ingathering of Jews to Israel from all corners of the earth. Name of 'One God' is very special and ineffable in Judaism, so Jews do not write it, or write G-D, for instance. The Jews use the word Hashem, meaning "The Name" when they talk about God. Like "Allah" in Islam, Yahweh/Jehovah is the name of God in Judaism. It seems to have originated from the Hebrew word "Haya/Bhayva," which is the verb "to be." in the sense of "the one who is, the existing." Another name of God is Elohim, which means the one strong enough to do everything. The three names (Yahweh, God and also Elohim) are so special that Orthodox Jews use these names only when they pray and read the Torah. When they are not praying or reading the Torah, they say "Hashem" (The Name) or "Eliakim" instead of Elohim.

RELIGIOUS TEXT:

The Sacred book of Judaism is the Tanakh, which is the Hebrew Bible. It contains the Torah, Nevi'im, and Ketuvim. The Torah covers the creation of the earth and the first humans, the Great Flood and the covenant, the enslavement of Hebrews and Exodus from Egypt, wandering through the desert till the death of Moses. The Nevi'im covers the time from the death of Moses until the Babylonian exile, and the Ketuvim covers the period after the return from the Babylonian exile.

Judaism is a fully organized religion with complete codification of Mosaic Law which is contained in their Holy Scripture TORAH, and Mishna-Jot (Oral doctrines and fables compiled in Talmud). The huge corpus of Talmud (38 volumes containing more than ten million words) contains lots of folklore of fabricated fantasies authored by many different rabbis over the centuries. Those folktales are inspirational fiction, and not part of canonized Torah.

The Jewish Talmud, in several ways, is similar to many thousand Traditions (Haditha, plural of Hadith) of Muslims, because the great majority of hadith was concocted by Muslim clergy, out of greed for money and influence, in the Umayyad and Abbasid caliphates, to provide religious cover to questionable orders of the caliphs. The fabricated folklores, contained in Talmud, though, are designed to solidify the belief, interest, and enthusiasm among illiterate Jews as they themselves could not read the canonized text written in Greek and Aramaic scripts. Talmud is not a part of the canonized and divinely inspired holy text of Torah. The illiterate Jews in the 7th century only knew the folkloric version narrated routinely in evening gatherings or at campfires, which was, as stated earlier, fabricated by rabbis over many centuries. Judaism is almost 4,000 years old by now. It requires belief in one Single, unique and transcendent God named Yahweh who is believed by Jews to have created the Universe.

The founder of Judaism is Prophet Abraham. He convinced his people that God (Yahweh) had revealed Himself to him in human form and spoke to him. Abraham was followed by many other prophets in his progeny like Moses, Jacob, Joseph, and others, who like Abraham, claimed that they received and passed on more instructions from God to the chosen Jewish people.

The five books of TORAH, written by Moses, are believed to be the words of God Almighty Himself, told directly to Moses. God made a covenant with Moses that his followers are the chosen people whose menfolk must enter that covenant with God by cutting off the foreskin of penis (circumcision) on the 8th day of their birth. Judaism offers a very comprehensive set of religious laws for individuals and the chosen people collectively, relating to all aspects of life, like protocol of worshiping, dietary restrictions, marriage and divorce, inheritance, funeral rites and burial, puberty, and pre-marital gender relationships.

Judaism says humans have two souls. One is Heavenly, as a tiny part of God's own soul, and the other is an earthly soul which stays with the body and suffers with it. The earthly soul can sin and suffer for it, but not beyond a 12-month period while it goes through a process of cleansing to finally join the Heavenly soul in Paradise. A great deal of Jewish religious observance is centered in the home. This includes daily prayers three times each day - in the morning (Shacharit), the afternoon (Micha), and after sunset (Ma'ariv or Arvit). Synagogues are for congregational prayer and study. On Mondays, Thursdays, the Sabbath, festivals, and High Holy Days.

Synagogue service includes readings in Hebrew from the Torah and the Prophets. The synagogue service can be led by any knowledgeable member of the congregation. However, this function is usually performed by a rabbi, an ordained religious teacher who has studied in a Jewish religious seminary (yeshiva). A rabbi is expected to conduct weekly or daily study sessions for members of the congregation. The rabbi can also be called upon to give informed decisions about the application of Jewish religious law and tradition to daily life. This may include adjudication of personal disputes. If more serious matters and disputes arise - such as religious divorce – they are referred to a Beit Din (House of Religion), which is a Jewish religious court.

Brit Mila

Health permitting, all Jewish boys are circumcised on the eighth day after birth. Practiced since the days of Abraham, the Brit Milah is a physical sign of the Covenant. The circumcision must be performed by a trained and certified mohel, while the baby is held by a selected person (known as a Sandek).

Bar and Bat Mitzvah

Bar and Bat Mitzvah are Jewish coming of age rituals. When a Jewish girl is 12, and a Jewish boy is 13, they become a full-fledged member of the Jewish community with the duties and responsibilities that come with it. On this occasion, the Bar Mitzvah boy is called up to read the Torah portion and the reading from the Prophets for the first time. In congregations where women participate in conducting the service, Bat Mitzvah girls are also called up to read from the Torah and the prophets. The Jews were relatively well to do, proud of themselves being the 'Chosen' people of God; had the most streamlined, codified and canonized religion. They were much respected by all others. They did not marry into other religions and mixed socially with Jews only.

(Ref.:(Audio-video-documentary)

https://www.YouTube.com/watch?v=0VAylWxDQfk&t=51s)

According to the Jewish Faith, the first day of Jewish calendar is the day the Universe was created by Almighty G-O-D or YHWH. That day, according to Jewish faith, is October

7, 3761 B.C.E. Hence the current Jewish year is 5783 which, according to Jews, denotes the age of the Universe.

Zoroastrianism:

Zoroastrianism, although the smallest of the major religions of the world in the number of its adherents, is historically one of the most important. Its roots are in the proto-Indo-European spirituality that also produced the religions of India. It was the first of the world's religions to be founded by an inspired prophetic reformer. It was influential on Mahayana Buddhism and especially on the Abrahamic religions of Judaism, Christianity, and Islam. To the latter three, Zoroastrianism bequeathed such concepts as a cosmic struggle between right and wrong, the primacy of ethical choice in human life, monotheism, a celestial hierarchy of spiritual beings (angels, archangels) that mediate between God and humanity, a judgment for each individual after death, the coming of a Messiah at the end of this creation, and an apocalypse culminating in the final triumph of Good at the end of the cycle of history.

History: Zoroast was the Persian Prophet, on whose teachings the ancient religion of Zoroastrianism is based. The name by which he is commonly known in the West is from the Greek form of his original name, Zarathushtra, which means "Shining Light".

Date of Zoroaster

Scholars differ considerably about the date of Zoroaster's birth. Greek sources place Zoroaster at 6000 years before the death of Plato, that is, about 6350 B.C. Archeological remains in Turfan, China, state that Zoroaster was born "2715 years after the Great Storm," placing his birth at 1767 B.C. The latest dates for his life come from Persian writings that place him 258 years before Alexander, that is, about 600 years B.C. Many other scholars place Zoroaster's birth between 1500 and 1200 B.C. According to Annie Besant in her lectures on Four Great Religions, the Esoteric Tradition dates the beginning of Zoroastrian teachings far earlier than any of those dates. That Tradition is based on two kinds of records. First, the Great Brotherhood has preserved the ancient writings, stored in underground temples and libraries. There are people today and have been those in the past who have been permitted to set eyes on these ancient writings. Second, there are the imperishable records of the Akasha itself.

According to these records, Zoroastrianism and Hinduism are the two oldest religions of our modern humanity. The Iranians, in their first migration into Iran, were led by the great teacher Zoroaster, who belonged to the same mighty Brotherhood as many of the Indic tradition and was a high Initiate of the same Great Lodge, taught by the same primordial Teachers, called the Sons of the Fire. From this great teacher came down a line of prophets, who superintended the early development of the Iranian peoples and all of them bore the name Zoroaster. The Zoroaster the Greeks refer to may have been the seventh Zoroaster in this line of prophets.

Birthplace of Zoroaster

Scholars are equally divergent about the birthplace of Zoroaster. They suggest such locations as eastern Iran, Azerbaijan (south of the Caspian Sea), Balkh (the capital of Bactria, in present day Afghanistan), Chorasmia and Sogdia (in present-day Tajikistan), or near the Aral Sea (in present-day Kazakhstan). Ref: "THE ZOROASTRIAN TRADITION", An Introduction to the Ancient Wisdom of Zarathushtra. Amazon.

Beliefs - Cosmology

In Zoroastrian cosmology, the head of the manifested universe is Ahura Mazda, the "Wise Lord." He is the universal and pervasive source and fountain of all life. But behind or beyond Ahura Mazda is Zurvan Akarana, 'Boundless Time and Boundless Space', the unmanifested absolute from which the manifested Logos, Ahura Mazda, came forth. Ahura Mazda is depicted in the Zoroastrian scriptures as a kind of trinity: "Praise to thee, Ahura Mazda, threefold before other creations." From Ahura Mazda came a duality: the twin spirits of Spenta Mainyu (the Holy or Bountiful Spirit) and Angra Mainyu (the Destructive or Opposing Spirit). The twin spirits are popularly thought of as good and evil, but rather they are two principles that represent all the opposites of life. In her lecture on "Zoroastrianism," Annie Besant has this to say of them: 'Good and evil may be said to only come into existence when man in his evolution develops the power of knowledge and of choice; the original duality is not of good and evil, but is of spirit and matter, of reality and non-reality, of light and darkness, of construction and destruction, the two poles between which the universe is woven and without which no universe can be. . . .

There are two names again that give us the clue to the secret, the "increaser" and the "destroyer," the one from whom the life is ever pouring forth, and the other the material side which belongs to form, and which is ever breaking up in order that life may go on into higher expression. After the trinity of Ahura Mazda and the twin spirits that emanated from him is a sevenfold expression of the divine reality. These seven are called the Amesha Spentas or Holy or Bountiful Immortals, the Highest Intelligences. They are sometimes thought of as archangels and sometimes as aspects of Ahura Mazda himself. These seven mighty intelligences are also guardians of various kingdoms of nature. They are as follows: Ahura Mazda himself. Just as the One Wise Lord is part of a trinity including also the twin spirits of bountiful increase and of destructive opposition, so too is he one of the sevenfold intelligences. The One Lord is present everywhere. Vohu Manah, Good Mind. It is divine wisdom, illumination, and love—the mental capacity to comprehend the next one of the Amesha Spentas, Asha Vahishta. Vohu Manah is associated especially with the animal kingdom. Asha Vahishta, Highest Truth. Often translated as "righteousness," the word Asha is etymologically the same as the Sanskrit term rta, and thus is the dharma or a planned system by which the world exists. Asha Vahishta is the order of the cosmos, the ideal form of the universe. It is associated with the element of fire.

Khshathra Vairya, Desirable Dominion, is the divine strength and the power of Ahura Mazda's kingdom. In theological terms, it represents the Kingdom of Heaven. In human terms, it represents the ideal society. Khshathra Vairya is associated with the sky and with the mineral kingdom. Human beings can realize the power of Khshathra Vairya when they are guided by the Good Mind and Highest Truth. Spenta Armaiti, Holy or Bountiful Devotion, theologically is the attitude of piety and devotion; ethically, it is the attitude of benevolence. It is associated with the element of earth. Haurvatat, Wholeness, is the state of perfection, complete well-being, spiritual and physical integrity. It is associated with the element of water. Ameretat, Immortality, is the state of immortal bliss. It is associated with the plant kingdom.

These seven can be thought of either as cosmic principles or as human principles (the macrocosm-microcosm). It is through human beings' use of a good mind (Vohu Manah), practicing love and devotion (Spenta Armaiti), and following the path of righteousness (Asha Vahishta) that humans can bring about the ideal state of things (Khshathra Vairya), in which ultimately perfection (Haurvatat) and immortality (Ameretat) will prevail. Human beings are not bystanders in life. People are the prime agents through whose actions the promise of Ahura Mazda will be fulfilled. With Ahura Mazda, humans are co-creators of the ideal world. Under the Amesha Spentas are other intelligences called Yazatas, sometimes compared to angels. Together with human beings, the Yazatas are the hamkars or helpers of Ahura Mazda.

Worldview

Zoroastrianism views the world as having been created by Ahura Mazda and as meant to evolve to perfection according to the law or plan of Asha, the divine order of things. The law of Asha is the principle of righteousness or "rightness" by which all things are exactly what they should be. In their most basic prayer, the "Ashem Vohu," repeated every day, Zoroastrians affirm this law of Asha: "Righteousness is the highest virtue. Happiness to him who is righteous for the sake of righteousness." This is the central concept in the Zoroastrian religion: Asha is the ultimate Truth, the ideal of what life and existence should be.

Duality exists as part of manifestation, but human beings also have free will to choose between the dual opposites. As they have the power of choice, they also have the personal responsibility of choosing well. Spenta Mainyu, the Bountiful Spirit, promotes the realization of Asha. Angra Mainyu, the Destructive Spirit, violates Asha. We have a choice between them, between spirit and matter, between the real and the unreal. Personal salvation is attained through making the right choice. And the salvation of the world, called "Frashokereti," is the restoration of the world to its perfect state, one that is in complete accord with Asha. As human beings make the right choices in the lives, they are furthering the realization of Frashokereti.

Life after Death

What happens after death? According to the Zoroastrian tradition, after the death of the body, the soul remains in this world for three days and nights, in the care of Sraosha, one of the Yazatas or angels. During this period, prayers are said, and rituals performed to assure a safe passage of the soul into the spiritual realm. At the dawn of the fourth day, the spirit is believed to cross over to the other world, where it arrives at the allegorical Chinvat Bridge.

At the Chinvat Bridge, the soul meets a maiden who is the embodiment of all the good words, thoughts, and deeds of its preceding life. If the soul has led a righteous life (one in accord with the divine Plan), the maiden appears in a beautiful form. If not, she appears as an ugly hag. This image, fair or foul, confronts the soul, and the soul acknowledges that the image is an embodiment of its own actions and thereby judges itself, knowing whether it is worthy to cross over the bridge to the other side or must return to earth to learn further lessons.

By another account, after the soul meets its own image, it appears before a heavenly tribunal, where divine justice is administered. Good souls go to a heaven called Vahishta Ahu, the Excellent Abode. Evil souls are consigned to a hell called Achista Ahu, the Worst Existence. One account reflects a belief in reincarnation; the other does not.

In the oldest Zoroastrian scriptures, heaven and hell are not places, but states of mind that result from right or wrong choices. Zoroaster spoke of the "druj demana" or "House of Lies" and the "garo demana" or "House of Song," to which souls are sent. Some say that the fall of the soul into the House of Lies means a return of the soul to earth, the realm of unreality or lies.

Burial Practices

Zoroastrianism places great emphasis on purity and not defiling any of the elements of Ahura Mazda's creation. For that reason, traditionally, neither burial nor cremation were practiced by Zoroastrians. Instead, dead bodies were taken to a Tower of Silence and laid out under the sun, where vultures devoured them. At the present time, there is great controversy about this practice.

Fire

Fire is the major symbol in Zoroastrianism and has a central role in the most important religious ceremonies. It has a special significance, being the supreme symbol of God and the divine Life. In Zoroastrian scriptures, Ahura Mazda is described as "full of luster, full of glory," and hence his luminous creations—fire, sun, stars, and light—are regarded as visible tokens of the divine and of the inner light. That inner light is the divine spark that burns within each of us. Fire is also a physical representation of the illumined mind.

Zoroastrian places of worship are called Fire Temples. In them an eternal flame is kept burning with sandalwood and frankincense. The first fire to be lit upon an altar is said to have been brought down from heaven by a Zoroaster with a rod.

When the Parsis fled from Iran and settled in India, fire was again brought down from heaven by lightning to create the sacred symbol of Ahura Mazda. The fire altar where that historic fire is still burning is an important pilgrimage site for the Parsis. Because the fire is such a sacred and holy symbol, the fire temples are open only to Zoroastrians.

Social Practices

Today, Zoroastrians do not proselytize, and consequently Zoroastrians are born to the faith. If a Parsi woman marries outside the religion, her children cannot be Zoroastrians, but if a man marries outside, his children can become Zoroastrians, although his wife cannot. No doubt these restrictions are later aberrations not befitting the lofty ideals and teachings of the religion.

Scriptures

The Zoroastrian scriptures are called the Avesta, and the ancient language in which those are written is called Avestan. That language is closely related to the Sanskrit of the ancient Vedic hymns. The term Zend Avesta refers to the commentaries made by the successors of Zoroaster on his writings. Later, commentaries to the commentaries were written in the Persian language of the Sasanian Empire, which is called Pahlavi. So, the Zoroastrian scriptures are in several languages and their composition spans vast periods of time. Yet they are fragmentary because of the destruction of written texts and the persecution of priest-scholars by foreign invaders. The oldest part of the Zoroastrian scriptures are the Gathas, which are the direct teachings of Zoroaster and his conversations with Ahura Mazda in a series of visions.

The Gathas are part of a major section of the Avesta called the Yasna, a term literally meaning "sacrifice," consisting of texts recited by priests during ceremonies. The Vendidad is a manual in the form of a catechism giving rules of purification and prevention of sins of both commission and omission. The Khordeh Avesta or "Little Avesta" includes invocations with beautiful descriptions of the Yazatas or angelic intelligences. Fundamental Moral Practices: The basic moral principles that guide the life of a Zoroastrian are three:

Humata, "Good Thoughts," the intention or moral resolution to abide by Asha, the right order of things.

Hukhta, "Good Words," the communication of that intention.

Havarashta, "Good Deeds," the realization in action of that intention.

Living these three principles is the way we exercise our freewill by following the law of Asha. These three principles are included in many Zoroastrian prayers, and children commit themselves to abide by them at their initiation ceremony, marking them responsible for entry into the faith as practicing Zoroastrians. They are the moral code by which a Zoroastrian lives.

(Ref.: (Audio-video documentary)

https://www.YouTube.com/watch?v=hl9QgeHdKYk&t=34s)

Hinduism or Hindu Mythology:

Native name Sanatana Dharma – is also 3,500 to 4,000 years old by now – Belief in one Single God 'Brahma(n)'. The 'n' in the end of Brahman is almost silent. Brahma(n) has many other manifestations as different gods with specific names. For this reason, most people consider it polytheism. 'Brahma(n)' has three main manifestations. Brahma (without an 'n' in the end) is the Creator of the universe, Vishnu is the Sustainer, and Shiva is the Destroyer of the Universe. Through these three manifestations the supreme god Brahma(n) operates a never-ending cycle of creation, sustenance, then destruction, repeating the three events, one after the other forever. Brahma, Vishnu, and Shiva together form the Hindu Trinity, Trimurti of Brahma(n). The creator god Brahma made different castes of Hindus in descending order of importance and duties. God Vishnu sustains the Universe every time it is created. Shiva started off as a minor deity, not even mentioned in the Rig Veda. But in the post Vedic literature, the Upanishads, and the great epic, Mahabharata, Shiva climbs higher, so he is now known as the destroyer, healer, afflicter, ascetic and hedonic, God of storms and dance.

(Ref.: Doris Srinivasan, "Vedic Rudra-Siva, "Journal of the American Oriental Society 103/3, 1983; 544-45.)

Ref: "HINDUISM' A Simple Guide to the Hindu Religion, Gods, Goddesses, Beliefs, History, and Rituals + A Hindu Meditation Guide. Crystal Moon. Amazon.

Interestingly, the three member gods of Trimurti are siblings, and their mother is goddess Durga. The biggest annual Hindu festival is "Durga Pooja" which is held as nine nights of celebrations of the victory of Durga over the demon king "Mahishasura" (Buffalo Devil').

Hinduism boasts a diverse collection of sacred writings. Can be summed up as: Brahm satya, jagat mithya Brahma means that reality is the cause of this material world. It always is. It is non changeable and limitless. That which cannot be destroyed. Jagat mithya means that which is impermanent and prone to change in name and form. Gold is Satyam and ornaments are mithya . You can change the design of jewelry but the foundation, the reality of gold stays.

Mitti is Satyam and the earthenware made from clay is mithya. You can change the shape and size of the earthenware, but you can't destroy mitti. So, that which changes name and shape is mithya but can't be destroyed is the reality. Human body is mithya. It grows old, sick and ultimately dies. But the soul lives forever. The jiv atma takes birth again. This is a thing for deep contemplation and study. We have learnt in physics that nothing can be destroyed. Ice changes to water and water changes to vapor. But it exists. Likewise, vapor condenses to water, which solidifies to ice. Only the manifestation changes.

Tatvamasi: Means you are that.

Hinduism believes in the divine manifestation of all that is. Everything that exists is divine. There is nothing but God. That is why everything is worthy of worship.

Everything that exists has five elements:

Bhumi   Earth element

Akash   Space element

Vayu   Air element

Agni   Fire Element

Jal   Water element

All that exists in the universe comprises these five elements. The only thing that makes man superior is the body, mind and intellect tools given to him/her. Because of which man can attain enlightenment and realize himself that he is just a tiny part of the grand scheme and everything that exists on the outside, exists within the human being. The aim is self-realization and rising above the confines of ego thus attaining nirvana (a state of being where one is without agitation and limitations of the mind and is one with Absolute Reality). This is a vast field of study and has no end.

Hinduism is a very concentrated study of Advaita, that is non-dual philosophy. A very deep spiritual study of Hindu seers. But it has all been explained symbolically and poetically hence the need of a guru. The guru first tests and then imparts the knowledge to a worthy seeker. This concept in many ways resembles the sufi practice, in which an accomplished sufi assesses an apprentice candidate for his capability and if the sufi is satisfied, he initiates the apprentice as his mureed, into an arduous training program spanning years. The sufi starts imparting spiritual guidance and training called Tarbiyat to the mureed (like a cadet) to help him to ascend up to higher levels of sufism. But the beauty is that these scriptures can be interpreted according to the state of mind of the seeker. Higher the state of mind, more subtle observations are made.

Therefore, these scriptures are timeless and can be applied by all in whichever mental capacity the seeker tries. Once the mind is polished, then one transcends all limitations, and an introverted mind can make his / her own poetical observations of the Supreme Reality by whatever name one calls God / Allah / Ishwar/ Waheguru. And every religion teaches that God is love. To reach that state of loved one must invoke the divinity within.

Sacred texts of Hindus are classified as either Shruti ("heard," meaning revelation) or Smriti ("remembered," meaning tradition). The former comprises Vedas, the oldest and most authoritative of Hindu scripture, which deals largely with rituals. The Brahmanas are commentaries on the Vedas; and the Upanishads, philosophical and metaphysical texts that have been central to the spiritual development of the tradition. together, the Shrutis form the corpus of Vedic thought and literature. The Smritis are the epics, like the Ramayana and the Mahabharata; mythological texts known as Puranas; theological treatises called Agamas; and philosophical texts are called Darshanas. Despite being a part of the larger Mahabharata, the Bhagavad Gita is widely considered Smriti, as it is believed to be the tradition's most powerful condensation of the broad spectrum of Vedic thought.

Contrary to common misperception, Hinduism was well known in Hejaz in the 7th century as Sanatana Dharma. The word Hindu had not been coined till that time. Hindu traders belonging to a Hindu caste called Vaishyas (traders or shop owners) were the only caste of Hindus allowed under Hindu mythology to travel beyond the shores of Bharat (India). They would take merchandise by boats to the coastline in Hejaz and then go overland by camel express to participate in the trading caravans, bartering goods in Hejaz, Yemen, Syria and Northern Arabia.

(Ref.:(Audio-video documentary)

https://www.YouTube.com/watch?v=xlBEEuYIWwY)

Sabaean Faith:

Sabaean dogma, or Mandaean Religion is written in their holy book "Ginza Rabba," or" The Holy Treasure." The book describes light as fighting against darkness or evil. White and other light tones are the favored colors of Sabaeans. Sabaeans claim their religion came with Adam, the first Man – Believe in one invisible deity - Creator and Governor of the universe.

The Sabaeans are Gnostic and God-Fearing. They performed an annual pilgrimage to Kaaba like Polytheist Pagans, by walking naked around it seven times. They complied with all of the associated rituals of Hajj performed by idol-worshiping Pagans. The Sabaeans also prayed seven times a day and called their prayers 'Salat'. They did ablution for cleansing themselves before offering 'Salat'. Sabaeans performed funeral prayers too which did not include 'Ruku' (bending at waist), or 'Sajdah' (prostration), unlike the ritualistic motions in prescribed sequence, during the routine seven daily 'Salat'. Muhammad poached the style and physical appearance of Sabaeans' Salat in his new Deen. The small community of Sabaeans, living in Iraq now, prays only three times a day, like the Jews. They fasted for five weeks in a year. The fasting was called 'Sawm'. Sabaeans were forbidden to eat or drink anything from before sunrise till after sunset during the five weeks of fasting. Early Muslim converts were mistakenly called 'New Sabaeans' because of rituals like Hajj, Salat and Sawm (Fasting) which were copy-pasted in Islam after minor adjustments by Muhammad and made mandatory for converts to Muhammad's Deen. The Sabaean Arabs practiced certain ritualistic traditions which too were inducted into Sharia of Muhammad's Deen. They did not marry both a mother and her daughter. They considered marrying two sisters simultaneously to be a most heinous crime. Sabaeans censured anyone who married his stepmother and called him 'daizan'. They washed themselves after having sex, clipped their fingernails, shaved pubic hair and performed circumcision of infant boys like the Jews. All of these features of

Sabaeanism was adopted by Muhammad in his Deen, saying that these were divinely revealed to him. Likewise, they cut off the right hand of a thief and stoned adulterers. These punishments too were inducted into Muhammad's Deen and included in Momineen's Shariah.

(Ref.: (Audio-video documentary)

https://www.YouTube.com/watch?v=QM5uRc8DJuQ)

Sabaeans must not be confused with Sabians. The Sabians live in a part of ancient Babylon, north of the Arabian Peninsula. They are Magians and worshippers of stars. Their religion is known as Sabianism. They worship the Sun, Moon, and three other stars as embodiments of divine beings. However, they too must not be confused with pseudo-Sabians of Harran who borrowed the name to protect themself from the threat of extermination by the Caliph al-Ma'mun in 830 C.E.

Christian Beliefs

Christianity is a monotheistic religion based on the life, death, and teachings of Jesus of Nazareth who lived about 2000 years ago in Palestine, then part of the Roman Empire. With 2.4 billion adherents or about one-third of the total world population, Christianity is the largest world religion. Much of Christianity's speedy growth in the early years was due to a Greek speaking Jew and a Roman citizen named Saul of Tarsus, later known as St. Paul (died around 65 AD). He preached and established churches in many parts of Europe and Asia.

Because Christians refused to worship the Roman Emperor as a 'divine entity', Romans severely persecuted Christians until the 4th century. At that time, Emperor Constantine converted to Christianity and made Christianity the official religion of the Roman State and thus started the era of Christians domination. Christians believe that Jesus was born in Bethlehem to Mary, a virgin, and Joseph, her betrothed and husband to be. Christians believe that Jesus was fully human and felt this world in the same way as other human beings of his time. Jesus was persecuted, tortured, and gave his life on the Cross. Christians believe Jesus rose from the dead on the third day after his crucifixion. Christians believe that Jesus Christ is the Son of God and the "Promised Messiah" who saves the world. Christians also believe that there is only one God, but this one God consists of 3 manifestations, God (the Father), God (the Son) and God (The Holy Spirit).

CRUCIFIXION:

Crucifixion is the killing of Jesus on The Cross. Crucifixion is the central part of Christian creed. According to the Gospels, Jesus was arrested and tried by the Sanhedrin (a Jewish judicial body) following his arrest in Jerusalem, and then convicted by Pontius Pilate (the 5th prefect/governor of the Roman province of Judaea, serving under Emperor Tiberius) to be punished, and finally crucified by the Romans. Jesus was removed of his clothes and was then hung between two convicted thieves and, according to the Gospel of Mark, died some 6 hours later. During this time, the soldiers attached a mark to the top of the cross mentioning "Jesus of Nazareth, King of the Jews" which, according to the Gospel of John, was written in 3 languages. They then divided his belongings among themselves and cast lots for his seamless robe, according to the Gospel of John.

RESURRECTION OF CHRIST: Resurrection of Jesus is also the central part of Christianity. The resurrection of Jesus is the Christian belief that God raised Jesus after his crucifixion, as also mentioned in verses of Gospel of Mark 16:5-6, Luke 24:6-7 and Matthew 28:5-6. In Christian theology, the death and resurrection of Jesus are the most significant events, a foundation of the Christian Creed, and celebrated by Easter. His resurrection is the guarantee that all the Christian dead will be resurrected at the 2nd coming of Christ.

ASCENSION:

Ascension is also the central part of Christian creed as mentioned in Book of Acts 1:9, Luke 24:50-51 and Mark 16:19. Ascension is the departure of Christ from Earth into the presence of God in heaven. In the Christian tradition God exalted Jesus after his death, raising Him as first of the dead, and taking Him to heaven, where Jesus took his seat at the right hand of God. It is mentioned in the Book of Acts1:3 and Acts 1:8, that before his Ascension, Christ spent forty days teaching the Apostles and disciples about the Kingdom of God. The Lord informed them that they would receive power from the Holy Spirit to be his witnesses to the ends of the earth. The Ascension occurred at Bethany on the Mount of Olives (Luke 19:29).

RESURRECTION & AFTER-LIFE:

Christians believe in bodily resurrection of all people and that Christians will be entered into eternal life in heaven and non-Christians to hell. Catholics Christians also believe in an intermediate state, "Purgatory". Those who die in a state of grace, but still carry venial sin go to a place called Purgatory where they undergo purification to enter Heaven. There is also a mention of a place called "Limbo" especially for Infants. Limbo was never recognized as a dogma of the Catholic Church but is said to be a place that unbaptized but innocent souls, such as those of infants and/or of individuals who lived before Jesus Christ, because they are not guilty of any personal sin. But they had not received baptism, so still bear original sin. They are generally seen as existing in this state, until the end of time. The attached link for watching a video of a lecture by world renowned religious scholars and academicians throws some significantly thought-provoking light on the holy scripture of Christianity called 'The New Testament'.

https://www.youtube.com/watch?v=zZ5cgQUJnrI

CHRISTIAN DENOMINATIONS:

Divisions and branches In Christianity.

Christianity is divided into four major branches: Catholics, Eastern Orthodox, Oriental Orthodoxy, and Protestantism. Roman or Latin Catholicism represents the continuation of the historical organized church as it evolved over the centuries and is headed by the Pope. However, if you see the narration below, there are other divisions also. The first split was in the 5th century after the Council of Ephesus in 431 AD. The Council agreed Nestorianism (which emphasized the disunity of the human and divine natures of Christ) was wrong. The Roman Catholic Church decreed Jesus to be "two natures in one person. The Assyrian Church of the East did not agree and split from the rest. Later after 20 years at the Council of Chalcedon, again there was a disagreement and the decision of the Council was to excommunicate all those not agreeing, and all such became the Non-Chalcedonian Orthodox, or in general, all these churches are known as Oriental Orthodox Churches. The Oriental Orthodox, also known as Old Oriental churches, acknowledge and recognize the first three ecumenical councils: Nicaea, Constantinople, and Ephesus, but reject the dogmatic definitions of the Council of Chalcedon. The third split happened in the 11th century. It is called the Great Schism. It was mostly based on personal disagreements between the Bishops of Rome and Constantinople resulting in Roman Catholicism and Eastern Orthodoxy respectively. It started when the Patriarch of Constantinople and the Pope excommunicated each other.

Eastern Orthodoxy includes the Greek, Russian Orthodox Churches, and several others. They differ from Catholicism in its refusal of allegiance to the Pope, its emphasis on the use of icons in worship, and the date it celebrates Easter. Other cultural, political, and religious differences exist as well. Christianity was little over six hundred years old when Muhammad announced his ministry. Christians believed in God Almighty as the Creator of the Universe, and Jesus as God's human manifestation.

The majority sect of Christianity called 'Catholics' believe in the Trinity (God, Jesus, and Holy Spirit). Trinitarians believe Jesus is the son of God. Mother of Jesus, Holy Virgin Mary gave birth to Jesus without a father. Holy Virgin Mary herself was conceived by her mother Hanna biologically but free from the blight of "Original Sin," as a miracle of 'Immaculate Conception'. This, the Christians say, was done by GOD the Lord, as Hanna's daughter Mary, having been conceived through Immaculate Conception, was chosen to give Virgin birth to Jesus without a father. (Ref.: (Audio-video documentary)

https://www.YouTube.com/watch?v=LvL3YXa0n2M)

Arab Paganism:

Arabian polytheism, the dominant religion in pre-Islamic Arabia, was based on veneration of deities and spirits. Worship was directed to various gods and goddesses, including Hubal and the goddesses al-Lāt, al-'Uzzā, and Manāt, at local shrines and temples such as the Kaaba in Mecca. Deities were venerated and invoked through a variety of rituals, including pilgrimages and divination, as well as ritualistic sacrifice. Many of the physical descriptions of the pre-Islamic gods are traced to idols, especially in and around the Kaaba, which is said to have contained up to 360 of them.

(Ref.: Robin, Christian Julien, "South Arabia, Religions in Pre-Islamic", in McAuliffe 2005, pp. 92)

All religions preach and promote, by far, the same code of conduct for the ultimate universal goal of peaceful co-existence. The Golden Principle "Do unto others as you wish others do unto you" permeates the essence of most religions. Therefore, all creeds, faiths and religious convictions are essentially headed in the same direction and emphasize righteousness. No religion or creed encourages dishonesty, infidelity, murder, thievery or cheating, back-biting or rudeness, arrogance, or cruelty while dealing with weak and infirm persons. Hence there is commonality of purpose in beliefs and faiths of all brands.

However, the world is a marketplace. The ideologues or wise guys, who initially introduced 'imagined realities' packaged as divine facts, are long gone. But the legatees of them are the clergy with lucrative franchises of different faiths to profit from. Hence the competition is raging on for market-share among the franchisees of different religions except Zoroastrianism and Judaism, and to great extent Hinduism, as they do not provide conversion to outsiders into their religion.

CHAPTER 5

Putting together a Counterfeit Deen.

Details of religions whose components were poached.

The exhaustive research brought forth a surprising fact to light that not a single belief, ritual, edict, or form of worship in Islam, is original or unique to Islam.

Muhammad put together a new Deen by copy-pasting religious edicts, forms ofworship, beliefs, and a complete set of laws and rituals by poaching all those from the preexisting faiths and religions being practiced in Arabia at that time.

This chapter discloses details of how 'each & every' component of Islam was poached from other prevailing creeds which have already been listed under "Religions practiced in Arabian Peninsula in the 7th century A.D.". The bottom line is that Muhammad himself contrived a new Deen.

Critics of Islam, for this reason, call it a counterfeit or synthetic Deen. Here you have the details of how and why Muhammad presented a new Deen as Allah's last and final religion, superior to all prevailing and previous religions, complete with a 'divine Scripture,' which was an orally recited ode (The word Quran literally means 'reciting an ode'). The new scripture (Quran) was claimed by Muhammad to be incorruptible and superior to the Torah of Jews, Avesta of Zoroastrians and Injil (New Testament) of Christianity, in its holiness and spirituality and wisdom.

Synthesis of the counterfeit 'Deen' was done by copying some rituals from one prevailing creed, e.g., mandatory daily prayers from one prevailing religion, Hajj and its associated rituals from another Faith, and so on: thus, making up a combination of complete code of religion for living life as a Momin. Muhammad named those components (copied, borrowed, or replicated, whatever you wish to call them.) as "Arkan-e-Deen" (Pillars of Deen).

The reason for borrowing some features from one religion, and other features from other religions, was not without a purpose. The purpose was to lead the prospective converts belonging to each religion, into developing an affinity, a sense of close connection with the new Deen due to the presence of a particular feature in it which they would find significantly familiar to them, being an important feature in their own current religion.

Those hand-picked features borrowed from other religions were kept as magnets to draw the believers of those religions, whose feature was poached by Muhammad for his new Deen. The new Deen being the latest arrival, and having an important ritual they were already familiar with, and headed by a living prophet, who was allegedly superior to their own previous prophets (like Abraham, Moses, Jesus or Zarathushtra), would coax and encourage the prospective converts to consider adopting Muhammads's deen as a new and improved version of their old and obsoleted religion. The followers of older faiths were warned by Muhammad that rejecting the new Deen would land them in the inferno of Hell for ever and ever, when they die.

One cannot help thinking that the so-called 'divine' revelations from Allah were claimed, only to forestall any doubts in Arabs' mind that Muhammad was putting together a new Deen on his own, or that Muhammad was NOT divinely ordained by Almighty God.

Details of how Muhammad contrived a New Deen

Muhammad had keenly observed and made a careful note of all the edicts and rituals of the prevalent religions practiced in Arabia. Muhammad gathered the information for many years.

The collected information of existing religions included some misinformation (uncanonized parts) which harmed Muhammad's cause to a great extent, as Muhammad was ignorant of the difference between canonized/codified and non-canonized/concocted components). Muhammad had kept collecting the information until he became 40 years old. The blunder occurred due to picking the brains of wrong people e.g., illiterate Jewish and Christian laborers and journeymen like himself, whose company he had had during years of working in trading caravans. Muhammad being an illiterate person, scholars of other religions were beyond his league. He gathered a plethora of knowledge, both accurate and inaccurate, about Judaism, Christianity, Zoroastrianism and Sabaean Faith. He already had all the information about the idol worshiping Pagans, as his clan was among the Pagans, and hence Muhammad grew up among them.

As a major part of his secret plan, Muhammad wished to put together a new Deen (Religion) by combining an assortment of beliefs, edicts, rituals, and religious laws of those other religions. However, the information gathered by him included some grave misinformation, because Muhammad's sources did not include any qualified, knowledgeable clerics and scholars of Old & New Testament, or of the Zend Avesta of Zoroastrians. The misinformation collected from illiterate sources, caused him much grief through loss of his image and ruining his personal brand, in years to come.

While Muhammad was an extremely talented person with extraordinary intelligence and insight, he was illiterate and limited in his knowledge and perception of the world beyond the vast desert of Arabian Peninsula. For instance, Muhammad did not have any idea about the Dravidians of India, the aborigines of Amazon or Australia, the pygmies of remote Pacific islands, the Nordic Vikings, the Red Indians of Americas, or the Eskimos of the Polar regions.

Muhammad worked with a limited amount of information relating to various religions practiced in Hijaz in his time, that too in layman's terms. He was unaware of the fact that he was using an incomplete and unsound knowledge base of illiterates among Jews, Zoroastrians, and Christians. He put together a new Deen, by combining and permuting the components he had collected from illiterate sources, like himself, over the years.

Hence Muhammad's Deen was tailor-made for the psyche of illiterate desert dwellers of Arabia. It related and made sense, within the confines of history, geography and wide-spread illiteracy of Arabian desert, its culture and tribal tradition.

The beliefs and convictions about the invisible gods and deities of each region of the world, are distinct, different, and grounded in the history, geography, culture, and tradition of each specific region. In other words, **one's mindscape is not independent of one's landscape.** Transposing one region's set of beliefs on the perception of the people of any other region is akin to pegging a square pole in a round hole. Muslims have been led to believe in the hoax of 'universality' of Muhammad's Deen due to ignorance and manipulation by their clergy. The cultural fruits of joy and horror grow like the fruits of harvest, according to the nature of soil, climate, rainfall and range of temperature and humidity of a region. An Indian's dream of a fruit of Paradise is a ripe, sweet, and juicy Mango or Lichi or Shareefa (Custard apple) or sweet ripe Guava. In Thailand, it would be a Sapota, Jack fruit or Papaya. It would not be Dates, olives, or figs, as in Arabia, or in Muhammad's Paradise in the Hereafter.... you get the drift. Muhammad did not know that products of Mother Nature vary from one climatic region to regions of other climates.

The whole experience, starting from the innovative creation of Muhammad's Deen, followed by its progression in subsequent generations through its equally ignorant preachers and hagiographers, right down to present day Muslim followers, reeks of a 'blind leading the blind'. That would be a precise description of Muhammad's Deen (Outside the Arabian Peninsula), which got labeled with a nametag of 'Islam', long after Muhammad's death.

Muhammad stuck to his claim of being the 'Exalted Prophet' of monotheistic religions despite facing many years of life-threatening opposition in Makkah. Muhammad claimed that his God Allah was the same as God of Judaism, Zoroastrianism and Christianity. But he rejected all deities and gods of Polytheism idol-worshipers and called their idols useless trash. Polytheists hated Muhammad for this reason and wanted him exterminated. Muhammad endured and surmounted every impediment in his path. We will go over his action plan and how marvelously he accomplished it, in the segment under 'Muhammad'.

Muhammad was highly impressed with the infrastructure of the Jewish faith. In hindsight, Muhammad seems to have planned to outdo and outshine Judaism on all levels, through a new religion put together by Muhammad, as an effective way of achieving his final goal of conquering and ruling the Arabian Peninsula. As a first step he planned to convert the Jewish people followed by others like Christians, Sabaeans and Pagans to his Deen. With that end in mind Muhammad decided to come up with a scripture of divine revelations like Torah and Bible (Gospel of Christians).

Since Muhammad was completely illiterate, revelations he claimed to have received from Allah, through the invisible and inaudible ArchAngel Gabriel, had to be oral and in the only dialect of Arabic lingo he knew. He expected to put it together as the world's greatest ode, to be memorized and recited devotionally. Muhammad had no clue that what he left as a bunch of verses of divine revelations over 22 long years, will be collected and compiled, as much as possible, in a book form, in a literary language, developed a couple of centuries after his death. That compiled contents were rephrased, paraphrased and transliterated to fit into a literary language, which was developed through an evolutionary process spread over 160 years beyond Muhammad's death.

Muhammad chose Allah, out of 360 deities worshiped in Kaaba, to be the God Almighty in Muhammad's new religion; perhaps because Allah is an Arabic word corresponding to Jews' Elah (Ilah) or Elohim (Plural form) in Aramaic, whom Muhammad seemed all set to outshine. The important point here is that Muhammad poached the name of Pagans' Moon God 'Allah', but not any frills or other details of Pagan's Allah, who had a wife Asherah, and three daughters Al-Lat, Al-Uzza and Al-Manat.

Muhammad's Allah was indescribable, with no beginning or end, free of time & space --- an Almighty God who could bring the entire Universe into existence just by willing it. By comparison the God of Jews and Christians took six days to build the Universe. Muhammad emphasized that Yahweh of Judaism, Jehovah of Christianity, and Allah of Muhammad's new Deen are one and the same, the Sole Creator God, whose name in Arabic language is Allah.

Muhammad had set his eyes on the Jewish community, who were held in highest esteem among Arabs, to convert to Muhammad's Deen and become his followers. He was determined to create a convincing impression among the Jews that the "Deen" (Religion) he was preaching was the latest and final version of Judaism itself. His plan was prompted by the fact that the Jews were the most organized, most resourceful, and most respected community, highest in the social classes of Arabs. Muhammad bent backward to convince the Jews that their God whose name Yahweh was ineffable and hence referred to as Iloh or Hashem etc. was the same entity as "Allah" of Muhammad's Deen, to be worshiped and obeyed by the entire mankind. By saying 'mankind', Muhammad was including all other communities too in the list of prospects whom he aimed to convert to his Deen.

The Jewish community was Muhammad's target number one, followed by Christians, Zoroastrians, Sabaeans and the idol-worshiping Polytheist Pagans.

This conclusion stands supported by the fact that Muhammad poached the following features from the Jews for his Deen:

1. Judaism's 'Temple on the Mount' as the 'Qibla' (Direction Muslims face while praying) in Muhammad's Deen.

2. The new Deen featured the circumcision of new-born boys, as in the Jewish tradition.

3. Copied with the dietary restrictions of Jewish doctrine of Kosher/non-Kosher, as 'Halal' and 'Haram' in Muhammad's Deen.

4. Copied 'Adhan' (Call for prayer) from the Jewish Chazahn.

5. Introduced the Arabic equivalent of the Jewish greeting "Shalom Aleichem," and its response 'Aleichem shalom', into the New Deen. Also introduced several other similar notions into his New Deen.

6. "Shema" the Jewish version of Shahada/Kalima, which means that 'there is no God but God', was copied to say the same affirmation in Arabic in Muhammad's Deen.

7. Above all of the aforementioned, it copied the concept of "Wahdaniyah" (Monotheism) from Judaism.

Muhammad had evidently planned to provide some hand-picked features of special attraction targeting each of the other communities, to help them choose Muhammad's Deen, as if the new Faith was the latest version of their own old religion. Later in the book, you will read what were the different tailor-made 'fish-hooks' implanted specifically for followers of each of those religions, to draw them into Muhammad's Deen.

1. Muhammad, for an undisclosed purpose, was also the first person to claim that Kaaba was built by Abraham and Ismail. The religious scriptures of Judaism and Christianity never mentioned Mecca, Kaaba, or Abraham ever being present in Mecca.

2. Muhammad, for the same secret purpose, was the first person to claim that Arbraham was offering his first son Ismail as a sacrificial offering to Almighty Allah, and NOT Isaac the younger son, which is clearly mentioned in the Jewish scripture.

3. Arabs believed for centuries that prophet Abraham was the ancestor of all monotheist prophets. Therefore, Muhammad had to claim that he too belonged to the bloodline of Abraham to make his claim of prophethood, to be above and beyond any doubt. That was Muhammad's scheme/trick to convince everyone in Makkah, that Muhammad too had the lineage and blood-line of Abraham, like other prophets before him.

The afore-mentioned six faiths were in clear focus of Muhammad. He poached some dominant components for his new Deen (religion) from each prevalent religion and used them as building blocks to put together a new Deen. The borrowed components collectively gave Muhammad's Deen the semblance of a full-fledged religion, having all required features, like a core concept, infrastructure, practice methodology, and rules of compliance; all nine yards.

The followers of the above-mentioned six faiths included a vast majority of idolatrous Pagan polytheists. Many idols of different gods/deities of idol-worshiping Pagans were housed in and around Kaaba. Muhammad viewed Pagans, Christians, Jews, Sabaeans and Zoroastrians as the prospective converts for his new Deen.

Evidently Muhammad's scheme and its planned execution were laser-focused on the followers of the said six religions in Hejaz and rest of the Arabian Peninsula, *but not beyond the peninsula.*

Muhammad's perception and thought process was ethnocentric, both fundamentally and in entirety. Muhammad being part of a tribal culture, clearly understood and successfully manipulated the calculus of how tribesmen think and act.

Muhammad's entire scheme of introducing a new religion, with himself as its leading star, worked within the confines of tribalism. He understood and successfully maneuvered the pathology of Arabs' faith in gods and deities. He had no knowledge of, or cared for, or planned for the people in faraway regions outside the Peninsula. After Muhammad's death however, the **four Rashidun Caliphs, and their successors kept on invading lands far beyond the Arabian Peninsula in their greedy pursuit of war booty (Maal-e-Ghanimat) and Jizya (The Annual Tax collected from infidels in the conquered areas, for providing protection), an income too attractive to pass.**

Muhammad declared that the validity of religions brought by his predecessors, stood expired, with immediate effect, due to the divine ordainment of Muhammad as the Final prophet by the same Creator of the Universe. In other words, he declared that all Jewish, Christian and Zoroastrians were required to give up their existing Faith and upgrade it by converting to the latest Deen brought by the latest Prophet, Muhammad bin Abdullah. Muhammad claimed that the Jews, Christians, Zoroastrians, Sabaeans and idolatrous Pagans were now duty-bound to start practicing the fresh and updated Deen preached by Muhammad.

The five foundational pillars of Muhammad's Deen, called "Arkan-e-Deen" (Pillars of Deen), have been harvested from:

Polytheism of idol-worshipers
Monotheism of Judaism
Trinity of Christianity
Duality of Zoroastrianism
Ancient Faith of Sabaeanism

The details of five 'Arkan-e-Deen' and from which religion each feature has been copied from, is charted below:

Arkan-e-Deen (Pillars Islam)	
Components of Muhammad's Deen	Copied From
1. 'Shahada' (Kalima) – Professing that there is no God but Allah'	Shahada has been copied from the Jewish declaration of faith called 'Shema' which essentially means exactly the same as 'Shahada' i.e., "Hear O Israel, Yahweh is our God, is one", Muhammad added an extremely important segment to it,'Muhammad Rasu Allah' to raise his personal brand to stellar height.
	The added segment means "Muhammad is the Messenger of Allah". Without the added segment, Shahada is incomplete.
2. 'Salat' is an offering of 5 times daily mandatory prayers facing 'Bayt al Maqdis' ('Temple of the Mount' in Jerusalem was the 'Qibla'). Qibla was poached from Jews and used for the first 13 years of the New Deen, and then changed to face Kaaba, for reasons explained later. Salaat, as a ritualistic prayer, was made mandatory for Muslims, to be offered 5 times daily while facing the prescribed direction called 'Qibla', after cleansing face, arms and feet with water. The preparatory cleansing, was called "Wudu" (Ablution)	Salat has been copied from the Sabaeans who offered Salat seven times a day. Prophet Muhammad inducted 5 of them as mandatory in Islam, as daily worship of submission to Allah, and incorporated the remaining two Salats as optional prayers for Muslims. Those 2 optional prayers are called "Tahajjud" and "Ishraq". He also borrowed Sabaeans' funeral prayer as a mirror image for prayer in the funeral rites of Muslims. The physical acts of Salat are a variation of how Jews acted while offering their Salat 3 times a day. Muslims' Wudu was also a variation of Jewish and Sabaean wudu.

	Muhammad incorporated, offering of Durood, i.e., acknowledging glory, divinity, and reverence for Muhammad and his progeny, in each and every salat offered by Momineen, 5 times a day. This virtually raises Muhammad to the position of an anthropomorphic God.
3. 'Sawm' is mandatory fasting, from before sunrise till after sunset, for one lunar month called Ramadan, of 29/30 days. Additional one week of fasting, after the month of Ramadan and one day of celebration called Eid, is 6 more days of fasting known as 'Sawm of Sitta Shawwal'. Those are optional fasts for scoring extra points of piety.	Sawm is actually a literal copy of the practice of Sabaeans who fasted every year for one lunar month plus the following week. Sabaeans ate or drank nothing at all from before sunrise till after sunset during fasting.
4. 'Zakat is paying religious tax yearly on wealth @2.5% of the net worth of the individual Momin	Zakat was copied from 'Zakut' of Jews, who are required to pay a portion of the income as religious tax every year. This was incorporated into Deen by the first Caliph Abu Bakr.
5. 'Hajj' is the annual holy pilgrimage of visitation to Kaaba in Mecca, including all of its associated rituals listed in this next column. Hajj is performed, dressed in one piece of unsewn cloth called 'Ihram' ; draped by men only. Women wear their usual modest clothes. The ritual is spread over ten days from the first day of the holy month "Zeeqad" to the 10th day of Zeeqaad.	The annual pilgrimage to Kaaba was regularly performed annually by idol worshiping polytheist Pagans and Sabaeans, for one thousand years before Muhammad incorporated it in his Deen along with its associated rituals. The mandatory rituals associated with Hajj are performed sequentially as described below: 'Tawaf' is the name of the ritual of walking briskly and barefoot around Kaaba seven times, in the anti-clockwise direction, while chanting prescribed prayers. Reverently kissing Hajr-e-Aswad (The Blackstone), installed outside the eastern corner of Kaaba, five feet above the ground, while making the rounds.

	'Saee' is jogging barefoot 7 times, between the two nearby hillocks, named in the early 8th century as 'Safa' and Marwa'.
	'Qiyam-e-Muzdalifa' is Camping and Praying from noon to sunset in the nearby open ground at Mina & Arafat and praying at night in Muzdalifah.
	'Rami al-Jamarat' is symbolic stoning of the devil by throwing pebbles at concrete towers, symbolizing 'Shaitan', built and rebuilt many times since the 8th century.
	Offering an animal sacrifice called Udhaiya.
	'Halq or Taqsir' is shaving of the head, or trimming of hair after completion of all rituals of Hajj, for men only.
	'Tawaf-e-Wida' means back to Kaaba to repeat item (i) above as bidding farewell to Kaaba, as a mark of completion of Hajj (Pilgrimage)

People persuaded and convinced by Muhammad to become 'Momin', had to at first confirm their belief in Arkan-e-Iman, a set of pre qualifying beliefs, before being formally initiated and admitted into Muhammad's Deen. These pre-qualifying beliefs were similarly harvested from numerous prevailing religions, and incorporated into the new Deen for serving the same purpose, i.e., act as strong magnets drawing the adherents of those religions to Muhammad's Deen.

The conclusive analysis of above data is that Islam was not 'Divinely revealed'; that Muhammad designed and synthesized it on his own and offered himself as the central figure for advancing his own agenda. History confirms that Muhammad had remarkable success in his endeavor.

Except for the change of Qibla, none of the edicts and religious rituals of Islam are innovations of Muhammad.

The 'Arkan-e-Iman,' were also copied from other existing creeds, and are as follows:

Arkan-e-Iman (Pillars of Faith)	
Components of Muhammad's Deen	Copied From
1. Tawheed – Belief in the existence and oneness of God (Allah)	This has been copied from Judaism, Sabaean Faith and Zoroastrianism. All of these religions preach belief in Oneness of the Sole Creator, with no other god(s) in existence.
2. Mala'ika – Belief in the existence of angels.	This too has been copied from Judaism, Zoroastrianism and Christianity.
3. Holy Scripture – Belief in the existence of the divinely/intuitively revealed books by Almighty God, which are mentioned below. The New Testament (Injil) revealed to Jesus. The Torah (Tawrait) revealed to Moses. Psalms (Zaboor) revealed to David. "Avesta" revealed to Zarathustra. "Kinzeraba" revealed to Sabaeans. "Quran", as direct words of Allah, communicated to Muhammad via ArchAngel Gabriel.	The belief in Holy Scripture(s) has been copied from Sabaean Faith, Judaism, Zoroastrianism and Christianity.

4. RISALAT – Belief in the existence of Allah's Prophets: Muhammad being the last of them, Jesus the penultimate, and many others sent before him. QIYAMAH – Belief in the Day of Judgement after complete annihilation of the world. On that day, humanity will be brought back to life by Allah, divided into two groups after examining the record of their deeds and intentions: Pious and righteous will be consigned to Paradise, and sinners to Hell. These groups are themselves composed of subgroups based on the quantity of good and bad deeds committed during their life on earth. TAQDEER – Belief in the existence of God's predestination, relating to all good and bad events.	Concept and belief of Risalat has been poached from Zoroastrianism, Judaism, and Christianity.

The above-mentioned "Arkan-e-Iman" are beliefs one must acknowledge and accept before formally becoming a Momin by taking an oath of "Shahada" as his official conversion to Muhammad's Deen.

Beside the above mentioned 'Arkan-e-Deen- and 'Arkan-e-Iman', all other Islamic concepts, detailed below, have been copied and pasted from the same set of other religions.

The Origin of the Other Key Edicts	
Components of Muhammad's Deen	Copied From
1. The Arabic word 'adhan' means "to listen." The ritual serves as a general statement of shared belief and faith for Muslims, as well as an alert that prayers are about to begin inside the mosque. The English translation of the text of Adhan is: God is Great! God is Great! God is Great! God is Great! I bear witness that there is no god except the One God. I bear witness that Muhammad is the messenger of God. I bear witness that Muhammad is the messenger of God. Hurry to the prayer. Hurry to the prayer. Hurry to the Salvation. Hurry to the Salvation. God is Great! God is Great! There is no god except the One God.	This has been copied from Jewish call for prayer which is named Chazzan, meaning calling out, "Hear ye hear ye O Israel! Bless the Lord, the Blessed One!" and the congregation responded, "Blessed is the Lord, the Blessed One forever and ever." The Chazzan then repeats the congregation's response, so as not to seem to be excluding their own selves. In the Jewish Chazzan, there is no mention of Abraham or Moses or any other Prophet of Jews. But Muhammad, as a part of building his godly status included his name in Adhan to remind his followers during daily prayers (Salat), five times a day, that he must be remembered and respected along with Allah.
2. Jannah (Paradise)	Concept of Paradise copied from Christianity, Judaism, and Zoroastrianism.
3. Jahannum (Hell)	Copied from Judaism and Zoroastrianism.
4. Soul (Life Force, whose presence in the body keeps the person alive	Copied from Zoroastrianism and Judaism
5. Khatna – Circumcision of infant boys called 'Khatna'.	Copied from the 'Brit milah' ceremony of the Jews, performed by a mohel ("Professional Circumciser") on the eighth day of the infant's birth as the formal acceptance and execution of Covenant with the Creator as a member of the 'Chosen people'.

6a. Isra (overnight instant journey from Mecca to the 'Temple on the Mount' in Jerusalem where Muhammad claimed he led all previous 124,000 prophets, like Adam, Abraham, Moses, Jesus etc. etc. who although had died many centuries ago, had come down miraculously from Heaven, to offer their worship to Allah in a congregational prayer called Salat (standing, bowing and prostrating, while chanting prescribed passages of Quran), led by Muhammad as their Imam (Lead worshiper), and the previous prophets as followers of Muhammad.	Muhammad himself seems to have picked the idea of his ride named Burraq used for Isra, from a Greek mythological creation named Pegasus, which was well known among Arabs of Hijaz as Greek folklore. According to Ibn Ishaq, the first biographer of Muhammad, 200 years after Muhammad's death, the Burraq transported Abraham when he visited Hagar and Ishmael in Mecca. Tradition states that Abraham lived with Sarah in Palestine, but the Burraq would transport him in the Morning to Mecca to see his family there and take him back in the evening.
6b. Mairaj (Journey from Temple Mount onwards to Heavens on a winged horse called "Burraq", sent from Heavens to fetch Muhammad to meet Allah).	The Mairaj was possibly copied from Prophet Zartusht's claimed travels to heavens on a winged horse sent by God to fetch him, (Also repeated later by a Zoroastrian priest named Arda Viraf) on invitation from God, to see for himself the fate of sinners in Hell, and pious people in Paradise, and narrate it as an eye-witness account to his followers upon returning to earth.
7. Halal and Haraam are the dietary restrictions	Copied from Kosher/Non-Kosher doctrine of Judaism
8. "Salam Alekum" is the word of greeting from one Muslim to another.	This has been copied from a similar greeting used by Jews which is "Shalom Aleichem". Both of these greetings mean "May there be peace with you".
9. "Bismillah" is the holy shibboleth uttered by Muslims before taking any minor or major action, which means "I begin to take this action with the name of Allah".	This has been copied from Jewish beginning of any task by saying "Beshem" or "Beismka" both of which mean "In the name of our Lord"
10. "Allah o Akbar" is a battle cry of the Muslims	Copied from "Deus Vult", (God wills it) battle cry of Roman Crusaders

My purpose for describing the fundamentals of other religions was to point out the original sources of the essential components of a new make-believe Deen. It would be stating the obvious that this synthesized Deen is the brainchild of Muhammad as a part of his mission to unite all Arabs under his command to fight and occupy the entire Arabian Peninsula as a territory ruled by Muhammad. Allah, Gabriel and revelations were mere facades to shore up the credibility of the new Deen, in the gullible and medieval brains of the largely illiterate Arabs of the seventh century..

To give an idea of what was extracted by Muhammad, from (1) Judaism, (2) Zoroastrianism, (3) Christianity, (4) Idol-worshiping Paganism, and even (5) Sabaean Faith, I have already given a synopsis explaining how all components of Muhammad's Deen had been poached by him from the pre-existing religions.

The Quran does not prescribe five daily prayers. One View is that they were borrowed from Persians (Ref.: Goldziher, ZDMG. 53 (1899), p. 385; Jewish Encyl., 'Islam', p.653).

The other view is that it is derived from the five prayers of Yom-kippur'. Another view confirms that Muslim prayers are replicas of Sabaean and Haneefs' daily prayers.

The Quran became appealing and a lot more appealing to many Arabs, after adopting existing Arab rituals in its legislation. Jewish prayers were three a day (6:11). In the Mecca period, three prayers a day were ordained in four passages (Ref.: Quran 11:116, 17:80 f., 50:38 f., 76:25f.) Like the Jews, Muhammad said a man must pray as often as he can. It may be curtailed in times of danger (Ref.: Quran 4:102), as in Mishna (ber. Iv, 4). The prayer must be said loudly (Ref.: Quran 17:110), as in Erub. 64a and Ber. 31a. A drunk man must not pray as in Ber ibid 4:46. Jewish law ordained, 'Grace before meal'. Muslims must say Bismillah (in the name of God) before meals (Lane, 'Manners and Customs', I, 183). Pagans offered tahlil (The ritual of making it 'Halal') over slaughtered animals. Muhammad ordered that too and, Eat of the lawful… Good food… thank the bounty of your Lord" (Ref.: Quran 16:115, 2:167, 5:6, 6:118 ff, 22:35 ff).

Mosque (masjid) is an old Aramaic word, common in Nabataean inscriptions, poached by Muhammad, to name the place of congregational prayers. Service in the mosque consists of prayer, reading from the Quran and an address by the Imam, part of which relates to existing conditions, is like the service at the synagogue. After Muhammad passed on, the prayer was given the more elaborate Christian form, especially after Muslims got control of Syria, Egypt, and Mesopotamia (Ref.: Becker in `Islam', 3, 384). Ramadan was probably adopted from Christian Lenten, though abstaining from food and drink from sunrise to sunset is Jewish and Sabaean. Beginning of a new day (Ref.: Quran 2:183) in the month of fasting is defined as "When a white thread can be distinguished from a black thread" as in the Rabbinical in the Mishna (Ber 1, 2), where it refers to the uttering of Shema. Permission for a man who is not well or traveling to keep fast another time is the same as 'little Passover' (Num. 2:180 0. The fast on the tenth of Muharram (Lane, 'Manners and Customs', II 148 f.) came about after Muhammad. Ashura is Aramaic and the fast coincided with the Jewish fast.

The Social Legislation:

The duty of the child and man to revere his parents was a core principle of the Arab family. But Muhammad turns to the Hebrew tradition for authority. In 17:24, "…that you should do good to your father and mother". One of the ten Commandments, the fifth was given special regard by the Jews, "Honor thy father and mother, "In Lev. 19:3, mother is placed before the father, in order with the environment of Palestine rather than Arabia. The Quran (31:13; 46:14) cites discomfort of pregnancy, the pain of childbirth, thirty months of nursing and care thereafter, to give precedence to the mother. Children must obey the parents (Beidawi's comments on Surah 4:35). The Talmud, Yebamoth 5 b, 6 a, a son must not obey a parental command if contrary to... divine ordinances. So does the Quran, "If your parents urge you to join...worship of other gods, do not obey them (29:7, 31:14)".

One of the five 'pillars of Islam' is alms giving; the practice is recognized in all civilized and semi-civilized people. But the terms used for it by Muhammad are borrowed from North-Semitic norms. Zakat is Aramaic ...Hebrew.... 58:14 distinguishes between zakat and sadaqa. Jews placed great value on alms giving (Daniel 4:24; the book of Tobit 4:7). Funds for support of the poor were voluntary at first, later made compulsory. Contribution to Muslim funds was essential from the very beginning, for the poor, for peaceful conditions and war. A part of war booty was assigned to the common fund (8:42). Kethuboth 50 a, "...not spend more than the fifth part (of property in charity)". The first prophet to legislate on part of the state in property was Joseph, "made it a statute in the land of Egypt...that Pharaoh should have a fifth part (Gen. 47:24-26). A fifth part of the wealth acquired by the state was to be handed over to 'Allah and his prophet.

"An eye for an eye and a tooth for a tooth" was accepted in most of the ancient world. In the early Semitic laws, Hammurabi Code, and the Law of Moses. Quran Verse 49, Sura 5:48, its source is believed to be the Torah, "We prescribed...life should pay for life, eye for eye, nose for nose..." The Quranic Kaffara (atonement) reminds of Ex. 21:30 in Mechita which is applied by Rabbi Isaac for minor injuries. Muhammad allowed payment instead of revenge, but not in case of deliberate murder. The law concerning Killing of a Muslim by another Muslim is based on ancient Arab custom. The Rabbis tended towards a milder interpretation of the law as they well realized that retaliation would keep the door of revenge open (Babba Qamma 83 b). Muhammad allowed payment... for every injury including murder...advised his followers to forgive...but the law of retaliation stayed in place

(Bokhari, ed. Krehl, II, 203 f.). On trade and business, questions such as-how to treat debtors, should Muslim charge interest from other Muslims on debt, could trade be pursued on Friday etc. had to be answered and Muhammad borrowed from Hebrew laws. Muhammad ordained written contracts with two male (or four female) witnesses in civil as well as in criminal cases (Quran Sura 2:282), though in ordinary bargains and loans, nothing in writing was required (Quran 2:283).

Dealing with delinquent debtors was difficult. They always resisted and their triumph was celebrated (Hamasa, ed. Cheikho, pp 263). Deuteronomy 15:1 f cancels all debt in seven years. The Quran (2:280), "If the debtor is in straitened circumstances...wait until easier times, but to remit debt as alms is better for you,". But in actual practice, they followed Hebrew usage, the debtor may be imprisoned (cf. Matt. 5:25), work in exchange, but could not be made a slave. As in Jewish law, a Muslim may not charge interest from a fellow believer (cf. 2:276-279 with Ex. 22:25 and Deut.23:19). As to business on Friday, Muhammad was closer to Christians, not like the Jewish Sabbath, it must cease only during the Friday service (Quran 62:11). On marriage, concubines, divorce, adultery, family relations, the main influence was of ancient Arabic practices. Quran Sura 4:26 gives a list of those relatives whom one may not marry, 24:31 in whose presence women may be unveiled agrees with Lev. 18:6-18. Muslims may marry Christian and Jewish women, without conversion to Islam but not pagan women. With slave women, the law is nearly the same as in Deut. 20:10-14. The law of divorce in Islam vastly favors men, man's dissatisfaction with his wife. Quran Sura 2, 226 is like Deut. 24:1; the right to divorce given only to men. The period of waiting after divorce is three months (Quran Sura 2:228; the Mishna, Yebamoth iv, 10), for giving suck to the baby two years (Quran Surah 2:233; cf. Kethuboth 60 a). Adultery is severely punishable, as generally in the ancient world. Quran prescribes flogging (Quran 4:30), the Mishna, Kerithuth ii, forty stripes for slave females, Quran raises it to fifty and for free men and women it is twice as many (Quran 24:2).

The earlier Quran Surah 33, "If a man and a woman of full age commit the crime...stone them relentlessly. The Sura was later abrogated. New Testament John 8:3-5, scribes say to Jesus, "This woman has been taken in adultery... Moses commanded us to stone such...what...sayest thou ". They know Mosaic law does not say so; has the verse been removed from the Pentateuch as in the Quran? The passage from John has also been removed from the Gospel. The emphasis on the care of orphans in Islam resembles that in the Old Testament. Muhammad elevates the status of women to much higher than Arabs did. Pagan Arabs regarded daughters as more inferior to boys than Jews did. Muhammad stopped the practice of burying newborn girls alive. Pagan Arabs had excluded daughters, widows, and other female relatives from inheriting any part of family property. In the Hebrew law the incident of the daughters of Zelophedad, Num. 27:1 ff., and the legislation in vss.8-11 specifying the successive heirs of one who dies leaving no son. The order of succession given in the Quran is the same as in Hebrew law. But Muhammad goes further in permitting the female relative to benefit in Quran Sura 4:14-15 and vs. 175. The sons and daughters of a female slave if acknowledged by the father may inherit in like manner.

The Semites have always treated slaves leniently as their laws from the code of Hammurabi bear witness. Among Muslims more than in the Jews the slave's religion was important in his treatment. A slave who had accepted circumcision shared in certain Jewish religious privileges. In a Muslim house the slave was very likely to be a Muslim though there was never lack of harsh and barbarous treatment, yet undue severity was the exception among both Muslims and Jews.

Muhammad borrowed laws dealing with food and drink from the Jews but conditions in Arabia required some differences and Muslim laws superseded the laws of Israel. In 6:147, he specifies,

"To those who were Jews we forbade everything that has a solid hoof: and of cattle and sheep we prohibited the fat, save that which is inside their backs or their entrails, or attached to the bone". He insists that these prohibitions were of the nature of the punishment (4:158, 3:87). In Quran 2:167, 6:146 and 16:116 Muhammad enumerates things forbidden to Muslims: flesh of what is found dead, blood, swine's flesh, food offered to idols. 5:4 adds to this list, "What has been tangled, killed by a blow or a fall, or by goring; that of which wild beasts have eaten and whatever has been slaughtered on heathen altars". Muhammad in Quran 2:168, 5:5, and 16:116, makes the exception that if a man is forced to eat some of those things driven by his sore need of food, it is no sin. The Talmud says the same.

The Islamic prohibition of drinking any intoxicating beverage has an interesting antecedent. The ancient Hebrews looked upon drunkenness as one of the serious evils. The story of Noah is an early example. The Hebrew ideal, however, was always the temperance by man's exercise of self-control. "Wine that makes the heart of man "is classed as a blessing. Such a saint as Rabbi Meir might become intoxicated without damage to his reputation. Fitz Simmonds, p. 1255: "These two aspects of wine, its use and its abuse, its benefits and its curse, its acceptance in God's sight and its abhorrence, are interwoven into the fabric of the [Old Testament] so that it may gladden the heart of man (Ps. 104:15) or cause his mind to err (Is. 28:7), it can be associated with merriment (Ec. 10:19) or with anger (Is. 5:11), it can be used to uncover the shame of Noah (Gn. 9:21) or in the hands of Melchizedek to honor Abraham (Gn. 14:18).... The references [to drinks that can contain alcohol] in the [New Testament] are very much fewer in number, but once more the good and the bad aspects are equally apparent....

In Quran surah 16:67-71 Muhammad gives a list of the special blessings given by God to men: water, milk, wine, and honey. Surah 47:16 assures the believers that they shall have plenty of wine in Paradise. But soon after this approval begins to be qualified as in Quran 2:216 and 5: 92f. In the later years of his career the prohibition was at first quite mild. Quran 2:216, "They will ask you about wine, and al-Maisir (a form of gambling), "Say: in them both is sin and profit to men; but the sin of both was recognized as imperfectly effective, " 0 you believer! Come not to pray when you are drunk, until you know what you are saying". This injunction may have had its origin in the Prophet's experience (reportedly they were talking and disturbing the sermon he was giving) or have been borrowed from the Mishnaic law, Ber. 31 a. One of the last Surah in Quran 5:92f has a much more decided sound, "0 you who believe! Verily wine and al-Maisir are an abomination of Satan's work; avoid them then. Satan desires to put enmity and hatred among you by wine and al-Maisir, and to turn you away from God ...After the Prophet's death the prohibition was sharpened specially under Caliph Omar.

Zoroastrian and Sabian Elements in Islam

Arab and Greek writers tell us that Persians exercised great influence over certain parts of the Arabian Peninsula.

By 612 C.E., 2 years after Muhammad declared him-self a prophet, the Persians had overrun Syria, Palestine, and Asia Minor. The Arabs in Muhammad's time were in 'The Time of Ignorance', while the Persians had been civilized for long. The Quran tells us ...legends...poetry of Persian... had great popularity among the Arabs...Muhammad was accused of...borrowing...imitating them. Ibn Hisham said "Muhammad had gathered an assembly... read the Quran to them, warned them...Nadir bin Ali Harith... By God Muhammad is not a better storyteller than I am".

The Persian fables are the ascension to heaven of Arda Viraf... Zoroaster before him, description of Paradise, Bridge of Chinvat... must have been known to Arabs. Abu'l Fida, informs us that, early in the seventh century of the Christian era, Khusran, or as the Arabs called him, Kisra' Anushiravan invaded the kingdom of Hirah on the banks of the Euphrates, dethroned the king Hirah, and placed upon the throne in his stead a creature of his own, named Mundhir Mai's Sama. Anushiravan, not too long after, sent an army into Yemen, under a general called Vahraz, to restore the Yarnanite prince Aba Saif to the throne of his ancestors. But the Persian force remained in the country, and its general ultimately himself ascended the throne.

Abu'l Fida goes on, the princes of the family of Mundhir who succeeded also ruled over the Arabian 'Iraq' but were merely governors under the kings of Persia. In Yemen four Abyssinian rulers and eight Persian princes held sway, before it acknowledged' Muhammad's sovereignty. There was much intercourse, even before Muhammad, between the North and West of Arabia and Persia. Naufal and Muttalab, brothers of Muhammad's great-grandfather, and the leading chiefs of the Quraish, made a treaty with the Persians, so the merchants of Makkah were permitted to trade with 'Iraq and Fars' , the ancient Persia. In the year 606 C.E., a party of merchants headed by Abu Sufyan reached the Persian capital and were received into the king's presence. By 612 C.E., when Muhammad declared himself a prophet, the Persians had overrun Syria, Palestine, and Asia Minor. By the year 626 C.E., the Byzantine Emperor Heraclitus had begun to reconquer the lands lost to the Persians who were obliged to sue for peace. In consequence, Badzan, the Persian governor of Yemen, was obliged to submit to Muhammad and agree to pay tribute (628 C.E.,). Within a few years of the Prophet's death, the armies of Islam had overrun Persia and converted the great mass of its people, most of them by the sword. The Arabs, in Muhammad's time, were in an unenlightened condition; in fact, their own writers speak of pre-Islamic ages as 'The Times of Ignorance." The Persians, as we learn from the Avesta, from the cuneiform inscriptions of Darius and Xerxes, from the still existing ruins of Persepolis, and from the evidence of Greek writers, had been highly civilized for a long time. It was only natural that the intercourse with them should enlighten the Arabs. The accounts of Arab historians and the Quran tell us that the romantic legends and the poetry of the Persians had obtained a very considerable degree of popularity among the Arabs. Some of these tales were so well known that Muhammad was accused by his enemies of having borrowed or imitated them in the Quran. Ibn Hisham says that one day when Muhammad, "Had gathered an assembly ... summoned them to God ... and read the Quran ... warned them what would befall the nations that remained destitute of faith, when Nadir bin Al Harith, who had followed him into haram, rose up and told them about Rustam the strong and about Isfandiyar and the kings of Persia and went on, "By God! Muhammad is not a better storyteller than I am, and his discourse is nothing but the Tales of the Ancients ... composed them just as I have composed them." On this God sent down the verse, "And they have said, Tales of the Ancients hath he written down ... are recited to him morning and evening. Say thou, He who knoweth what is secret in the heavens and the earth hath sent it down verily He is forgiving and merciful." And on his account, this also came down.

"When verses are recited to him, he hath said, Tales of the Ancients!" And this also descended for his benefit, "Woe unto every sinful liar that heareth God's verses read to him; then he persisted in being proud, as if he did not hear them! Therefore, give him good news of a sore punishment" Muhammad's answer to the charge was not altogether satisfactory to his audience. The stories of 'Rustam and Isfandiyar and the Kings of Persia' referred to by Nadir, have survived and are among those which, some generations later Firdausi, the most celebrated of the epic poets of Persia, learnt from the collection which he tells us a Persian villager had made, 'The Shahnama by Firdausi. But the authority of a work, which is later than Muhammad's time, might not be deemed sufficient. The Avesta and other books of the

Parsis or Zoroastrians offer information which cannot be called into question on the ground of antiquity. The Arabs had heard of 'Rustam and Isfandiyar' and are unlikely to have been quite ignorant of the story of Jamshid. The Persian fables regarding the ascension to heaven of Arda Viraf and of Zoroaster before him, their descriptions of Paradise and the Bridge of Chinvat and tile tree Hvapah, the legend of Ahriman's coming up out of primeval darkness, and many other such tales, must have been known to the Arabs. So, it was natural that Muhammad would have made some use of them, as he did of Christian and Jewish legends. Some of them were part of the religions and intellectual heritage of both Persia and India and when the Persians and the Hindus left their ancient common home - the Airyanem Viejo near Herat, to go separately to Persia and India, and were carried away in the minds of both peoples.

The 'Night Journey' is thus referred to in a verse " (Surah XVII., Al Asra' - also called Surah Bani Israil' - 1) - "Praise be to Him who caused His servant to journey by night from the Sacred Mosque to the Farther Mosque, whose enclosure We have blessed, that We might show him of our signs. Not all the commentators on the Quran are in agreement with regard to this verse, some opine that Muhammad merely dreamt that he made the journey, others take it in a literal sense and add many details from Tradition, and still others explain it in a mystical or figurative sense. Ibn lshaq giving the authority of the traditions, tells us that Muhammad's wife 'Ayesha used to say, "The body of the Apostle of God did not disappear, but God took his spirit on the journey by night."

According to another Tradition Muhammad himself said, "My eye was sleeping, and my heart was awake." The celebrated mystical commentator Muhiyyu'd Din accepted the whole account only in a metaphorical sense.

It is certain that a great number of Muhammadan commentators and Traditionalists believe that Muhammad actually went from Mecca to Jerusalem and also visited the heavens. They give long accounts, of deep and abiding interest to Muslims, regarding what he did and what he saw. The main features of this tradition can be traced to earlier legends and Zoroastrian sources.

Quoting Ibn Ishaq's account which is the earliest that has reached us as given by Ibn Hisham, his editor, "Muhammad, we are informed, asserted that Gabriel came and awoke him twice to go on the 'Night Journey,' but he fell asleep again- Then he continued, "Accordingly he (Gabriel) came to me the third time: then he touched me with his foot, and I sat up. He seized me by my arm, and I stood up with him. He then sent forth to the door of the Mosque: and lo! a white animal, (in appearance) between mule and an ass; on its flanks were two wings, ... When I approached it to mount it, it stepped back. Accordingly, Gabriel placed his hand upon its mane and said, "O Buraq, art thou not ashamed of what thou art doing I swear by God, O Buraq, there never mounted thee before Muhammad a servant of God more honored with God than he is". "Accordingly (Buraq) became so ashamed that he poured forth sweat. Then he stood still till I mounted him."

Al Hasan in his Tradition has said, "The Apostle 0f God went, and Gabriel went with him, until he reached the Holy House (Jerusalem) ... There he found Abraham and Moses and Jesus amid a band of the prophets ... the Apostle of God acted as the leader (Imam) of them in worship, and prayed with them, thereupon (Gabriel) brought two vessels, in one of which there was wine and in the other milk. Accordingly, the Apostle of God took the vessel of milk and drank of it and left the vessel of wine. Therefore, Gabriel said to him, "Thou hast been guided to Nature and thy people have been guided to Nature, O Muhammad, and wine is forbidden you." Then the Apostle of God departed, and when it was morning, he went to the Quraish and gave them this information. They said ..., "By God! This matter is clear: by God! a caravan takes a month from Mecca to Syria, and a month in returning, and does that fellow Muhammad go within one-night time and come back to Mecca?'

Later traditions amplify the journey considerably, however, professing to give the account which the reciter declared came from Muhammad himself. In the Mishkat Ul Masabih the following story is given, "The Prophet of God related... While I was asleep... lo! a comer came to me: then he opened what is between this and this... and he took out my heart. Then I was brought a golden cup full of faith. My heart was washed, then it was replaced, then I came to myself... Then I was brought an animal smaller than a mule and taller than a donkey, and white: it is called Buraq, and places its front feet at the far end of its range of sight. Then I was set upon it and Gabriel carried me off until I came to the lowest heaven. He demanded admittance. It was said, 'Who is that?' He said, 'Gabriel' It was said, 'And who is with thee?' He said 'Muhammad.' It was said, 'And was he sent for?' He said, 'Yes.' It said, welcome to him, and very good is his coming.' Then it opened. Accordingly, when I entered, lo! Adam was there. Gabriel said, "This is thy father Adam, therefore salute him." Accordingly, I saluted him, and he returned the salute. Then he said, 'Welcome to the good son and the good prophet.".

The story goes on with repetition of much the same account. In the second heaven Muhammad was introduced to John the Baptist and Jesus, in the third to Joseph, in the fourth to Idris, in the fifth to Aaron, in the sixth to Moses. The latter wept, and when asked why, replied that the cause of his tears was the knowledge that more of Muhammad's followers than of his own people would enter Paradise. In the seventh heaven Muhammad met Abraham, and the usual greeting took place. "Afterwards I was carried aloft to the Sidratul Muntaha, and lo its fruits were like the pots of a potter, and lo its leaves were like the ears of an elephant. He said, "This is the Lotus or the Boundary." Then lo! four rivers, two interior rivers and two exterior rivers. I said, "What are these two, O Gabriel?" He said, "The two interior ones are two rivers in Paradise, but the two exterior ones are the Nile and the Euphrates."

In the popular works from which modern Muslims obtain their knowledge, the account of the Mairaj is even more full of marvels. When he had reached the Lotus of the Boundary, beyond which Gabriel dared not advance with him, the angel Israfil took charge of Muhammad and led him to his own realm, whence the prophet advanced to the very Throne of God, being bidden by God's own Voice not to remove his sandals, since their touch would honor even the court of God. After a few more details, we are told that Muhammad entered behind the veil, and that God said to him, "Peace be upon thee, and the mercy of God, and His blessing, O Prophet."

It is very possible that the legend as related by Muhammad himself was based upon a dream; if we consider Surah LIII., 13-18, to be of later date, it does not seem to have any account of an ascension. The narrative contained in the Traditions, on the other hand, enters into very precise details regarding the Mairaj or ascent. The story may have derived elements from many quarters, but it seems to be based mainly upon the account of the ascension of the Zoroastrian priest Arta Viraf contained in a Pahlavi book called "The Book of Arda Viraf," which was composed, according to the Zoroastrian, in the days of Ardashir Babagan, King of Persia, some 400 years before Muhammad's Hijrah.

Finding that the Zoroastrian faith had to a great extent lost its hold upon the minds of the people of the Persian Empire, the Magi priests determined to support by fresh proof the restoration of the faith which the zeal of Ardashir had undertaken to carry out ... they selected a young priest of saintly life, and prepared him by ... ceremonial purifications for an ascent into the heavens, ... he might see what was there and bring back word whether it agreed or not with the account contained in their religious books ... When this young Arda Viraf was in a trance, his spirit ascended into...the heavens under the guidance of an archangel named

Sarosh, and passed from one storey to another ... ascending until he reached the presence of Ormazd himself. Arda Viraf had thus beheld everything in the heavens ... the happy state of the inhabitants, Ormazd commanded him to return to the earth as His messenger and to tell the Zoroastrians what he had seen. All his visions are fully related in the book which bears his name.

A few quotations to show how it served as a model for the Muhammadan legend of the ascent of Muhammad. In the Arda Viraf Namak (cap. vii, 4§§ 1-4) we read, "And I take the first step forward unto the Storey of the Stars, in Humat ... And I see the souls of those holy ones, from whom light spreads out like a bright star. And there is a throne and a seat, very bright and lofty and exalted. Then I inquired of holy Sarosh and the angel Adhar:

What place is this, and who are these people? "It should be mentioned that the 'Storey of the Stars' is the first or lowest 'court' of the Zoroastrian Paradise. Adhar is the angel who presides over fire. Sarosh is the angel of obedience, and is one of the 'Eternal Holy Ones', 'Amesha-spentas later Amshaspands' or archangels of the Zoroastrian faith. He guides Arta Viraf through the different heavens, just as Gabriel does Muhammad.

Arda Viraf reached the Storey of the Moon, or the second storey, and then the Storey of the Sun, which is the third of the celestial mansions. He was led on and on, through every one of the heavens, until he was introduced into Ormazd's presence, and had the interview which is detailed in cap. xi in these words, "And finally up rose from his throne overlaid with gold the archangel Bahman, and he took my hand and brought me to Humat and Hukht and Hurast, amid Ormazd and the archangels and the other holy ones and the Essence of Zoroaster the pure-minded... and the other faithful ones and chiefs of the faith .... And Bahman said, "This is Ormazd." And I wished to offer a salutation before Him. And he said to me, "Salutation to thee, O Arda Viraf!

Welcome! Thou hast come from that perishable world to this undefiled bright place." And he commanded holy Sarosh and the angel Adhar ``Carry off Arda Viraf visited Paradise and hell, and what he saw in each. After his visit to hell the tale goes on, "At last holy Sarosh and the angel Adhar took my hand and brought me forth from that dark, dreadful and terrible place, and they bore me to that place of brightness and the assembly of Ormazd and the archangels. I, who am Ormazd, am here. Whoever speaks rightly and truly, I hear and know. Speak thou to the wise ones.' And when Ormazd spoke thus, I remained astounded, for I saw a light and did not see a body, and I heard a voice, I knew that this is Ormazd".

Great is the resemblance between this and the legend of Muhammad's Mairaj. The Zartosht-Namak, a work probably composed in the thirteenth century C.E., relates a legend that Zoroaster himself, centuries earlier than Arda Viraf, ascended up to heaven, and afterwards obtained permission to visit hell also. There he saw Ahriman, who closely corresponds with the Iblis of the Quran?

In Sanskrit also we have similar tales, the Indraloka Gamanam, or 'Journey to the World of Indra' the god of the atmosphere. There the hero Arjuna made a journey through the heavens, where he saw Indra's heavenly palace, named Vaivanti, which stands in the garden called Nandanam. The Hindu books tell us that ever-flowing streams of water the fresh, green plants that grow in that beautiful place, and in its midst, there stands a tree called Pakshajati, bearing a fruit styled' Amrita' (Immortality), of the Greek poets, of which whoever eats never dies. Beautiful flowers of varied hues adorn that tree; and whoever rests under its shade is granted the fulfillment of whatever desire he may conceive in his heart.

The Zoroastrians also have an account of the existence of a marvelous tree, called Hvap in the Avesta and Humaya in Pahlavi, the meaning in each case being possessed of good water,' 'well-watered." In the Vendidad it is described in these words, " In purity do the waters flow from the sea of Puitika into the sea of Vourukasha, to the tree Hvapa: there grow all plants and of all kinds."Hvapa and Pakshajati are identical with the Tuba' or tree of "goodness" of the Muhammadan paradise. Similar legends are found in certain Christian apocryphal works, especially in the 'Visio Pauli' and the 'Testament of Abraham'. In the 'Visio Pauli Paul ascended to the heavens and beheld the four rivers of Paradise and Abraham also viewed the wonders of the heavens in his legendary 'Testament,' each returning to earth to relate what he had seen, just as Arta Viraf and Muhammad are said to have done. Of Abraham it is said, "And the archangel Michael descended and took Abraham up upon a cherubic chariot, and he raised him aloft into the ether of the sky, and brought him and sixty angels upon the cloud and Abraham were traveling over the whole inhabited earth upon a conveyance. This 'cherubic chariot' assumes another form in the Muhammadan legend, for Muhammad rides upon an animal called Buraq. The word Buraq is probably derived from the Hebrew baraq, 'Lightning,' which in Arabic is barq.

The Book of Enoch contains a long account of the wonders of earth, hell, and sky which Enoch saw in his vision. On the 'Tree of Life' in the Garden of Eden the Jews have many marvelous legends, which may have been borrowed from the Accadian tales about the 'Sacred Tree of Eri Tu,' mentioned in some of the earliest inscriptions at Nippur by Dr. Hilprecht. There is a great similarity between all such legends and the simple narrative contained in Genesis. The Jewish legends have affected the Muhammadan account of the heavenly Paradise; they therefore transfer to the heavenly Paradise much that the Jews have related about the earthly. In this respect they may have been led into error by the Christian apocryphal books. The four rivers of Eden that Muhammad saw are identical with those of the Visio Pauli. Whether the biblical account of the ascension of Enoch, Elijah,

Jesus, and the 'catching up to the third heaven' of the person whom some have supposed to be St. Paul, have not been the original sources of all the fables given above, would be a good question.

The Muhammadan Paradise with Huris:

Huris, along with the Ghilman, the Angel of Death; and the Dharratu'l Kainat. In the following passages of the Quran are given descriptions- Surah LV., Ar Rahman, 46 sqq. "And for him who feareth the tribunal of his Lord there are two gardens dowered with branches. In each of them two fountains flow. In each of them there are two kinds of fruit. They recline upon couches of which the inner lining is of brocade; and the fruits of the two gardens hang low. In them are [maidens] restraining their glances, whom neither man nor demon hath approached before them. They are as if they were rubies and pearls. And besides these two there are two [other] gardens, with similar Huris"

Similar accounts of the delights reserved in Paradise for the "Companions of the Right Hand," are In Surah LVI., Al Waqi'ah, II sqq. Upon them wait immortal youths (the Ghilman), "With goblets and beakers and a cup from a spring of wine". They do not suffer from headaches, nor do they become intoxicated. The derivation of the idea of the Huris is from the ancient Persian legends about the Pairakas, called by the modern people of Iran, Parees. They are described by the Zoroastrians as female spirits living in the air and closely connected with the stars and light.

They are so alluring that they captivate men's hearts. The word Hur, by which these damsels of Paradise are called in the Quran, is generally supposed to be of Arabic derivation, and to mean "black-eyed." But it is perhaps more likely a Persian word, derived from the word which in Avestic is 'hvare', in Pahlavi 'hur', originally denoting 'light,' 'brightness,' 'sunshine, and finally 'the sun'. Firdaus itself, one of the words in the Quran for Paradise, is a Persian word. The beings the word Huris intended to express, are of distinctly Aryan origin, as are the Ghilman. The Hindus believe in the existence of both, calling the Huris in Sanskrit Apsaras, and the Ghilman Gandharvas. They dwelled principally in the sky, though often visited the earth.

There are many tales told by Muslim historians on how much the prospect of receiving a welcome from the Houris in Paradise cheered many an ardent young Muhammadan warrior to rush boldly to his death in battle. The belief is very similar to the ancient Aryan idea to reward those who died on the field with all their wounds in front. For Manu says in his Dharmasastra, "Earth-lords contending in battles, mutually desirous of killing one another, not averting their faces, thereafter through their prowess go to heaven." In the Nalopakhyanam, Indra says to the hero Nala, "Just guardians of the earth i.e., kings, warriors who have abandoned (all hope of) life, who in due time by means of a weapon, go to destruction without averting them faces-theirs is this imperishable world "- the heaven of Indra. The ancestors of the people of the north used to believe in heathen days that the heavenly Valkyries, or 'Selectors of the Slain,' would visit the field of battle and bear thence to the heaven of Odhin, to Valhalla, the "Hall of the Slain," the spirits of brave warriors who fell in the strife

The Jinns, a kind of evil and malicious spirits which have great power, are a source of terror in the Muslim world. They were the subject of Solomon, and they are frequently mentioned in the Quran that they were made of fire, as were the angels and the demons. The word itself seems to be Persian, for the singular Jinni is the Avestic Jaini, a wicked (female) spirit. The black figures were the spirits of Abraham's descendants as yet unborn. They are generally termed 'The Existent Atoms' (adu dharratu'l kainat). They differ from the beings mentioned in the 'Testament of Abraham' in the fact that, in the latter book, Abraham sees the spirits of his descendants who had died, while in the Muhammadan tradition he sees those of men not yet born, in the form of 'Existent Atoms.' The name by which these beings are known in Muhammadan religious works is a purely Arabic one.

The Muslims, like the Jews, speak of the Angel of Death very much, though the latter say that his name is 'Sammael', while the former call him 'Azrail'. 'Azrail' is not Arabic but Hebrew, showing the extent of the influence exercised by the Jews upon Islam. This angel's name is not mentioned in the Bible, so what the Jews and the Muslims say about him must be borrowed from some other source. This is probably Persian, for the Avesta tells us of an angel called Astovidhotus or Vidhatus, 'the divider,' whose duty it is to separate body and spirit. It was the Angel of Death, Vidhatus.

The Ascent of 'Azazil from Hell. 'Azazil, according to the Muslim tradition, was the original name of Satan or Iblis. The name is Hebrew and occurs in the original text of Leviticus (xvi. 8, 10, 26). But the tale of his origin is almost Zoroastrian, as shown by a comparison between the Muslim and the Zoroastrian legends. In the Qisas Anbiya (p. 9), we read, "God Most High created 'Azazil. Azazil worshiped God Most High for a thousand years in Sijjin.

Then he came up to the earth. On each storey he worshiped God Most High for a thousand years until he came up upon the surface," the highest story, on which men dwell. God then gave him a pair of wings made of emerald, with which he mounted up to the first heaven. There he worshiped for a thousand years, and thus was enabled to reach the second heaven, and so on, worshiping for a thousand years at each stage of his ascent, and receiving from the angelic inhabitants of each heaven a special name. In the fifth heaven he was, for the first time, called 'Azazil. He thus ascended to the sixth and the seventh heaven, and then had performed so much adoration that he had not left in earth or heaven a single spot as large as the palm of a man's hand on which he had not prostrated himself in worship. Afterwards for the sin of refusing to worship Adam he was cast out of Paradise. The 'Arais al Majalis tells us that, "Being then called Iblis, he remained for three thousand years at the gate of Paradise in the hope of being able to inflict some injury on Adam and Eve, since his heart was full of envy and ill-will towards them".

The Zoroastrians give the account of the same matter in the Bundahishn, a Pahlavi work, the name of which means 'Creation.' In Pahlavi the Evil Spirit is called Ahriman, which is derived from Auro Mainyus ('the destroying mind'), the name by which he is known in the Avesta. In the first and second chapters of the Bundahishn we read, "Ahriman was and is in darkness, and after-knowledge and the desire of inflicting injury ... And that injuriousness, and that darkness too are a place which they call the dark region". Ormazd in his omniscience knew that Ahriman existed, because he That is, Ahriman', "Excites himself and intermingles himself with the desire of envy even unto the end ..." They (Ormazd and Ahriman) were for three thousand years in spirit, that is, they were without change and motion. ...The injurious spirit, on account of his after-knowledge, was not aware of the existence of Ormazd. At last, he rises from that abyss, and he comes to the bright place; and, since he saw that brightness of Ormazd ... because of his injurious desire and his envious disposition he became busied in destroying.

There is a definitive difference in form between the legend among the dualistic Zoroastrians and that among the Monotheistic Muslims. In the former, the Evil Principle is not a creature of Ormazd, who does not at first know of His existence, whereas in the latter he is one of the creatures of God. In the Muhammadan legend he gradually ascends higher and higher by his piety, while in the Zoroastrian account piety has nothing to do with the matter. In both cases, however, the Evil Spirit at first dwells in darkness and ignorance and comes up to the light, and in both cases, he sets himself to work to destroy God's creatures through envy and ill-will. According to Zoroastrianism, the twelve thousand years during which the contest between good and evil goes on, is divided into four periods of three thousand years each. It accords with the three thousand years during which 'Azazil (Iblis) lies in wait for Adam's destruction.

In both the Muhammadan and the Zoroastrian legend The Peacock has some connection with the Evil Spirit. In the Qasas Ul Anbiya, when Iblis was seated in ambush before the gate of Paradise, watching for an opportunity to enter and tempt Adam and Eve to sin, the Peacock was sitting on the wall, on top of one of the battlements, and saw Iblis most piously engaged in repeating the loftiest names of God Most High. Struck with admiration for so much piety, the Peacock inquired who this ardent devotee might be. Iblis replied, "I am one of the angels of God; may He be honored and glorified!" When asked why he sat there, he replied, "I am looking at Paradise, and I wish to enter it." The Peacock was acting as watchman, so he replied,"I have no orders to admit any one to Paradise while Adam is in it." But Iblis bribed him to grant him admission by promising to teach him a prayer, the repetition of which would keep him from ever growing old, from rebelling against God, and from ever being driven forth from Paradise. On this the Peacock flew down from the battlement and told the Serpent what he had heard. This led to the fall of Eve and afterwards of Adam. When, therefore, God Most High cast Adam, Eve, the Tempter and the Serpent down from Paradise to the earth, He hurled down the Peacock 'knowledge' with them. For Zoroastrians also there is a connection between Ahriman and the Peacock. TheArmenian writer Ezniq tells us that the Zoroastrians of his day said that Ahriman said, "It is not that I cannot make anything good, but I will not. In order to prove what he said, he made the Peacock." The Peacock in the Zoroastrian legend is a creature of Ahriman, no wonder he helped Iblis in the Muhammadan one, and was the 'Light of Muhammad' legend:

Though not mentioned in the Quran, which shone on his forehead and was his re-existent essence, occupies a very important place in the Traditions. In the Raudhatul Ahbab we read that, "When Adam was created, God placed that light upon his forehead, and said, 'O Adam, this light which I have placed upon thy forehead is the light of the noblest and best son of thine, and it is the light of the chief of the prophets who shall be sent; the light passed on from Adam to Seth, and from Seth to the noblest of his descendants in each generation, until in due course it reached 'Abdullah ibn Al Muttalab. From him it passed to Aminah when she conceived Muhammad". It is likely that Muhammadans have intended in their account of this light of Muhammad to exalt their master so as to match what is said of Christ in John 4, 5 (cf. xii. 41). The details are actually borrowed from the Zoroastrian legend. In the Pahlavi khirad (Mini), which was composed in the days of the early Sasanian kings of Persia, Ormazd created this world and all His creatures, and the archangels, and the Heavenly Reason, out of His own special light, with the praise of Zarva I Akarana or 'Endless Time.'

The Avesta mentions in connection with the great Yima Khshaeta or Yima 'the Brilliant,' who from its possession derived his name, afterwards corrupted into the modern Persian Jamshid. He is identical with the Sanskrit Yama, who in the Rig Veda is spoken of as the first of men, as in vain tempted to sin by his twin sister Yami, and as after death ruling the shades of the dead.

In Persian tradition Yima is the founder of Persian civilization. His father's name is the same as the Vivanhvat of the Indian legend, who is the Sun, and is the father of Yima. On Yuma's brow shone the Kavaem Ilvareno or 'Royal Brightness,' an emanation from the Divine glory, until through sin he lost it. The description is given in the Avesta, "The mighty Royal Brightness for a long time adhered to Jamshid, master of the good herd, while he reigned on the seven-climbed earth, over divs and men, magicians and Parees, evil spirits and soothsayers and wizards …

Then, when he conceived in mind that false and worthless word, the visible brightness departed from him in the form of a bird ... He who is Jamshid, master of the good herd, Jam, no longer seeing that brightness, became sorrowful; and he, having become troubled, engaged in working hostility upon earth. The first time that brightness departed from Jamshid, the brightness departed from Jam, son of Vivanhvat, like a fluttering bird ... Mithra took that brightness. When the second time that brightness departed from Jamshid, that brightness (departed) from Jam, son of Vivanhvat, it went away like a fluttering bird: Faridun, offspring of the Athwiyani tribe, the brave tribe, took that brightness, since he was the most victorious man among victorious men. When the third time that brightness departed from Jamshid, that brightness departed from Jam, son of Vivanhvat, like a fluttering bird, Keresa spa took that brightness, since he was the mightiest among mighty men." We see that, just as in the Muhammadan legend, the light passes on from generation to generation, to the worthiest man in each generation.

The Bridge of the Dead:

In the Muhammadan Traditions it is called As-Siraat or 'The Way.' It is said to be finer than a hair and sharper than a sword and stretches right over the abyss of hell and is the only way of passing from earth to heaven on the Judgment Day. All have to cross it. The pious Muslim will do so without difficulty; but the unbeliever, unable to cross, will fall headlong into hell fire.

The word Siraat is used in the Quran in the metaphorical sense of a way, ('the Right Way,' Surah I., Al Fatihah, et passim), but it is not an Arabic word. The word comes from no Arabic or Semitic root, but is the Persian Chinvat in Arabic letters, since the Arabic language, not having any character to represent the sound ch' (as in church), replaces it by the letter, the first letter in Sirat. Chinvat in Persian means a collector, one that sums up or assembles (cf. Sanskrit) or takes account. Hence it is only by contraction that the Arabic Sirat gets its meaning, for the Avesta speaks, not of Chinvat but of Chinvato-peretus, "The bridge of him that reckons up" good deeds and bad. This bridge reaches over hell. Each man's spirit, as soon as certain funeral ceremonies have been performed, reaches the bridge, and has to cross it. When he has crossed the bridge, he is judged by Mithra, Rashnu, and Sraosha in accordance with the account of his deeds, good and bad. Only if his good deeds exceed his evil ones can the gate of Paradise be opened to admit him. If his deeds are preponderantly evil, he is cast into hell: but if the good are equal to the bad, the spirit of the dead has to await the last judgment (vulaiti), which will take place at the close or the final struggle between Ormazd and Ahriman.

The origin of the word Sirat of the Muhammadan doctrine is in the translation of the passage from the Pahlavi book called the Dinkart, "I flee from much sin, and I keep pure my conduct by keeping pure the six powers of life – act and speech and thought and intellect and mind and understanding-by thy desire, O mighty Causer of good deeds". We also find many references to the same belief in the Avesta, among others the passage in which it is said of good men and women, "Whom too I shall lead through the prayer of such as you: with all blessings shall I guide them to the bridge of Chinvat."

The Aryan Origin of this Belief

The ancient Scandinavian mythology contains mention of Bifrost, generally styled the bridge of the gods, by which they cross over from their abode in Asgard (in heaven) to the earth. It is the rainbow. This explains the natural basis on which the legend of the bridge is founded, and shows how ancient it is, as the Scandinavians brought the idea with them to Europe. It must therefore have been common to them and the Persians in very ancient times.

In Greece the rainbow becomes the messenger of the gods (Iris) in the Iliad, but the idea of a bridge connecting heaven and earth seems to have been lost.

The Other Persian Ideas Borrowed.

One other point of some importance besides the ones referred to above, is the Muslim belief that every prophet before his death foretold the coming of his successor. The Muhammadan theory is most likely borrowed from a Zoroastrian work called the Dasatir i Asmani. This work claims to be of very great antiquity and is believed by many of the modern Parsis to be 'composed in the language of heaven'. Accompanying the text is an interlinear translation into the old Dari dialect of Persian which is said to have been discovered in Persia early in the last century and was edited by Mulla Firuz of Bombay. It consists of fifteen tractates which are supposed to have been revealed to fifteen successive prophets, the first of whom is styled Mahabad and the last Sasan, from whom probably the Sasanian dynasty is supposed to trace their descent.

The Dari translation is said to date from the time of Khusrau Parviz (C.E., 590-5), so that the original must be of some antiquity. The second verse of every one of these tractates runs thus, "In the name of God, the Giver, the Forgiver, the Merciful, the Just." These words are closely related to those which form the introduction to every Surah of the Quran except the ninth, "In the Name of God, the Compassionate, the Merciful." Probably the Quran has been borrowed from the Zoroastrian book, the 'Bundahishn' which has a similar clause, "In the Name of Ormazd the Creator."

Jewish Origin:

In the Tradition one of the Hanifs, Ummiyyah, a poet belonging to Taif, taught this formula to the Quraish, having learnt it from his intercourse with Jews and Christians during his journeys in Syria and elsewhere as a merchant. Muhammad may have heard it in this way and adopted it. But it is more probably of Zoroastrian origin than of Jewish, and Ummiyyah might have learnt it from the Persians whom he met on his mercantile expeditions.

Tradition offers the possibility of the Zoroastrian ideas and legends as one of the sources from which Islam has derived very much of what is contained in certain parts of the Quran and the Traditions. Raudat ul Ahbab tells us that it was Muhammad's habit to speak a few words in their own language to people that came to him from different nations, and that, since on one or two occasions he spoke Persian to such visitors, a few Persian words in this way found an entrance into the Arabic language.So, Muhammad had at least some slight acquaintance with Persian, if with no other foreign tongue.

The Siratul Rasul of Ibne Ishaq and Ibn Hisham tell us that there was one Persian convert, called Salman, a man of education and ability. It was on his advice that Muhammad in February, 627 C.E., defended Medina against the Quraish with the celebrated ditch, a method which the Arabs had not previously used. By Salman's advice Muhammad is also said to have used a catapult at the time of his campaign against Taif (630 C.E.,).

Salman was likely the person whom Muhammad's enemies are said to have accused the Prophet of using as his assistant in the composition of certain parts of the Quran; for in Surah XVI., An Nahl, 105, we read, "Truly we know that they say, 'Verily a human being teacheth him.' The tongue of him at whom they aim is Persian, and this [book] is Arabic, clear."

We see that Persian fables were well known enough in Arabia to be recognized by some of the Arabs when incorporated into the supposed Divine Revelation. The charge affected the matter and not the language of the Quran. Muhammad's concept of the world was limited to the Arabian Peninsula and its neighboring regions, but not the far-away places on Earth. Also, he was not the last adventurer to build another religion based on imagined realities. Many after him during the past fourteen centuries following his death, came up with new Beliefs, Convictions and fully formed Religions, making him one of the many in the "Also Ran" category of religion-founders. Here's a long chart of the founders of religions, both before and after Muhammad, with their brief descriptions.

THE BIG RELIGION CHART

The Religion Facts ``Big Religion Chart" is an attempt to summarize all the complexities of religions and belief systems into tiny little boxes on a single, quick-reference comparison chart. Yes, this is impossible. As we always warn with our comparison charts, this is no substitute for reading about religions in greater detail, talking with religious adherents, etc. But this religion comparison chart can (hopefully be a useful and accessible way to "get the gist" of some unfamiliar groups and compare basic beliefs and practices of the world's religions and belief systems.

Despite the chart's simplistic title, we have been very inclusive with what is regarded as a "religion" for purposes of this comparison chart. Basically, the grounds for any group's inclusion is that it provides a set of teachings and/or rituals that deal with the traditionally "religious" issues of ultimate reality, the meaning of life, and/or how to find fulfillment, spiritual health, or salvation. Also, all the groups listed below can be found in dictionaries of religion.

Inclusion of a group on this list does not mean that the group is a "religion" per se (note that atheism is listed) or a "true religion" or that "[one listed group] is just as much a religion as [another listed group]. "Similarly, if a group does not appear on this chart, it doesn't mean it's not a religion or doesn't matter, the chart is not comprehensive and is continually growing. In addition, listing groups separately does not mean they are mutually exclusive, nor does grouping them together mean that they are basically the same thing. This is not an authoritative list of religions, simply a resource on some worldviews and ways of life that hopefully some will find useful.

Religion/Sect/ Belief System	Origins & History	Adherents Worldwide (Approx.)	God(s) and Universe	Human Situation and Life's Purpose	Afterlife	Practice	Texts	More Info
Aladura	Various prophet-healing churches founded since c.1918, West Nigeria.	1 million	Generally monotheistic; a mix of Anglican, Pentecostal, and traditional African beliefs	Strong emphasis on healing and salvation in this life through prayer, fasting and other rituals.	Not emphasized; views vary.	Spiritual healing is central. Mix of Anglican and African rituals; a prophet plays a prominent role.	None	ReligionFacts article
Asatru	Revival of Norse and Germanic paganism, 1970s Scandinavia and USA.	Unknown	Polytheistic, Norse gods and goddesses, Norse creation myths.	Salvation or redemption not emphasized Fatalistic view of universe.	Valhalla (heaven) for death in battle; Hel (peaceful place) for most, Hifhel (Hell) for the very evil.	Sacrifice of food or drink, toast to the gods, shamanism (less frequently), celebration of solstice holidays. Nine Noble Virtues is a moral code.	Eddas (Norse epics); the Havamal (proverbs attributed to Odin)	ReligionFacts article Asatru Alliance Wikipedia
Atheism	Appears in history, but especially after the Enlightenment (19th cent)	1.1 billion (this figure includes agnostic and non-religious, which tend to be grouped on surveys)	There is no God or divine being. Beliefs about the universe generally based on latest scientific findings.	Only humans can help themselves and each other solve the world's problems.	None	None	Influential works include those by Marx, Freud, Feuerbach, and Voltaire	The Secular Web BBC Religion Wikipedia

Religion	Founded	Adherents	God / Deity	Purpose	Afterlife	Practices	Texts	Links
Bahá'í Faith	Founded by Bahá'u'lláh, 1863, Tehran, Iran.	5-7 million	One God, who has revealed himself progressively through major world religions.	The soul is eternal and essentially good. Purpose of life is to develop spiritually and draw closer to God.	Soul separates from the body and begins a journey towards or away from God. Heaven and hell are states being.	Daily prayer, avoidance of intoxicants, scripture reading, hard work for social justice and equality.	Writings of Bahá'u'lláh and other Bahá'í leaders	ReligionFacts section; The Bahá'í World
Bön	Indigenous religion of Tibet.	100,000	Non Theistic Buddhism, but meditation on peaceful and wrathful deities.	Purpose is to gain enlightenment.	Reincarnation until gain enlightenment.	Meditation on mandalas and Tibetan deities, astrology, Monastic life.	Bonpo canon	ReligionFacts section; Tibet.com
Buddhism	Founded by Siddharta Gautama (the Buddha) in c. 520 BC, NE India.	360 million	Varies: Theravada atheistic; Mahayana more polytheistic Buddha taught nothing is permanent.	Purpose is to avoid suffering and gain enlightenment and release from the cycle of rebirth, or at least attain a better rebirth by gaining merit.	Reincarnation (understood differently than in Hinduism, with no surviving soul) until gain enlightenment.	Meditation, mantras, devotion to deities (in some sects), mandalas (Tibetan)	Tripitaka (Pali Canon); Mahayana sutras like the Lotus Sutra; others	ReligionFacts section; BuddhaNet

	Origin	Adherents	God / Deities	Purpose	Afterlife	Practices	Texts	Links
Cao Dai	Founded in 1926, Vietnam by Ngo Van Chieu and others based on a séance.	4-6 million	God represented by the Divine Eye. Founders of Buddhism, Taoism, Hinduism, Islam, and Christianity venerated, and saints including Victor Hugo.	Goal is peace and harmony in each person and in the world. Salvation by "cultivating self and finding God in self."	Reincarnation. Bad karma can lead to rebirth on a darker planet; good karma to better life on earth. Eventual attainment of nirvana or heaven.	Hierarchy similar to Roman Catholicism. Daily prayer. Meditation. Communication with spirit world (now outlawed in Vietnam).	Cao Dai canon	ReligionFacts article / CaoDai.org
Chinese Religion	Indigenous folk religion of China	394 million	Dualistic yin and yang; mythological beings and folk deities.	Purpose is a favorable life and peaceful afterlife, attained through rituals and honoring of ancestors.	Judgment, then reincarnation or temporary hell until gain a Buddhist-type paradise.	Ancestor worship, prayer, longevity practices, divination, prophecy and astrology, feng shui.	None	ReligionFacts section / Chinese Cultural Studies
Chopra Center	Founded by Deepak Chopra in 1991, California	Unknown	Monism – God or Supreme Reality pervades all things; all is unity	Humans have limitless potential but do not recognize this. Health and success can be had by focusing on whole self (mind, body, Spirit).	Reincarnation	Yoga, meditation, massage, nutrition, mindfulness, detox sessions, positive thinking.	Deepak Chopra's many books, such as the *Seven Spiritual Laws of Success*	ReligionFacts article / Official Website

	Founded	Adherents	God / Deity	Purpose / Salvation	Afterlife	Practices	Texts	Links
Christianity (Catholic, Protestant, Orthodox)	Founded by Jesus Christ in c. 30 AD, Israel	2 billion	One God who is a Trinity of Father, Son, and Holy Spirit	All have sinned and are thereby separated from God. Salvation is through faith in Christ and, for some, sacraments, and good works.	Eternal heaven or hell (or temporary purgatory).	Prayer, bible study, baptism, Eucharist, church on Sundays, numerous holidays.	The Holy Bible (Old and New Testaments)	ReligionFacts section / Wikipedia / BBC Religion
Christian Science	Founded by Mary Baker Eddy in 1879, Massachusetts.	150,000 – 400000	One God. No Trinity (in the traditional sense). Matter and evil do not exist.	Salvation is "Life, Truth, and Love understood and demonstrated as supreme over all; sin, sickness and death destroyed."	Heaven is "not a locality, but a divine state of Mind in which all the manifestations of Mind are harmonious and immortal."	Spiritual healing through prayer and knowledge, Sunday services, daily *Bible and Science & Health* reading.	Christian Bible / *Science and Health with key to the Scriptures*	ReligionFacts article / Official Website
Confucianism	Founded by Confucius (551-479 BC), China	5-6 million	Not addressed	Purpose of Life is to fulfill one's role in society with propriety, honor, and loyalty.	Not addressed	Honesty, politeness, propriety, humaneness, perform correct role in society, loyalty to family, nation	*Analects*	ReligionFacts article / Wikipedia

Deism	Especially popularized in the 18th-century Enlightenment under Kant, Voltaire, Paine, Jefferson, and others	Unknown	One Creator God who is uninterested in the world. Reason is basis for all knowledge	Not addressed	Not addressed	None prescribed, although some deists practice prayer.	*Thomas Paine's The Age of Reason* and similar texts	World Union of Deists Wikipedia
Druze	Al-Darazi in the 11th century, Cairo, Egypt. Roots in the Isma'iliyah sect of Shia Islam.	500,000	Universal Intelligence (*al-Aql al-kulli*) or Divine Essence (akin to Neoplatonism), of which al-Hakim is believed to be an incarnation.	Live a good life for a favorable reincarnation. Await the re-appearance of al-Hakim (a Fatimid caliph who disappeared in 1021), who will usher in a Golden Age for true believers.	Reincarnation Heaven is a spiritual existence when one has escaped reincarnation. Hell is distance from God in lifetime after lifetime.	Modest lifestyles, fasting before Eid al-Adha. Beliefs and practices are hidden for protection from persecution. Special group of initiates called *uqqal*.	*Al-Naqd al-Khafi* (Copy of the Secret); *Al-Juz Al-Awwal* (Essence of the First)	Wikipedia Lexicorient
Eckankar	John Paul Twitchell in 1965, Las Vegas.	50-500,000	The Divine Spirit, called "ECK"	"Each of us is Soul, a spark of God sent to this world to gain spiritual experience." Salvation is liberation and God-realization.	Reincarnation. The Soul is eternal by nature and on a spiritual journey. Liberation possible in a single lifetime.	Spiritual Exercises of ECK: mantras, meditation, and dreams. These enable Soul travel and spiritual growth.	*Shariyat-Ki-Sugmad and books by Harold Klemp*	ReligionFacts article Official Website

Epicureanism	Epicurus in c. 300 BC, Athens.	Unknown	A deistic sort of polytheism: the gods exist, but take no notice of humans	Materialism: everything is made of atoms, including gods and the soul.	No Afterlife. The soul dissolves when the body dies.	Pursue the highest pleasures (friendship and tranquility) and avoid pain.	Letters and *principal* Doctrines of Epicurus	ReligionFacts article Epicurus.net
Falun Gong	Li Hongzhi in 1992 in China	10 million	Countless gods and spiritual beings, Demonic aliens.	The Falun (wheel) is an energy source located in the navel. Goal is spiritual transcendence, achieved by practicing Falun Gong.	Not Addressed	Five exercises to strengthen the Falun. Cultivation of truthfulness, benevolence, and forbearance. Meat eating is discouraged.	*Zhuan Falun* and other writings by Master Li	ReligionFacts article Falundafa.org
Gnosticism	Various teachers including Valentinus, 1st-2nd cents. AD	Ancient form extinct; small modern revival groups	The supreme God is unknowable; the creator god is evil and matter is evil.	Humans can return to the spiritual world through secret knowledge of the universe	Return to the spiritual world.	Asceticism, celibacy	Gnostic scriptures including various *Gospels* and *Acts* attributed to apostles	Wikipedia Gnosis.org

	Origin	Adherents	God	Human Condition	Afterlife	Practices	Texts	Links
Greek Religion	Variety of religions of ancient Greeks	Ancient form extinct	Olympic pantheon (Zeus, etc.) mixed with eastern deities like Isis and Cybele	Human life is subject to the whim of the gods and to Fate; these can be controlled through sacrifice and divination.	Beliefs varied from no afterlife to shadowy existence in the underworld to a paradise-like afterlife (mainly in mystery religions	Animal sacrifice, harvest offerings, festivals, games, processions, dance, plays, in honor of the gods. Secret initiations and rituals in mystery religions.	Epic poems of Homer and Hesiod.	ReligionFacts section Wikipedia Ancient Greek Religion
Hare Krishna	Bhaktivedanta Swami Prabhupada, 1966, USA (with roots in 15th-century Hindu movement)	250,000-1 million	Krishna is the Supreme God.	Salvation from this Age of Kali is by a return to Godhead accomplished through Krishna-Consciousness.	Reincarnation until united with the Godhead.	Chanting, dancing, evangelism, vegetarianism, temple worship, monastic-style living.	*The Bhagavad-Gita As It Is*	ReligionFacts article iSKCON.com Krishna.com
Hinduism	Indigenous religion of India has developed to the present day.	900 million	One Supreme Reality (Brahman) manifested in many gods and goddesses	Humans are in bondage to ignorance and illusion, but are able to escape. Purpose is to gain release from rebirth, or at least a better rebirth.	Reincarnation until gain enlightenment.	Yoga, meditation, worship (puja), devotion to a god or goddess, pilgrimage to holy cities, live according to one's dharma (purpose/role)	*The Vedas, Upanishads, Bhagavad Gita, Ramayana, etc.*	ReligionFacts section BBC Religion

Religion	Founder / Origin	Adherents	God	Humans / Purpose	Afterlife	Practices	Scriptures	Links
Islam	Muhammad, 622 AD, Saudi Arabia	1.3 billion (Sunni: 940 million)	One God (Allah in Arabic)	Humans must submit (islam) to the will of God to gain Paradise after death.	Paradise or Hell.	Five Pillars: Faith, Prayer, Alms, Pilgrimage, fasting, Mosque services on Fridays. Ablutions before prayer. No alcohol or pork. Holidays related to the pilgrimage and fast of Ramadan.	Qur'an (Scripture); hadith (tradition)	ReligionFacts section; BBC Religion; IslamiCity
Jainism	Mahavira, c. 550 BC, eastern India	4 million	The universe is eternal; many gods exist. Gods, humans, and all living things are classified in a complex hierarchy.	The soul is uncreated and eternal and can attain perfect divinity. Purpose is to gain liberation from the cycle of rebirth, by avoiding all bad karma, especially by causing no harm to any sentient being.	Reincarnation until liberation.	Monasticism under the Five Great Vows (Non-Violence, Truth, Celibacy, Non-Stealing, Non-Possessiveness); worship at temples and at home. Meditation and mantras.	The teachings of Mahavira in various collections.	ReligionFacts section; BBC Religion; Jainworld.com
Jehovah's Witnesses	Charles Taze Russell, 1879, Pittsburgh	6.5 million	One God, Jehovah. No Trinity – Christ is the first creation of God; the Holy Spirit is a force.	Salvation is through faith in Christ and obeying Jehovah's laws. The End of the World is soon.	Heaven for 144,000 chosen Witnesses, eternity on new earth for other Witnesses. All others were annihilated. No hell.	No Blood transfusions, no celebration of holidays, no use of crosses or religious images. Baptism, Sunday service at Kingdom Hall, strong emphasis on evangelism.	New World Translation of the Scriptures.	ReligionFacts section; Official Website; BBC Religion

	Origin	Adherents	Deity	Beliefs	Afterlife	Practices	Texts	Sources
Judaism	The religion of the Hebrews (c. 1300 BC), especially after the destruction of the Second Temple in 70 AD.	14 million	One God, Yahweh.	Obey God's commandments, live ethically. Focus is more on this life than the next.	Not historically emphasized. Beliefs vary from no afterlife to shadowy existence to the World to Come (similar to heaven).	Circumcision at birth, bar/bat mitzvah at adulthood. Synagogue services on Saturdays. No pork or other non-kosher foods. Holidays related to historical events.	*Bible (Yanakh), Talmud*	ReligionFacts section, Judaism 101, BBC Religion
Mayan Religion	c.250 AD (rise of the Mayan civilization)	Historically up to 2 million. Some survival today	Many gods, including Itzamná, Kukulcán, Bolon Tzacab, and Chac	Appease and nourish the gods; determine luckiest dates for various activities.	The soul journeys through dark and threatening underworld; but sacrificial victims and women who die in childbirth go to heaven.	Astronomy, divination, human sacrifice, elaborate burial for royalty, worship in stone pyramid-temples	Dresden, Madrid, and Paris codices; *Books of Chilam Balam; Popol Vuh; The Ritual of the Bacabs*	ReligionFacts article
Mormonism (LDS)	Joseph Smith, 1830, New York	12.2 million	God the Father, the Son Jesus Christ, and the Holy Ghost are three separate individual beings	Humans existed as spirits before this life, salvation is returning to God. Salvation by faith in Christ, good works, ordinances, and evangelism.	All return to spirit world for period of instruction before resurrection Mormons to heaven with God and families; others rewarded but not with God; hell for those who reject God after death.	Abstinence from alcohol, tobacco, coffee and tea; baptism for the dead; eternal marriage; temple garments under daily clothes; active evangelism.	Christian Bible, *Book of Mormon, Doctrine and Covenants,* and *Pearl of Great Price*	ReligionFacts section, Official Website, BBC Religion

	Founders / Origin	Adherents	View of the Divine	Key Beliefs	Afterlife	Practices	Texts	Links
New Age	Helena Petrovna Blavatsky and Annie Besant in the 19th C, Alice A. Bailey (1880-1949), flourished in 1970s and 80s	5 million (very approximate)	The Divine is an impersonal life force that pervades all things	Dawning of a New Age of heightened consciousness and international peace. Individuals can obtain a foretaste of the New Age through spiritual transformation ("Ascension"). More emphasis on the latter now. Evil comes from ignorance.	Reincarnation based on karma	Astrology; mysticism; use of crystals; yoga; tarot readings; holistic medicine; psychic abilities; angelic communications; channeling; amulets; fortune-telling	Works of a variety of New Age writers	Beliefnet, Religious Movement Homepage
New thought	Phineas Parkhurst Quimby (1802-66) and others, late 19th century, USA.	160,000	Generally monism (all is One), but members might be theist, pantheists or panentheist. God is immanent; the universe is essentially spiritual.	Man is divine, essentially spirit, and has infinite possibility. Mind can control the body. Sin and sickness cause by incorrect thinking. Man can live in oneness with God in love, truth, peace, health, and prosperity.	"Life is eternal in the invisible kingdom of God."	Emphasis on spiritual and mental healing, but without rejection of modern medicine. Worship services; prayer for the sick; discussion of New Thought authors and ideas	Writings of Quimby (such as the *The Quimby Manuscripts*) and other New Thought authors	ReligionFacts article, International New Thought Alliance

	Founding	Adherents	God	Human nature / Salvation	Afterlife	Practices	Texts	Links
Rastafari	Teachings of Marcus Garvey (1920s, Jamaica) and coronation of Haile Selassie (1930, Ethiopia)	1 million	God is Jah, who became incarnate in Jesus (who was black) and Haile Selassie	Humans are temples of Jah. Salvation is primarily in this world and consists of liberation from oppression and return to Africa.	Some Rastas will experience "everliving" (physical immortality). Heaven is a return to Eden, which is in Africa.	Many practices based on Jewish biblical Law. Abstinence from most or all meat, artificial foods, and alcohol. Use of Marijuana in religious rituals and for medicine. Wearing of dreadlocks.	Holy Piby (the "Blackman's Bible). The Ethiopian Epic Kebra Nagast also revered.	ReligionFacts article; The Afrocentric Experience; Jamaicans.com
Scientology	L. Ron Hubbard, 1954, California	70,000 or several million, depending on the source	God(s) not specified; reality explained in the Eight Dynamics	Humans consist of body, mind and thetan; capable of great things. Gain spiritual freedom by ridding the mind of engrams.	Reincarnation	Auditing, progressing up various levels until "clear". Focus on education and drug recovery programs.	Writings of Hubbard, such as *Dianetics* and *Scientology*	ReligionFacts section; Official Website; Beliefnet
Seventh-day Adventists	Rooted in Millerite movement; Ellen White was main leader; founded 1863 in New England	10 million	One God who is a Trinity of Father, Son, and Holy Spirit	Second Coming of Christ is imminent; salvation is by faith in Christ; emphasis on quality of life both now and in afterlife	A "peaceful pause" after death until the coming of Christ, then resurrection to judgment and eternity in heaven or hell	Sabbath observance on Saturdays; healthful lifestyle; baptism by immersion	Bible only; but later prophets like Ellen White are authoritative when tested against Scriptures	ReligionFacts article; Official Website; Beliefnet

Name	Origin/Founder	Adherents	Theology	Purpose	Death/Afterlife	Practices	Texts	Links
Shinto	Indigenous religion of Japan	3-4 million	Polytheism based on the kami, ancient gods or spirits.	Humans are pure by nature and can keep away evil through purification rituals and attain good things by calling on the kami	Death is bad and impure. Some humans become kami after death.	Worship and offerings to kami at shrines and at home. Purification rituals.	Important texts are *Kojiki* or 'Records of Ancient Matters' and *Nihon-gi* or 'Chronicles of Japan'	ReligionFacts article, Wikipedia, Japan Guide, BBC Religion
Sikhism	Guru Nanak, c. 1500 AD, Punjab, India.	23 million	One God (Ik Onkar, Nam)	Overcome the self align life with the will of God, and become a "saint soldier," fighting for good.	Reincarnation until resolve karma and merge with God.	Prayer and meditation on God's name, services at temple (gurdwara), turban and five Ks. Balance work, worship, and charity. No monasticism or asceticism.	*Adi Granth (SRI Guru Granth Sahib)*	ReligionFacts section, Sikhs.org, SikhNet.com
Stoicism	Zeno in c. 313 BC, Athens.	Unknown	Pantheism: the logos pervades the universe.	Purpose is happiness achieved by virtue i.e., living reasonably.	Possible continued existence of the Soul, but not a personal existence.	Ethical and philosophical training, self-reflection, careful judgment and inner calm.	Fragments of founders plus later writers like Seneca, Epictetus, Marcus Aurelius	ReligionFacts article, Encyclopedia of Philosophy

	Founder/Origin	Adherents	Deity	Purpose/Salvation	Afterlife	Practices	Texts	Links
Taoism	Lao-Tzu, c. 550 BC, China	20 million (394 million adherents of Chinese religion)	Pantheism – the Tao pervades all. Yin-yang – opposites make up a unity.	Purpose is inner harmony, peace, and longevity. Achieved by living in accordance with the Tao.	Revert back to the state of non-being, which is simply the other side of being.	General attitude of detachment and non-struggle, "go with the flow" of the Tao. Tai-chi, acupuncture, and alchemy to help longevity.	*Tao Te Ching* *Chuang-Tzu*	ReligionFacts section / Taopage.org / Beliefnet
Unification Church	Sun Myung Moon, 1954, South Korea	Over 1 million (3 million acc. to official sources)	Monotheism, with the duality of God (esp. masculine and feminine) emphasized. No Trinity doctrine.	Purpose is true love and world peace instead of selfish love. True love and the kingdom of God on earth will be restored by the creation of "true families."	Eternal life in a spirit world.	Blessing Ceremony	*The Divine Principle* (1954) by Rev. Moon	ReligionFacts article / Official Website
Unitarian Universalism	Formal merger of Unitarians and Universalists in 1961, USA.	800,000	Not specified. Members might believe in one god, many gods, or no God.	Salvation is "spiritual health or wholeness." Members seek "inner and outer peace." Insight, health, compassion and strength.	Not specified. Some believe in an afterlife, some do not. Very few believe in hell – "Universalism" indicates the belief that all will be saved.	Ceremonies for marriages, funerals, etc. Church services have elements from various religions. Emphasis on civil rights, social justice, equality and environment. Most UUs are anti-death penalty and pro-gay rights.	Many sacred texts are revered by various members; some none at all. The Bible is the most commonly used text.	ReligionFacts article / UUA.org

Wicca	Based on ancient pagan beliefs, but modern form founded in the early 1900s. Founder generally said to be Gerald Gardner.	1-3 million	Polytheism, centered on the Goddess and God, each in various forms; also a belief in a Supreme Being over all	"if it harms none, do what you will."	Reincarnation until reach the Summerland	Prayer, casting a circle, Drawing Down the Moon, reciting spells, dancing, singing, sharing cakes and wine or beer	No sacred text; foundational texts include *The Witch Cult in Western Europe* and *The God of the Witches*	ReligionFacts article, Wicca.org, Wikipedia
Zoroastrianism	Zoroaster in c.6th cent. BC, Persia. Official religion of ancient Persia. May have influenced Judaism and Vedic religion.	c. 200,000	One God, Ahura Mazda, but a dualistic worldview in which an evil spirit, Angra Mainyu, is almost as powerful.	Humans are free to do good or evil, and must choose the side of good.	Judgment followed by heaven or hell. Hell is temporary until final purgation and return to Ahura Mazda.	Good deeds, charity, equality, hard work.	*Zend Avesta*	ReligionFacts article, BBC Religion, WZO

CHAPTER 6
Allah

Who invented God? When, why, and where? **Thomas Römer** seeks to answer these questions about the deity of the great monotheisms — YHWH, God, or Allah — by tracing Israeli beliefs and their context from the Bronze Age to the end of the Old Testament period in the third century BCE.

That we can address such enigmatic questions at all, may come as a surprise. But as Römer makes clear, a wealth of evidence allows us to piece together a reliable account of the origins and evolution of the god of Israel. Römer draws on a long tradition of historical, philological, and exegetical work and on recent discoveries in archaeology and epigraphy to locate the origins of YHWH in the early Iron Age, when he emerged somewhere in Edom or in the northwest of the Arabian Peninsula as a god of the wilderness and of storms and war. He became the sole god of Israel and Jerusalem in fits and starts as other gods, including the mother goddess Asherah, were gradually sidelined. But it was not until a major catastrophe—the destruction of Jerusalem and Judah—that Israelites came to worship YHWH as the one God of all, creator of heaven and earth, who nevertheless proclaimed a special relationship with Judaism.

A remarkable forensic work and exposition by one of the world's leading experts on the Hebrew Bible, The Invention of God casts a clear light on profoundly important questions that are too rarely asked, let alone answered.

Muhammad borrowed, like everything else, a name from polytheist Pagans of Makkah for his monotheist God '**ALLAH**'. Allah was the name of one of the several more significant deities of Pagans. Muhammad poached that name for his 'One & Only'

Supreme Creator, Almighty God. However, Muhammad insisted that Ahura Mazda -- God of Zoroastrians, Yahweh -- God Almighty of Judaism, and Jehovah – God Lord of Christians, were the different older names of the same God Allah.

Allah, Jehovah, Yahweh, Ahura Mazda, Brahma(N), supreme deity of Sanatana Dharma (Hinduism) --- all belong to same category --- an **IMAGINED REALITY**, abbreviated for convenience as **IR** for our discourse.

Simply put, IR is a concept existing in imagination ---- an imagined god as provider of Infinite pleasure to the obedient and faithful persons, and provider of infinite pain to the outlaws, renegades, and dissidents.

Nothing ever happens unless IR wills it, starts it, or stops it.

IR brings things into existence just by willing it, and makes things vanish into non-existence, also by just willing it.

The human mind has come a long way in its cognitive abilities. After several millennia, it managed to distinguish between a factual REALITY and an IMAGINED REALITY. The logical and rational minds now know that IR is the meanest ever **'ScareCrow'** and mightiest ever **'Sugar Daddy'**. Mother Nature tops IR any day without blinking an eye. Nature can, and does, cause immeasurable death and destruction by volcanic eruptions, floods, tsunamis, wildfires, famines, and various other pandemics and calamities. All such misfortunes are dismissively misappropriated by believers as wrath of IR. In reality though, all actions of Nature fall under the "Cause & Effect" phenomenon.

Human nature too often tops IR --- racism, nationalism, tribalism, greed, fear, cruelty and unkindness of the strong over the weak and oppressed; all these are manifestations of human nature. There is no dearth of events of reality topping the IR. There are a lot of residual remains of beastly nature in humans, whose evolution towards fully developed humanity still has a significant distance to cover.

Muhammad planned his mission carefully, and as a first step he chose Allah, because it came close to 'Iloh' or 'Eloh', the pronouns for God of Judaism, in the Jewish language. Muhammad transformed Allah from its less significant status as one of the 360 deities of Pagans connected with the pantheon of Kaaba, to the ultimate position of 'One and Only' God, Creator of Universe and all that it holds, Omni-Potent, Omniscient and Omni-Present. The Pagan deity Allah was the husband of mother-goddess Asherah, and father of al-Laat, goddess of fortune, and al-Manat, the Sun goddess. Muhammad just chose Allah alone and dropped off His family, while completely excluding and rejecting all other gods/goddesses in Kaaba, as useless non-entities.

Muhammad's strategy was based entirely on using the two useful perceptions of Allah --- the fiercest 'scare crow' and the ultimate 'sugar daddy' --- to apply the proverbial carrot & stick formula to make the tribal minds submit worshipfully to Allah's pronouncements, thereby promoting Muhammad's mission.

A stream of revelations from Allah was announced by Muhammad, at ideally timed intervals, to first establish Allah's status as the Creator, Governor, and Master of Universe, far superior to the perceived power of all other mighty gods of former prophets. Followed by other revelations furthering Muhammad's planned mission. Here are a few such 'Aya' (Revelations) which are presented as supplications of previous prophets, showing that Allah, the God of Muhammad, is the real God Almighty and that is why all previous prophets of Judaism and Christianity also prayed to Muhammad's God Allah.

These revelations serve the dual purpose; firstly, establishing Allah, being above and beyond any comparison with how Yahweh, Ahura Mazda or Jehovah, God the Lord were ever perceived. Secondly, installing Muhammad as the Regent of Allah, His mouthpiece, and his anthropomorphic personation in flesh and blood, and to be so treated by mankind, in **Deed**, but not in **Word**.

The Supplications of Previous Prophets from Adam to Jesus

1. Prophet Adam (the first man and first prophet)

Surah Yusuf, 12-101:

اَنْتَ وَلِيّ فِى الدُّنْيَا وَالْأخِرَةِ ۚ رَبِّ قَدْ اٰتَيْتَنِىْ مِنَ الْمُلْكِ وَ عَلَّمْتَنِىْ مِنْ تَأْوِيْلِ الْاَحَادِيْثِ ۚ فَاطِرَ السَّمٰوٰتِ وَالْاَرْضِ تَوَفَّنِىْ مُسْلِمًا وَّاَلْحِقْنِىْ بِالصّٰلِحِيْنَ

"My Lord! You have bestowed dominion upon me and have taught me to comprehend the depths of things. O Creator of heavens and earth! You are my Guardian in this world and in the Hereafter. Cause me to die in submission to You, and join me, in the end, with the righteous."

Surah Al-Araf, 23-7:

قالا ربنا ظلمنا أنفسنا و إن لم تنير لنا و ترحمنا لتكون من الخاسرين

"Our Lord, we have wronged ourselves, and if you do not forgive us and have mercy upon us, we will surely be among the losers."

2. Prophet Noah

Surah Hud 11-47:

قَالَ رَبِّ اِنِّىْٓ اَعُوْذُ بِكَ اَنْ اَسْئَلَكَ مَا لَيْسَ لِىْ بِه عِلْمٌ وَاِلَّا تَغْفِرْ لِىْ وَتَرْحَمْنِىْٓ اَكُنْ مِّنَ الْخٰسِرِيْنَ

'My Lord! I take refuge with You that I should ask You for that concerning which I have no knowledge. And if You do not forgive me and do not show mercy to me, I shall be among the losers.

Surah Al-Mu'minun, 23-29:

و قل رب أنزلني مثلا بركًا و أنت خير المنزلين

"And say, 'My Lord, let me land at a blessed landing place, and You are the best to accommodate [us]."

Surah Al-Mu'minun, 23-23:

وَلَقَدْ اَرْسَلْنَا نُوحًا اِلٰى قَوْمِهٖ فَقَالَ يٰقَوْمِ اعْبُدُوا اللّٰهَ مَا لَكُمْ مِنْ اِلٰهٍ غَيْرُهٗ اَفَلَا تَتَّقُوْنَ

"We sent Noah to his people, and he said: 'My people! Serve Allah; you have no deity other than He. Do you have no fear?'"

Surah Al-Nuh 71:28:

رَبِّ اغْفِرْ لِى وَلِوَالِدَىَّ وَلِمَن دَخَلَ بَيْتِىَ مُؤْمِنًا وَلِلْمُؤْمِنِينَ وَالْمُؤْمِنَاتِ وَلَا تَزِدِ الظَّالِمِينَ إِلَّا تَبَارًا

"My Lord, grant pardon to me, and to my parents, and to everyone who enters my home as a believer, and to all the believing men and believing women, and do not increase the wrongdoers but in ruin."

3. Prophet Ibrahim

Surah Al-Baqarah:127:

وَإِذْ يَرْفَعُ إِبْرٰهِۧمُ الْقَوَاعِدَ مِنَ الْبَيْتِ وَإِسْمٰعِيلُ رَبَّنَا تَقَبَّلْ مِنَّا إِنَّكَ أَنتَ السَّمِيعُ الْعَلِيمُ

"When Ibrahim was raising up the foundations of the House, along with Ismaīl (Ishmael) (supplicating: "Our Lord accepted (this service) from us! Indeed, You - and You alone - are the All-Hearing, the All-Knowing!"

Surah Ibrahim 14:41:

رَبَّنَا ٱغْفِرْ لِى وَلِوَٰلِدَىَّ وَلِلْمُؤْمِنِينَ يَوْمَ يَقُومُ ٱلْحِسَابُ

"Our Lord, forgive me and my parents and all believers on the day when reckoning shall take place."

Surah-Al saffat 37:100:

رَبِّ هَبْ لِى مِنَ ٱلصَّٰلِحِينَ

"O my Lord, bless me with a righteous son."

4. Prophet Shuaib

Surah Al A'raf 7:89:

قَدِ ٱفْتَرَيْنَا عَلَى ٱللَّهِ كَذِبًا إِنْ عُدْنَا فِى مِلَّتِكُم بَعْدَ إِذْ نَجَّىٰنَا ٱللَّهُ مِنْهَا ۚ وَمَا يَكُونُ لَنَا أَن نَّعُودَ فِيهَا إِلَّا أَن يَشَاءَ ٱللَّهُ رَبُّنَا ۚ

وَسِعَ رَبُّنَا كُلَّ شَىْءٍ عِلْمًا ۚ عَلَى ٱللَّهِ تَوَكَّلْنَا ۚ رَبَّنَا ٱفْتَحْ بَيْنَنَا وَبَيْنَ قَوْمِنَا بِٱلْحَقِّ وَأَنتَ خَيْرُ ٱلْفَٰتِحِينَ

We will be forging a lie against Allah if we were to turn to your faith after Allah has saved us from it. It is not for us that we turn to it unless Allah, our Lord, so wills. Our Lord has encompassed everything with His knowledge. In Allah we place our trust. Our Lord, decide between us and our people, with truth, and You are the best of all judges."

5. Prophet Younus

Surah Al-Anbiya 21:87:

وَذَا ٱلنُّونِ إِذ ذَّهَبَ مُغَضِبًا فَظَنَّ أَن لَّن نَّقْدِرَ عَلَيْهِ فَنَادَىٰ فِى ٱلظُّلُمَٰتِ أَن لَّآ إِلَٰهَ إِلَّآ أَنتَ سُبْحَٰنَكَ إِنِّى كُنتُ مِنَ ٱلظَّٰلِمِينَ

"And (remember) Dhunnūn (the man of the fish, namely Yūnus X), when he walked away in anger and thought that We would never put him to trouble. Then, he called (Us) in depths of darkness saying, 'There is no god but You. Pure are You. Indeed, I was among the wrongdoers.'"

6. Prophet Ayub

Surah Al-Anbiya 21:83:

وَأَيُّوبَ إِذْ نَادَىٰ رَبَّهُۥٓ أَنِّى مَسَّنِىَ ٱلضُّرُّ وَأَنتَ أَرْحَمُ ٱلرَّٰحِمِينَ

"And (remember) Ayyūb (Job), when he called his Lord saying, 'Here I am, afflicted by pain and You are the most merciful of all the merciful.'"

7. Prophet Yousuf

Surah- Al-Yousuf 12:101:

رَبِّ قَدْ ءَاتَيْتَنِى مِنَ ٱلْمُلْكِ وَعَلَّمْتَنِى مِن تَأْوِيلِ ٱلْأَحَادِيثِ ۚ فَاطِرَ ٱلسَّمَٰوَٰتِ وَٱلْأَرْضِ أَنتَ وَلِىِّۦ فِى ٱلدُّنْيَا وَٱلْءَاخِرَةِ ۖ تَوَفَّنِى مُسْلِمًا وَأَلْحِقْنِى بِٱلصَّٰلِحِينَ

"My Lord! You have indeed bestowed on me sovereignty and taught me the interpretation of dreams; The (only) Creator of the heavens and the earth! You are my Wali (Protector, Helper, Supporter, Guardian, etc.) with the righteous."

8. Prophet Musa

Surah - Al-A'raf 7:151:

قَالَ رَبِّ ٱغْفِرْ لِى وَلِأَخِى وَأَدْخِلْنَا فِى رَحْمَتِكَ ۖ وَأَنتَ أَرْحَمُ ٱلرَّٰحِمِينَ

"My Lord! Forgive me and my brother and admit us into Your mercy. You are the most Merciful of all the merciful."

Surah - Al-Qasas 28:24:

فَسَقَىٰ لَهُمَا ثُمَّ تَوَلَّىٰٓ إِلَى ٱلظِّلِّ فَقَالَ رَبِّ إِنِّى لِمَآ أَنزَلْتَ إِلَىَّ مِنْ خَيْرٍ فَقِيرٌ

"So, he watered (their flocks) for them, then he turned back to shade, and said: 'My Lord! Truly, I am in need of whatever good that You bestow on me!'"

Surah - Al- Taha 20:25

قَالَ رَبِّ ٱشْرَحْ لِى صَدْرِى

"O my Lord! Open my chest (grant me self-confidence, contentment, and boldness)."

9. Prophet Sulaiman

Surah Al-naml, 27:19:

فَتَبَسَّمَ ضَاحِكًا مِّن قَوْلِهَا وَقَالَ رَبِّ أَوْزِعْنِىٓ أَنْ أَشْكُرَ نِعْمَتَكَ ٱلَّتِىٓ أَنْعَمْتَ عَلَىَّ وَعَلَىٰ وَٰلِدَىَّ وَأَنْ أَعْمَلَ صَٰلِحًا تَرْضَٰهُ وَأَدْخِلْنِى بِرَحْمَتِكَ فِى عِبَادِكَ ٱلصَّٰلِحِينَ

"My Lord! Inspire and bestow upon me the power and ability that I may be grateful for Your Favors which You have bestowed on me and on my parents, and that I may do righteous good deeds that will please You and admit me by Your Mercy among Your righteous slaves."

10. Prophet Zakariya

Surah Al-Anbya, 21:89:

وَزَكَرِيَّآ إِذْ نَادَىٰ رَبَّهُ رَبِّ لَا تَذَرْنِى فَرْدًا وَأَنتَ خَيْرُ ٱلْوَٰرِثِينَ

"And (remember) Zakariya (Zachariah), when he cried to his Lord: 'O My Lord! Leave me not single (childless), though You are the Best of the inheritors.'"

11. Prophet Eesa

Surah Al-Maida, 5:116:

وإذ قال الله ياعيسى ابن مريم ، أأنت قلت إلى ايمان و أمي الهين من دون الله قال شبخنگ ما يكون إلى أن تعلم أقول ما ليس لى * بحق ص إن كنث قئ فقد علقت ما فين فين و لا أعلم ما في نفيگ انک انت علام الغيوب

"And [beware the Day] when Allah will say, 'O Jesus, Son of Mary, did you say to the people, 'Take me and my mother as deities besides Allah?' He will say, 'Exalted are You! It was not for me to say that to which I have no right. If I had said it, you would have known it. You know what is within yourself, and I do not know what is within Yourself. Indeed, it is You who is Knower of the unseen.'"

يَـٰٓأَيُّهَا ٱلَّذِينَ ءَامَنُوٓا أَوْفُوا بِٱلْعُقُودِ
أُحِلَّتْ لَكُم بَهِيمَةُ ٱلْأَنْعَٰمِ إِلَّا مَا يُتْلَىٰ عَلَيْكُمْ
غَيْرَ مُحِلِّى ٱلصَّيْدِ وَأَنتُمْ حُرُمٌ إِنَّ ٱللَّهَ يَحْكُمُ مَا يُرِيدُ

"O you who believe! Fulfill (your) obligations. Lawful to you (for food) are all the beasts of cattle except that which will be announced to you (herein), game (also) being unlawful when you assume Ihram for Hajj or 'Umrah (pilgrimage). Verily, Allah commands that which He wills."

Importance and purpose of 'Tawheed' and 'Shirk' in the new Deen

The indivisible and unique 'oneness' of Allah is called "Tawheed". Muhammad's purpose behind enforcing Tawheed is explained below.

'Shirk' is the mechanism to indirectly safeguard and perpetuate the high office of Muhammad as the one and only human being **'Next-to-Allah, the Supreme'**. For lack of an appropriate word, Muhammad assumed the status of an **Anthropomorphic** God in all respects, albeit without admitting it.

The concept of 'Tawhid' (Oneness of Allah) was thus weaponized through the infamous Blasphemy Laws in Shariah which forbid any disparaging remarks against any of the three most important things i.e., Allah, Rasul, or Kitab, directly or implied. It carries a death sentence for blasphemer.

The sin called 'Shirk' would chip away the ultimate supremacy of Allah in people's perception and consequently hurt the unique and infinitely high status of Muhammad.

Muhammad, first of all gave an infinite face-lift to a semi-significant Pagan deity called Allah and up-graded Allah as the 'ONE & ONLY' supreme deity and Creator of Universe. Simultaneously, *Muhammad dismissed and trashed all other gods and deities worshiped by Polytheists.*

Through this action Muhammad was firmly set on shaping Bedouin Arabs' perception that as Almighty Allah's designated Messenger and His Most Exalted Prophet he deputized Allah in all His glory. Any infringement in Allah's supreme status would put a dent in Muhammad's importance as the Messenger of a lesser god. For this reason, attaching any of Allah's powers or attributes to any other deity was pronounced the greatest crime called 'Shirk' and an unpardonable sin in the new Deen. (Ref.: Aya from Quran about Shirk listed at the end).

Here's a long list of verses in Quran which emphasize on importance of Tawhid (Oneness of Allah) and seriously warn against the sin of 'Shirk' (Assigning or sharing any of Allah's powers and virtues with any other person, deity, or God of any denomination)

Quranic verses on Tawheed

Monotheism or belief in one Allah alone is the strongest Faith upon which Muhammad's Deen is based. Muslims believe worship is the exclusive right of Allah and owed to Him alone. Monotheism is such an important part of Faith that Muhammad during the thirteen years of His preaching in Makkah focused on Tawheed (Oneness of Allah) mainly and called people upon Tawheed by forbidding any partners to Allah. The 'divine' revelations are full of this concept of Monotheism and most of the verses are about Monotheism.

Every Prophet, Muhammad said, taught people the same lesson:

"Indeed, We sent Nuh (Noah) to his people and he said: "O my people! Worship Allah! You have no other *Ilah* (God) but Him. Certainly, I fear for you the torment of a Great Day!" [**Al-A'raf** 7: 59]

"And verily, We have sent among every *Ummah* (community, nation) a Messenger (proclaiming): "Worship Allah (Alone), and avoid (or keep away from) all false deities" Then of them were some whom Allah guided and of them were some upon whom the straying was justified. So, travel through the land and see what the end of those who denied (the truth)." [**An-Nahl** 16:36]

The basis of Creation of mankind is to worship Allah:

"And I (Allah) created not the jinn and mankind except that they should worship Me (Alone)." [**Az-Zariyat** 51:56]

"And your Lord has decreed that you worship none but Him…" [**Al-Isra'** 17:23]

"Say (O Muhammad P.B.U.H): "Come, I will recite what your Lord has prohibited you from: Join not anything in worship with Him…." [**Al-An'am** 6:151]

Every Muslim in His Five Prayers confirms this Belief:

"You (Alone) we worship, and You (Alone) we ask for help (for each and everything)" [**Al-Fatihah** 1:5]

Some of the verses that mention Monotheism are:

1. "And indeed, when we heard the Guidance (this Quran), we believed therein (Islamic Monotheism), and whosoever believes in his Lord shall have no fear, either of a decrease in the reward of his good deeds or an increase in the punishment for his sins" [**Al-Jinn** 72:13]

2. "Say (O Muhammad): "Who provides for you from the sky and the earth? Or who owns hearing and sight? And who brings out the living from the dead and brings out the dead from the living? And who disposes of the affairs?" They will say: "Allah." Say: "Will you not then be afraid of Allah's punishment (for setting up rivals in worship with Allah)?" [**Yunus 10:31**]

3. "Has he made the *Alihah* (gods) (all) into One *Ilah* (God – Allah). Verily, this is a curious thing!" [**Surah Sad 38:5**]

4. "That is Allah, your Lord! There is no god but He, the Creator of all things. Then worship Him, and He has power to dispose of all affairs" [**Al-An'am 6:102**]

5. "And verily if you ask them: "Who created the heavens and the earth?" Surely, they will say: "Allah (has created them)." Say: "tell me then, the things that you invoke besides Allah – if Allah intended some harm for me, could they remove His harm? Or if He (Allah) intended some mercy for me, could they withhold His Mercy?" Say: "Sufficient for me is Allah; in Him those who trust (i.e., believers) must put their trust." **[Az-Zumar 39:38]**

6. "Were they created by nothing? Or were they themselves the creators? Or did they create the heavens and the earth? Nay, but they have no firm Belief." **[At-tur 52:35,36]**

7. "And they say: "There is nothing but our <u>life</u> of this world, we die, and we live and nothing destroys us except *Ad-Dahr* (time). And they have no knowledge of it: they only conjecture." **[Al-Jathiya 45:24]**

8. "This is the creation of Allah. So, show Me that which those (whom you worship) besides Him have created. Nay, the Zalimun (polytheists, wrongdoers and those who do not believe in the Oneness of Allah) are in plain error." **[Luqman 31:11]**

9. "Say (O Muhammad): "Think about all that you invoke besides Allah? Show me. What have they created on the earth? Or have they a share in (the creation of) the heavens? Bring me a Book (revealed before this), or some trace of knowledge (in support of your claims), if you are truthful!"" **[Al-Ahqaf 46:4]**

10. "[Musa (Moses)] said: "Verily, you know that these signs have been sent down by none but the Lord of the heavens and the earth (as clear evidence i.e., proofs of Allah's Oneness and His Omnipotence.). And I think you are, indeed, O Fir'aun (Pharaoh) doomed to destruction!"" **[Al-Isra 17:102]**

11. "And they rejected those signs in iniquity and arrogance, though their souls were convinced there of…" **[An-Naml 27:14]**

12. "O mankind! Worship your Lord (Allah), Who created you and those who were before you so that you may become Al-Muttaqun (the pious).

13. Who has made the earth a resting place for you, and the sky as a canopy, and sent down water (rain) from the sky and brought forth fruits as a provision for you? Then do not set up rivals unto Allah (in worship) while you know (that He Alone has the right to be worshiped)" **[Al-Baqarah 2:21,22]**

14. "And (remember) when Ibrahim (Abraham) said to his father and his people: "Verily, I am innocent of what you worship, Except Him (i.e., Allah Alone) Who did create me; and verily He will guide me**." [Az-Zukhruf 43:26-7]**

15. "There is no compulsion in religion. Verily, the Right Path has become distinct from the wrong path. Whoever disbelieves in *Taghut* and believes in Allah, then he has grasped the most trustworthy handhold that will never break. And Allah is All-Hearer, All-Knower**." [Al-Baqarah 2:256]**

16. "Then anyone who violates his oath does so to the harm of his own soul. And anyone who fulfills what has been covenanted to Allah; Allah will soon grant him a great reward" **[Al-Fath 48:10]**

17. "And I have followed the religion of my fathers, – Ibrahim (Abraham), Ishaq (Isaac) and Ya'qub (Jacob) [A.S], and never could we attribute any partners whatsoever to Allah. This is from the Grace of Allah to us and to mankind, but most men do not (i.e., they neither believe in Allah, nor worship Him)**." [Yusuf 12:38]**

18. "And those who believe and whose offspring follow them in Faith: to them shall We join their offspring, and We shall not decrease the reward of their deeds in anything. Every person is a pledge for that which he has earned." **[At-Tur 52:21]**

19. "And indeed, we sent Nuh (Noah) to his people, and he said: 'O my people! Worship Allah! You have no other Ilah(God) but Him. Will you not then be afraid (of Him and His punishment)?'" **[Al-Mu'minun 23:23-4]**

20. "And recite to them the story of Ibrahim (Abraham). When he said to his father and his people: "What do you worship?" They said: "We worship idols, and to them we are ever devoted." He said: "Do they hear you, when you call on (them)? "Or do they benefit you or do they harm (you)?" They said: "(Nay) but we found our fathers doing so."" **[As-Shu'ara 26:69-74]**

21. "Those who took partners (in worship) with Allah would say: "If Allah had willed, we would not have taken partners (in worship) with Him, nor would our fathers, and we would not have forbidden anything (against His Will)." Likewise believed those who were before them, (they argued falsely with Allah's Messengers), till they tasted Our Wrath. Say: "Have you any knowledge (proof) that you can produce before us? Verily, you follow nothing but guess and you do nothing but lie." **[Al-An'am 6:148]**

22. "And they said: "If it had been the Will of the Most Gracious (Allah), we should not have worshiped them (false deities)." They have no knowledge whatsoever of that. They do nothing but lie!" **[Az-Zukhruf 43:20]**

23. "And We did not send any Messenger before you (O Muhammad P.B.U.H) but We revealed to him (saying): *Lâ ilâha illa Ana* [none has the right to be worshiped but I (Allah)], so worship Me (Alone and no one else)." **[Al-Anbiya 21:25]**

24. "And ask (O Muhammad P.B.U.H) those of Our Messengers whom We sent before you: "Did We ever appoint Gods to be worshiped besides the Most Gracious (Allah)?"" [**Az-Zukhruf 43:45**]

25. "Surely the religion (i.e., the worship and the obedience) is for Allah only. And those who take Protectors (helpers, lords, gods) besides Him (say): "We worship them only so that they may bring us near to Allah." Verily Allah will judge between them concerning that wherein they differ. Truly, Allah guides not him who is a liar, and a disbeliever." [**Az-Zumar 39:3**]

26. "And they worship besides Allah things that harm them not, nor profit them, and they say: "These are our intercessors with Allah." Say: "Do you inform Allah of that which He knows not in the heavens and on the earth?" Glorified and Exalted is He above all that which they associate as partners (with Him)!" [**Yunus 10:18**]

27. Who is he that can intercede with Him except with His permission?" [**Al-Baqarah 2:255**]

28. "And there are many angels in the heavens, whose intercession will avail nothing except after Allah has given leave for whom He wills and is pleased with" [**An-Najm 53:26**]

29. "Verily! I am Allah! *Lâ ilâha illa Ana* (none has the right to be worshiped but I), so worship Me, and perform *As-Salât* (*Iqâmat-as-Salât*) for My Remembrance" [**Surah Ta-Ha 20:14**]

30. "And whoever invokes (or worships), besides Allah, any other God, of whom he has no proof; then his reckoning is only with his Lord. Surely! The Disbelievers will not be successful." [**Al-Mu'minun 23:117**]

31. "False worship (shirk) is indeed the highest wrongdoing" [**Luqman 31:13**]

32. "Verily, Allah forgives not that any partners should be set up with Him (in worship), but He forgives anything else to whom He wills; and whoever sets up partners with Allah in worship, he has indeed invented a tremendous sin" [**An-Nisa 4:48**]

33. "Whoever assigns partners to Allah, it is as if he had fallen from the sky, and the birds had snatched him, or the wind had thrown him to a faraway place." [**Al-Hajj 22:31**]

CHAPTER 7:
Muhammad bin Abdullah

To get a clear idea of the 'Time & Space' where Muhammad made history, in terms of When, Why, and How, a brief review of the following facts will be helpful.

Facts relating to Arabian Peninsula at the dawn of Islam in 610 A.D.

Brief historical background:

The Pre-Islam Status of Arabs in the Near East.

By 530 CE, Sasanians and Byzantines had set up satellite states on their Southern frontiers. Emperor Justinian nominated Harith of Banu Ghassan, the ruler of a kingdom in Southern Syria. They converted to Monophysite Christianity and helped out their co-religionists in the region. For the next seven decades they participated in the intrigues of the Empire too. The phylarch in the Ghassanid area pleaded with Justinian and had the king Mundhir invited to the Monophysite synod in Constantinople in 580. Banu Lakhan in the East were rivals of Banu Ghassan and were involved in Sasanian affairs.

In the beginning of the 6th CCE, South Arabia was an independent country ruled by the last of the Himyarite rulers Dhu Nuwas, who was Jewish.

Monophysite Abyssinians invaded Yemen in 513 CE, Dhu Nawas did not like it and attacked the Christian settlement of Najran in 515 CE and again in 523 CE, with a massacre. Negus Ella Asbeha, the Abyssinian ruler invaded and defeated Dhu and left behind General Abraha and a deputy. In 533 CE Abraha got rid of the deputy and became the autonomous ruler and controlled the state for forty years till, 570 CE, the year of birth of Muhammad, when he died during the course of a failed invasion of Makkah. According to legend, his army had few elephants. Tiny birds threw stones at it, the elephants panicked and crushed their owners, thus that year is called 'The year of the elephant'.

None of the above took center stage in the 7th CCE; it was the relatively isolated Arabs of the Hijaz. And many Arabs especially in Syria and Iraq remained true to their patrons in Byzantine and Sassanid Empires.

But the Arabs had been deeply influenced by the civilizations around them in which Christianity and Judaism had a firm foothold.

The Arabian Peninsula, which encompasses present day Saudi Arabia, Yemen, Kuwait, Bahrain, UAE, Qatar, and Oman, had been a vast desert and wasteland of 12.5 million square miles. It was an arid land of sand dunes, frequent sandstorms, devoid of verdure, and few and far between oases. In its south is the Red Sea, and in the north the Arabian Gulf (Iranians call it 'Persian Gulf'). Maximum length from eastern tip to extreme west is 1900 miles, and maximum width north to south is 1300 miles. In the north of the Arabian Gulf was the Persian Empire, and in its northwest, the Roman Empire, during Muhammad's lifetime. The total population of the entire peninsula in the 7th century A.D. is not known as no indication is found in any historical or oral accounts. The best guesstimate is under one million.

Tribes in the Arabian Peninsula c. 600 CE: Approximate locations of some of the important tribes of the Arabian Peninsula before the dawn of Islam. Family groups called clans formed larger tribal units, which reinforced family cooperation in the difficult living conditions on the Arabian Peninsula and protected its members against other tribes.

Nomadic Tribes in Pre-Islamic Arabia

Until recently, the majority of Muslims were, and some still are, unaware of the environment and over-all living conditions that existed in the sixth and seventh century Arabia, except in passing. Here are some bullet points for readers to understand.

- **Bedouin:** a predominantly desert-dwelling Arabian ethnic group, traditionally divided into tribes or clans.

- Nomadic Bedouin tribes dominated the Arabian Peninsula before the rise of Islam.

- Family groups called clans formed larger tribal units, which reinforced family cooperation in the difficult living conditions on the Arabian Peninsula and protected its members against other tribes.

- The Bedouin tribes were nomadic pastoralists who relied on their herds of goats, sheep, and camels for meat, milk, cheese, blood, fur/wool, and other sustenance.

- The pre-Islamic Bedouins also hunted, served as bodyguards, escorted caravans, worked as mercenaries, and traded or raided to gain animals, women, gold, fabric, and other luxury items.

- Until Muhammad gained prominence in the first quarter of 7th century C.E. and declared that he was a direct descendent of Abraham, Bedouins never thought or believed that they were bani-Ismail i.e., progeny of Abraham's first-born Ishmael (Ismail in Arabic), son of Abraham's concubine Hager.

- Arab tribes began to appear in the south Syrian deserts and southern Jordan around 200 CE but spread from the central Arabian Peninsula after the rise of Islam in the 630s CE.

The whole region had no formal government, neither an administrative infrastructure nor a central authority to govern the region.

Most Muslims do not have a clear understanding of the quality of life, availability of economic opportunities, health-care facilities, environmental hygiene, general standard of living and the level of literacy that existed in the Arabian Peninsula when Muhammad announced his divine ordainment as the 'Final Rasul (Messenger) of Allah'.

The Arabian Peninsula was in an age of complete ignorance and darkness, compared to their northern and western neighbors in Persian and Roman Empires. Illiteracy among Arabs was overwhelming. Ability to read and write Hebrew, Aramaic,' Avestan' (Predecessor of primitive Persian), or Greek was considered literacy. The Arabic language till then, was just an oral means of communication, having a bunch of dialects – still in the very early stage of dealing with borrowed alphabets for developing a script for writing in one standardized Arabic language.

Neither the Persians, nor Romans had any interest in owning, occupying, or having anything to do with the unproductive desert or its inhabitants whom they considered savage, extremely backward and uncivilized; better stayed away from.

Homes in the Hejaz region were simply tents made with hides. There was no concept of latrines, running water and sewerage systems. Men, women, and children would go for bowel movement in the wilderness of desert and cover the feces with sand. Water from wells, few and far between, a pond, or collected from meager rainfall, was in short supply, hence a precious commodity.

As a result of endemic illiteracy, the collective pool of knowledge in the vast wasteland of Arabian Peninsula consisted of information perceived by the five basic senses of humans i.e., seeing, hearing, tasting, smelling, and feeling an object by touching. The gaps in organic knowledge were filled with fanciful imagination. That led to many cults with numerous imagined gods for the polytheist Pagans who made idols of those imagined gods and worshiped them. Stories filled with fantasies were concocted and orally passed down from generation to generation as a norm. Those imagined narratives and fictional tales were treated as facts simply because they fulfilled a human need of satisfying their imagination. In the absence of formal education and awareness, the only alternative, however poor in quality, was to sustain the collective psyche and natural curiosity with a generous dose of imagined realities.

1. People in the Roman and Persian empires by comparison, were intellectually advanced, refined, and sophisticated. They professed belief in organized religions and possessed duly canonized and codified scriptures in Greek, Hebrew, and Aramaic languages. They too would not doubt, or question, their own religious beliefs, or demand empirical verification. Most glaring examples of strong belief in imagined realities were the stories of miraculous transformation of burning embers into a cool bliss by prayer of first Jewish prophet Abraham, or parting of the Red Sea on a command of another Jewish Prophet Moses. Similarly, the fantasies of a virgin birth of Jesus among Christians, without a biological father, or the fanciful story of Arda Viraf (Viraz, in some texts) a Zoroastrian priest who had claimed that he was invited in spirit to Heavens by the Creator of Universe for a sight-seeing tour of Heaven and Hell to describe to his followers, on his return to Earth, how the sinners were being punished in Hell and pious rewarded in Paradise. All those fantastic claims were readily believed by their respective followers. Faithful till this day, believe in such fantasies as true gospels.

Here's an interesting commentary on Abrahamic faiths by an unknown satirist.

"Abraham invented God. Moses and his people owned that God. Jesus claimed he was the son of that God. Muhammad did prevaricate and presented himself as GOD's mouthpiece and regent on Earth"

In short, that was the prevailing intellectual level of the people of Arabian Peninsula, in the 7th century A.D.

The cultural values of Arabs revolved around hospitality, appreciation for poetry and poets (long odes and poems were the only means of recording the past events, in the oral era), bravery in battles, sword fights, archery and expertise in horse-riding.

Coalescence of oral storytelling, poetry recital, and performative music and dance were long-standing traditions in Arabs' cultural heritage. One outstanding feature was desert dwellers' ability to navigate in the vast desert by watching the position of stars in the clear sky at night and using them as a natural compass for charting the direction of their travels accurately for required destinations. (Ref.: Khouri, Malek (2010). The Arab National Project in Youssef Chahine's Cinema. American Univ in Cairo Press. ISBN 9789774163548.)

Some of the social behaviors were very strange from today's standards. For instance, the Arab tribesmen would steal or snatch property, cattle or women and children of other tribes, without guilt or remorse, whenever they could, hesitating rarely sometimes, due to fear of reprisal and revenge lasting several generations in future. This was a tribal norm for making a living. Muhammad and his earliest converts practiced this type of snatch & grab raids for several years in the beginning in Medina, after emigrating from Makkah. Those way-laying raids on other tribes were called "*Razzia*". They way-laid caravans of non-Medinan tribes, such as trading caravans of Meccans. When under Muhammad's command, a *Razzia* would be called a "Ghazwa" (Plural "Ghazwat").

The same practice was sanctified in Muhammad's new Deen in the name of "*Jihad fi sabil Allah*" (Struggle dedicated to Allah) as armed aggression over other regions, with the booty of war as incentive and collecting annual protection tax called *Jizya from the defeated and occupied tribes. A detailed explanation about what Jizya is, will follow later in the book.*

Culturally, it was considered shameful, embarrassing, and cowardly to attack any individual from behind, or stab an adversary in the back, except in the chaos of a battle. Once an enemy was challenged to a fight and killed in the battle, the killer would decapitate the enemy and stick a spear in the severed head and hoist it around as a trophy of victory. A soldier would carry the decapitated head of his kill, hoisted on his spear, and carry it to the chief of the tribe and throw it at Chief's feet to earn kudos from him. Women and children of the vanquished enemy would be hand-tied at the back, and feet tied with a short rope, just enough to let them take small steps, to preclude escape by running away. A famous example of this custom of hoisting an enemy's severed head is the killing of Hussain ibne Ali, grandson of Muhammad at Karbala, whose head was severed and hoisted on a spear. It was a routine tribal custom, made famous, as if an isolated case, in the Muharram Majalis of the Shia sect.

Muhammad, born in 570 A.D., had an unenviable start in life as an orphan grandson of a poor tribal chief, who himself was a humble trader. He lost his father Abdullah before he was born. Lost his mother Amenah at 6, lost his guardian grandfather Abdul Mottalib at 8, and became a ward of his uncle Abi Taleb. Being a parentless poor lonely kid, he had to fend for himself 24/7. He grew up being extra careful and extra cautious in all activities of daily existence, completely devoid of any material or moral support, normally provided by parents and older siblings. Nature had endowed him with a brilliant mind, perceptiveness, insight, fore-sight and far-sight. The paranoia heightened and sharpened the senses. All he did in his pre-teen years was shepherding the goats and sheep. Never received any coaching to learn reading or writing any numbers, or alphabets. Muhammad started working for his uncle Abi Taleb as an attendant of camels in trading caravans, at 12 or 14. Despite being completely illiterate he had an exceptional knack for communicating very convincingly, both with individuals and larger groups of people. These rare traits, skills and talents, came very handy when he rose up the ladder of career in trading caravans. From an insignificant existence as a camel attendant, he worked his way up to become a commercial deal maker of excellence. He was undoubtedly a rare example of a highly talented but illiterate desert dweller, with supreme qualities of revolutionary leaders.

Muhammad's mission in life, carefully assessed in hindsight, was unarguably the following:

Conquering the entire Arabian Peninsula and ruling it as an autocrat, to amass power and influence for himself and his clan. The purpose, also viewed in hindsight, was quite evident; ridding himself of insecurity, paranoia and vulnerability, to shake off the insignificance of a weak, insecure and paranoid orphan he once was. This was a dream only a person like Muhammad could have dreamt and actually bring it to fruition with his rare and unique talents. He built a strategy and worked on it with perseverance and determination. This is an awesome story of dedication to his mission.

All manipulations and maneuvering Muhammad did, is numbered in red, to count the number of hoops he jumped through to reach his goal.

His first milestone to achieve was *building an outstanding personal 'Brand'*, in today's lexicon, to gain prominence, power and influence. Building that iconic personal brand was a lengthy process, and not without purpose. He wished to create a personal image of a prominent individual of importance and authority, like a respected community leader, and eventually a special prophet of God Almighty.

As a first step in that direction, he excelled and made quite a name in the art of arbitrating between two strong individuals, or warring tribes, with both sides feeling very satisfied with Muhammad's handling of arbitration.

(1) To add spiritual aura, awe and devotional respect to his image, he decided to contrive and declare a new Deen (Religion) and present himself as 'Prophet' of God Almighty.

(2) One stumbling block though, in pursuing this objective was his blood line of ancestry. All monotheist prophets before him, like Abraham and the long list of prophets in Abraham's

progeny such as Moses Jacob, Joseph, Lot etc. etc. were natives of Israel, belonging to the same clan in the bloodline of Abraham. To satisfy the expectation of the tribal perception of a prophet's ancestry, Muhammad had to, somehow, establish that he too belonged to the bloodline of Abraham.

(3) With this end in mind, Muhammad tweaked the biblical story 'Aqēdat Yīshaq' in which Abraham takes his second son Isaac to offer him as a sacrifice to God almighty on Mount Moriah. It's the same mount where the Temple on the Mount was later built in Jerusalem.

(4) Muhammad switched Isaac by Ismail, Abraham's first born son, from his concubine Hager.

(5) Muhammad then switched the spot of sacrifice from mount Moriah in Jerusalem to Mount Hira near Makkah.

(6) Muhammad also switched the place where Abraham, according to legend, deserted Ismail and Hager in the Paran part of Sinai desert, 1200 miles northwest of Makkah, To Makkah itself.

(7) The story of Ismail thus becoming progenitor of Arabs in Hejaz was crafted to portray Muhammad as a direct descendant of Abraham.

Here's a chart pointing out the importance of being a progeny of Abraham's clan and blood line.

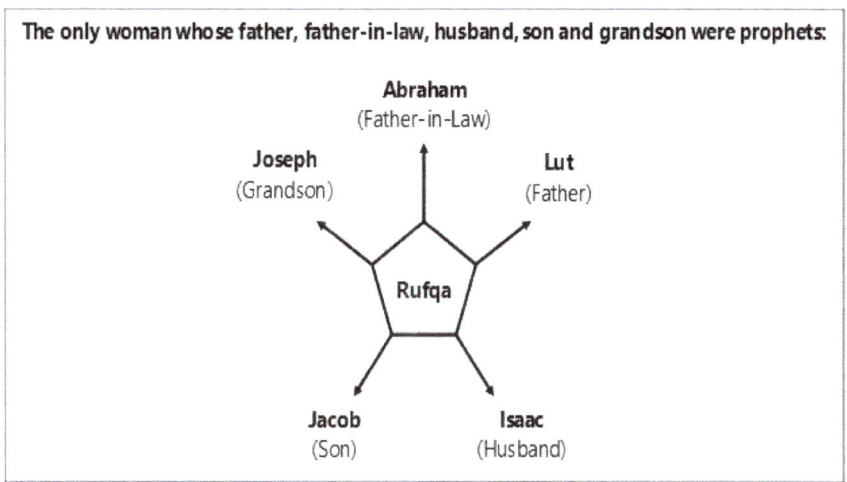

"*There is no historical evidence whatsoever showing that Ishmael was the progenitor of the Arabs, or that Abraham was ever in Mecca. The Ishmaelites were probably Canaanite-speaking, not an early form of Arabic, but a dialect similar to Hebrew. In time they disappeared or were absorbed into other groups, like so many other ancient peoples. Much later Josephus invoked Ishmael's name* **to conjure up a genealogy for the Arabs**. *He has a lot to answer for. The rest, as they say, is history*".

Ref.1. (**Dr. Mark Durie** *is an academic, human rights activist, a Stillman-Ginsburg Writing Fellow at the Middle East Forum, and Adjunct Research Fellow of the Arthur Jeffery Centre for the Study of Islam at Melbourne School of Theology.*

Ref. 2. Eph'al, I., 1976. "Ishmael" and the "Arab(s)": A transformation of ethnological terms'. Journal of Near Eastern Studies, 35(4): 225-235.)

Here's one more narrative of a renowned Biblical Scholar Nicholas Jagdeo , Blogger at The Times of Israel (2010-present). "Mecca has no place in Jewish religious history. The story of the

Kaaba is revisionist history - definitely a myth propagated by Muhammad as an attempt to legitimize himself and his imagined version of history. Muhammad appropriated the Jewish narrative to (1) give himself and his Arab brethren a supposed link to Abraham through Ishmael (this link has never been verified, except for say-so of Muhammad) by changing the main characters in the *'Aqēdat Yīṣḥaq* story - from Isaac to Ishmael, and (2), to change the location from the Jewish-centric Jerusalem to Arab-centric Mecca.

Before Muhammad gained prominence, no Arabs in Hejaz had any inkling of being the "Ishmaelite" race, or descendants of Abraham. The character of Abraham was Arabized to Ibrahim and the character of Ishmael (Isma'il) was inserted to include Arabs in the lineage of Abraham in order to counter the Jewish narrative. It was a masterful stroke of marketing genius from Muhammad and is a very early example of cultural appropriation.

That was a story of forced validation for Muhammad to act as an ordained prophet of Monotheist God Almighty with an Arabic name "Allah". All this manipulation of legend was done to convince the 7th century Bedouins that Muhammad too belonged to the clan of Abraham like all other prophets before him.

Tribal antecedence of Muhammad. (Ref.: https://www.youtube.com/watch?v=e4N4MzTCM6w)

The progeny of Ismail and his mother Hager (Hajirah in Arabic) were known as Hagarines and they actually lived in   the Northwestern Arabia known as the Musta'riba or the "Arabized Arab". It was Josephus, a Jewish historian, writing in the first century CE, who first advanced the idea that Ishmael was the ancestor of the Arabs in Musta'riba. In *"The Antiquities of the Jews"* Josephus stated that Ishmael was "the founder" of the Arabian nation, and Abraham was "their father". From Josephus, this assumed connection between the Arabs and Abraham, through Ishmael, passed into the historical consciousness of Christians, and then made its way in next few millennia into early Islam by Muhammad, to push his own agenda.

The original progeny of Ismail (Bani Ismail) had been the natives of Paran desert. Being nomadic in character, over a couple of millennia, some of them traveled as far as central regions of Arabian Peninsula and got amalgamated with other populations of the peninsula including the natives of Hejaz region.

(8) Muhammad poached a less significant god known as Allah from Pagans' pantheon i.e., Kaaba in Makkah, and upgraded Allah for his new Deen, as a lot more powerful, resourceful and knowledgeable God than the supreme gods of Judaism, Christianity and Zoroastrianism.

Once he created that outstanding image for himself as the final and ultimate prophet ever, he would start the Herculean task of uniting the feuding, infighting Arabian tribes, as his next milestone. He had to accomplish the unity among feuding tribes to be able to raise a large, unified army to conquer and occupy the entire Arabian Peninsula. However, he could not make any headway in that direction in Makkah due to overwhelming opposition from Pagans of Makkah.

Almost all tribes were mired in blood-feuds for generations, due to their traditional and aggressive activities provoking hostile reactions from other tribes. That was the normative way of tribal life among Bedouins of the Arabian Peninsula.

To create the desired unity and brotherhood, Muhammad needed the infighting tribes to completely submit to Muhammad's will. To that end, Muhammad proffered Allah as the 'One & Only God'. The converts were required to completely surrender and submit to Allah's 'Will' under all circumstances.

(9) The Will of Allah was, by design, received by Muhammad alone, through 'Divine Revelations', and announced to the followers, by Muhammad. This was the brilliant mechanism for Muhammad to present his own will, dressed as Allah's Will for fail-proof compliance. Ref. A list of Aya from the Quran is attached emphasizing the importance of complying with Allah's Will, conveyed through divine messages from Allah. The divine messages also warn the followers about the very dire punishments if the Will of Allah is not obeyed. These Aya were obviously composed for the consumption of Arabs to make them submit completely to the Will of Allah (which in fact was the will of Muhammad).

Muhammad had two powerful protectors. His rich and influential wife Khadijah and his uncle Abi Taleb, head of Banu Hashem clan, and chief of the al-Quresh tribe. When Muhammad announced that God Almighty Allah had ordained him as the 'Most Exalted' and Final Prophet for the mankind, for preaching the latest version of Allah's 'One & Only' Deen, he pointed out that his Deen was also preached earlier by all prophets, from Adam to Jesus. Muhammad did not deny the prophethood of the prophets of Judaism, or prophethood of Jesus Christ. Therefore, the Jews and Christians were not as hostile to Muhammad, in the beginning, as the Pagan polytheism idolaters, whose deities Muhammad rejected altogether as trash. The great majority of Pagan population of Makkah, therefore, became deadly against Muhammad and his ministry. If they could, they would kill Muhammad. The protective support from Muhammad's wife, coupled with protective support he had from his uncle, the chief of the tribe, kept him protected from Pagans' wrath.

Khadijah and Abi Taleb, Muhammad's two protectors, died within 8 months of each other in 621 A.D. and Muhammad was left with no protection. The danger to his life forced Muhammad to seek protection in exile as soon as possible. The details of

Muhammad's migration to Medina in 622 A.D., and details of its background are as follows:

Yethrib was inhabited by both Arabs and Jews. The Arabs consisted of two tribes–the Banu Aws and Banu Khazraj. The Aws and Khazraj were constantly at war with each other, and this made traditional rules for maintaining law and order dysfunctional, and, without a neutral man with considerable authority over things, stability seemed unlikely. It is also accepted by modern historians of Arabia that the Arabs of Medina, erstwhile Yethrib, had heard from their Jewish fellow citizens of the coming of a prophet.

al-Tabari (839-923) explained it this way:

"One of the things which God had done for them [the Khazraj] *in order to prepare them for Islam was that the Jews lived with them in their land. The Jews were people of scripture and knowledge, while the Khazraj were polytheists and idolaters. They had gained mastery over the Jews in their land, and whenever any dispute arose among them the Jews would say to them, "A prophet will be sent soon. His time is at hand. We shall follow him, and with him as our leader we shall kill you as 'Ad and Iram were killed." When the Messenger of God spoke to this group of people* [the Khazraj] *and called them to God, they said to one another, "Take note! This, by God, is the prophet with whom the Jews are menacing you. Do not let them be before you in accepting him."*

These six accepted Islam because they believed that Muhammad was the prophet with whom the Jews had been threatening them. These six men of the Khajraz wanted to be the first to join with that prophet.

These six new converts returned to Medina and started converting others to Muhammad's Deen; the converts in Medina later became known as *Ansaars* [Helpers]

Groups of the *Medinan converts* came to Mecca and met with Muhammad in 621 and again in 622. In that second meeting the Ansar took an oath of allegiance to Muhammad. This oath of allegiance included a pledge to wage war against all of mankind:

"When they gathered to take the oath of allegiance to the Messenger of God, al-'Abbas b. 'Ubadah b. Nadlah al-Ansari…said, "People of the Khazraj, do you know what you are pledging yourselves to in swearing allegiance to this man?" "Yes," they said. He continued, "In swearing allegiance to him you are pledging yourselves to wage war against all mankind."

This oath of allegiance also meant that the Ansar would have to sever their ties with the Jews of Medina. One of the Ansar said to Muhammad:

"O Messenger of God, there are ties between us and other people which we shall have to sever (meaning the Jews). If we do this and God gives you victory, will you perhaps return to your own people and leave us?" The Messenger of God smiled and then said, "Rather, blood is blood, and blood shed without retaliation is blood shed without retaliation. You are of me, and I am of you. I shall fight whomever you fight and make peace with whomever you make peace with."

During Dhu al-Hijjah of the year 620 CE, Muhammad convened with some members of the Banu Khazraj tribe from Medina near the al-'Aqabah Hill in Mina just outside of Mecca, propounded to them the doctrines of his Deen, and recited portions of the 'divine' revelations. Impressed by this, they embraced Muhammad's Deen, and during the pilgrimage of 621, five of them brought seven others with them. These twelve informed Muhammad of the beginning of gradual development of the new Deen in Medina, and took a formal pledge of allegiance at Muhammad's hand, promising to accept him as a prophet, to worship none but one God, and to renounce sins including theft, adultery, and murder, in what is now known as the First Pledge of al-'Aqabah. At their request, Muhammad sent with them Mus'ab ibn 'Umair to teach them the instructions of the new Deen. The following year, in 622, a delegation of around 75 Momineen consisting of members of both the Aws and Khazraj from Medina restated the terms of the First Pledge and also assured Muhammad of their full support and protection if the latter would migrate to Medina as an arbitrator to reconcile among the Aws and Khazraj. This is known as the Second Pledge at al-Aqabah, and was a religio-political success that paved the way for the Medinan Hegira. Following the pledges, Muhammad encouraged his followers to migrate to Yethrib, later called Medina, and in a span of two months, nearly all the Momineen of Makkah migrated to the city of Medina. Once he settled in Medina, Muhammad proceeded with his plan to unite all infighting and feuding tribes.

1. Muhammad had already announced a new religion and proclaimed the position of the Final Prophet of "ONE & ONLY" God Allah, about 12 years ago in Makkah.

He upgraded himself as the "Most Exalted Prophet" of Allah to proselytize and unite all the infighting tribes under his 'Divine and Spiritual' leadership. (Quran 21:107 affirms Muhammad to be "Most exalted" among all prophets of Allah as a "Mercy" to the entire Universe)

Muhammad's character, conduct and reputation, as the greatest ever demagogue of mankind.

Muhammad planned and successfully executed it, by building a stellar, nay a **godly Brand** of himself as an **anthropomorphic God**, which has endured for a millennium and a half so far. It is a magnificent proof of his brilliance, his insight, fore-sight and far-sight.

The initial lessons of life he was forced to learn by circumstance, are to fend for himself, and avail all opportunities he came across, to secure himself and benefit from.

(10) How Muhammad built a godly image, and a supreme brand with the help of appropriately worded 'Divine Revelations' given below.

The Quran Chapter 21:108

وَ مَآ اَرْسَلْنٰكَ اِلَّا رَحْمَةً لِّلْعٰلَمِيْن

"And We have sent thee not but as a mercy for all peoples."

The Quran Chapter 33:56

اِنَّ ٱللَّهَ وَمَلٰٓئِكَتَهُ يُصَلُّونَ عَلَى ٱلنَّبِيِّ ۚ يٰٓأَيُّهَا ٱلَّذِينَ ءَامَنُوا۟ صَلُّوا۟ عَلَيْهِ وَسَلِّمُوا۟ تَسْلِيمًا

"Indeed, Allah and his Angels send blessings on the Messenger. O you who believe, send your blessings upon him and salute him with appropriate salutation."

"There is no one in creation more worthy of an example of the Quranic verse; indeed, Allah loves those who are Muhsins — those who do beautiful things (2:195), than Prophet Muhammad (pbuh, abbreviation for "Peace be upon him")."

"O ye who believe! Obey Allah, and obey the Messenger, and those charged with authority among you...." (Known as the obedience verse) ... Say, 'Obey Allah and the Messenger.'" 4:69

"And whoever obeys Allah and the Messenger - those will be with the ones upon whom Allah has bestowed favor of the **prophets.**

The Quran 9:128.

لَقَدْ جَاءَكُمْ رَسُوْلٌ مِنْ اَنْفُسِكُمْ عَزِيْزٌ عَلَيْهِ مَا عَنِتُّمْ حَرِيْصٌ عَلَيْكُمْ بِالْمُؤْمِنِيْنَرَءُوْفٌ رَحِيْمٌ

Surely, a Messenger has come unto you from among yourselves; grievous to him is that you should fall into trouble; *he is* ardently desirous of your *welfare*; and to the believers *he is* compassionate, merciful.

The Quran 33:22

لَقَدْ كَانَ لَكُمْ فِىْ رَسُوْلِ اللهِ اُسْوَةٌ حَسَنَةٌ لِمَنْ كَانَ يَرْجُوا اللهَ وَ الْيَوْمَ الْاٰخِرَ وَ ذَكَرَ اللهَ كَثِيْرًا

"Verily you have in the Prophet of Allah an excellent model, for him who fears Allah and the Last Day and who remembers Allah much."

The Quran Chapter 33:41

مَا كَانَ مُحَمَّدٌ اَبَآ اَحَدٍ مِّنْ رِّجَالِكُمْ وَ لٰكِنْ رَّسُوْلَ اللهِ وَ خَاتَمَ النَّبِيّنَ ۭ وَ كَانَ اللهُ بِكُلِّ شَىْءٍ عَلِيْمًا

"Muhammad is not the father of any of your men, but *he is* the Messenger of Allah and the Seal of the Prophets; and Allah has full knowledge of all things."

The Quran Chapter 33:46

يَٰٓأَيُّهَا ٱلنَّبِىُّ إِنَّآ أَرْسَلْنَٰكَ شَٰهِدًا وَّ مُبَشِّرًا وَّ نَذِيْرًا

"O Prophet, truly We have sent thee as a Witness, and Bearer of glad tidings, and a Warner."

The Quran Chapter 33:47

وَّ دَاعِيًا إِلَى ٱللهِ بِإِذْنِهِ وَ سِرَاجًا مُّنِيْرًا

"And as a Summoner unto Allah by His command, and as a Lamp that gives *bright* light."

The Quran Chapter 33:57

إِنَّ ٱللهَ وَ مَلَٰئِكَتَهُ يُصَلُّوْنَ عَلَى ٱلنَّبِىِّ يَٰٓأَيُّهَا ٱلَّذِيْنَ أَمَنُوْا صَلُّوْا عَلَيْهِ وَ سَلِّمُوْا تَسْلِيْمًا

"Allah and His angels send blessings on the Prophet. O ye who believe! you *also* should invoke blessings on him and salute *him* with the salutation of peace."

The Quran Chapter 48:29

هُوَ ٱلَّذِىٓ أَرْسَلَ رَسُوْلَهُ بِٱلْهُدَى وَ دِيْنِ ٱلْحَقِّ لِيُظْهِرَهُ عَلَى ٱلدِّيْنِ كُلِّهِ وَ كَفَى بِٱللهِ شَهِيْدًا

"He it is Who has sent His Messenger, with guidance and the Religion of truth, that He may make it prevail over *all other* religions. And sufficient is Allah as a Witness."

The Quran Chapter 68:05

وَ إِنَّكَ لَعَلَى خُلُقٍ عَظِيْمٍ

"And thou dost surely possess high moral excellence."

Quran 2:195

"There is no one in creation more worthy an example of the Quranic verse; emphatically, Allah loves those who are Muhsins — those who do beautiful things, as done by Prophet Muhammad (pbuh)."

Quran 4:69

وَمَن يُطِعِ ٱللَّهَ وَٱلرَّسُولَ فَأُو۟لَـٰٓئِكَ مَعَ ٱلَّذِينَ أَنْعَمَ ٱللَّهُ عَلَيْهِم مِّنَ ٱلنَّبِيِّـۧنَ وَٱلصِّدِّيقِينَ وَٱلشُّهَدَآءِ وَٱلصَّـٰلِحِينَ ۚ وَحَسُنَ أُو۟لَـٰٓئِكَ رَفِيقًا

"O ye who believe! Obey Allah, and **obey the Messenger,** and those charged with authority among you...." (Known as 'The obedience' **verse**) ... Say, 'Obey Allah **and the Messenger.**'" 4:69 "And whoever obeys Allah **and the Messenger** - those will be with the ones upon whom Allah has bestowed favor of the **prophets** ..."

Quran 9:128

لَقَدْ جَآءَكُمْ رَسُولٌ مِّنْ أَنفُسِكُمْ عَزِيزٌ عَلَيْهِ مَا عَنِتُّمْ حَرِيصٌ عَلَيْكُم بِٱلْمُؤْمِنِينَ رَءُوفٌ رَّحِيمٌ

"Surely, a Messenger has come unto you from among yourselves; grievous to him is that you should fall into trouble; he is ardently desirous of your welfare; and to the believers he is compassionate, merciful."

Quran 21:108

وَ مَآ اَرْسَلْنٰكَ اِلَّا رَحْمَةً لِّلْعٰلَمِيْنَ

"And We have sent thee not but as a mercy for all peoples."

Quran 33:22

لَقَدْ كَانَ لَكُمْ فِىْ رَسُوْلِ اللهِ أُسْوَةٌ حَسَنَةٌ لِمَنْ كَانَ يَرْجُوا اللهَ وَ الْيَوْمَ الْآخِرَ وَ ذَكَرَ اللهَ كَثِيْرًا

"Verily you have in the Prophet of Allah an excellent model, for him who fears Allah and the Last Day and who remembers Allah much."

Quran 33:41

مَا كَانَ مُحَمَّدٌ أَبَآ أَحَدٍ مِنْ رِجَالِكُمْ وَ لٰكِنْ رَسُوْلَ اللهِ وَ خَاتَمَ النَّبِيّنَ ۖ وَ كَانَ اللهُ بِكُلِّ شَىْءٍ عَلِيْمًا

"Muhammad is not the father of any of your men, but he is the Messenger of Allah and the Seal of the Prophets; and Allah has full knowledge of all things."

Quran 33:46

يَآأَيُّهَا النَّبِىُّ إِنَّآ أَرْسَلْنٰكَ شَاهِدًا وَّ مُبَشِّرًا وَّ نَذِيْرًا

"O Prophet, truly We have sent thee as a Witness, and Bearer of glad tidings, and a Warner."

Quran 33:47

وَّ دَاعِيًا إِلَى اللهِ بِإِذْنِهِ وَ سِرَاجًا مُّنِيْرًا

"And as a Summoner unto Allah by His command, and as a Lamp that gives bright light."

Quran 33:57

اِنَّ اللهَ وَ مَلٰٓئِكَتَهٗ يُصَلُّوۡنَ عَلَى النَّبِیِّ ۚ يٰۤاَيُّهَا الَّذِيۡنَ اٰمَنُوۡا صَلُّوۡا عَلَيۡهِ وَ سَلِّمُوۡا تَسۡلِيۡمًا

"Allah and His angels send blessings on the Prophet. O ye who believe! you also should invoke blessings on him and salute him with the salutation of peace."

Quran 48:29

هُوَ الَّذِیۡۤ اَرۡسَلَ رَسُوۡلَهٗ بِالۡهُدٰی وَ دِيۡنِ الۡحَقِّ لِيُظۡهِرَهٗ عَلَى الدِّيۡنِ كُلِّهٖ ؕ وَ كَفٰی بِاللهِ شَهِيۡدًا

"It is He Who has sent His Messenger, with guidance and the Religion of truth, that He may make it prevail over all other religions. And sufficient is Allah as a Witness.

Quran 68:04

وَ اِنَّكَ لَعَلٰی خُلُقٍ عَظِيۡمٍ

"And thou dost surely possess high moral excellences."

Quran 33:21

لَقَدۡ كَانَ لَكُمۡ فِیۡ رَسُوۡلِ اللَّهِ اُسۡوَةٌ حَسَنَةٌ لِّمَنۡ كَانَ يَرۡجُوا اللَّهَ وَالۡيَوۡمَ الۡاٰخِرَ وَذَكَرَ اللَّهَ كَثِيۡرًا

Most exemplary character: "Indeed, in the (Prophetic) Messenger of Allah you have an excellent example (to follow) for him whose hope is in Allah and the Last Day and remembers Allah much."

Quran 68:4

"And most surely, you have an exalted moral character."

Quran 4:65

فَلَا وَرَبِّكَ لَا يُؤْمِنُونَ حَتَّىٰ يُحَكِّمُوكَ فِيمَا شَجَرَ بَيْنَهُمْ ثُمَّ لَا يَجِدُوا فِى أَنْفُسِهِمْ حَرَجًا مِّمَّا قَضَيْتَ وَيُسَلِّمُوا تَسْلِيمًا

Final judge and arbiter: "But, nay, by your Lord, they do not have (real) Faith until they make you judge of what is in dispute between them and find within themselves no dislike of that which you decide but submit with full submission."

Quran 24:51

إِنَّمَا كَانَ قَوْلَ الْمُؤْمِنِينَ إِذَا دُعُوا إِلَى اللهِ وَرَسُولِهِ لِيَحْكُمَ بَيْنَهُمْ أَنْ يَقُولُوا سَمِعْنَا وَأَطَعْنَا وَأُولَٰئِكَ هُمُ الْمُفْلِحُونَ

"The response of the believers when summoned to Allah and His (Prophetic) Messenger that he may judge between them is only that they say: "We hear, and we obey". And it is those who are successful."

Quran 24:52

وَمَنْ يُطِعِ اللهَ وَرَسُولَهُ وَيَخْشَ اللهَ وَيَتَّقْهِ فَأُولَٰئِكَ هُمُ الْفَآئِزُونَ

"Those who obey Allah and His Messenger and fear Him and avoid disobeying Him: such, indeed, shall triumph."

Quran 69:40

إِنَّهُ لَقَوْلُ رَسُولٍ كَرِيمٍ

Honored, Noble: "It (the Quran) is indeed the Word (of Allah, brought) by an honored (Prophetic) Messenger."

Quran 4:174

يَٰٓأَيُّهَا ٱلنَّاسُ قَدْ جَآءَكُم بُرْهَٰنٌ مِّن رَّبِّكُمْ وَأَنزَلْنَآ إِلَيْكُمْ نُورًا مُّبِينًا

He is Burhan (Clear Proof): "O mankind! Surely, there has come to you a Clear Proof (Prophet Muhammad) from your Lord and We have sent down to you a clear Light (the Quran)."

Quran 21:107

ٱقْتَرَبَ لِلنَّاسِ حِسَابُهُمْ وَهُمْ فِى غَفْلَةٍ مُّعْرِضُونَ

Mercy for all the worlds: "And We have sent you not except as a mercy for all the worlds."

Quran 47:2

وَالَّذِينَ آمَنُوا وَعَمِلُوا الصَّالِحَاتِ وَآمَنُوا بِما نُزِّلَ عَلى مُحَمَّدٍ وَهُوَ الحَقُّ مِن رَبِّهِمْ كَفَّرَ عَنهُم سَيِّئَاتِهِم وَأَصلَحَ بالَهُم

His name is Muhammad (Meaning the Most Praised One): "And those who believe and do good deeds and believe in that which is revealed to Muhammad, and it is the Truth from their Lord, He (Allah) removes from them their ill-deeds and improves their state."

Quran 4:113

وَلَوْلَا فَضْلُ اللَّهِ عَلَيْكَ وَرَحْمَتُهُ لَهَمَّت طَّائِفَةٌ مِّنْهُمْ أَن يُضِلُّوكَ وَمَا يُضِلُّونَ إِلَّا أَنفُسَهُمْ ۖ وَمَا يَضُرُّونَكَ مِن شَيْءٍ ۚ وَأَنزَلَ اللَّهُ عَلَيْكَ الْكِتَبَ وَالْحِكْمَةَ وَعَلَّمَكَ مَا لَمْ تَكُن تَعْلَمُ ۚ وَكَانَ فَضْلُ اللَّهِ عَلَيْكَ عَظِيمًا

Possessor of Allah's Grace: "But for the Grace of Allah upon you (O beloved Prophet), and His Mercy, a party of them had resolved to deceive you, but they misled no one except themselves and they will not hurt you at all. And Allah has sent down to you the Scripture (the Quran) and the Wisdom, and has taught you what you did not know, and the Grace of Allah toward you has been very great."

Quran 3:164

لَقَدْ مَنَّ اللَّهُ عَلَى الْمُؤْمِنِينَ إِذْ بَعَثَ فِيهِمْ رَسُولًا مِّنْ أَنفُسِهِمْ يَتْلُوا عَلَيْهِمْ ءَايَتِهِ وَيُزَكِّيهِمْ وَيُعَلِّمُهُمُ الْكِتَبَ وَالْحِكْمَةَ وَإِن كَانُوا مِن قَبْلُ لَفِى ضَلَلٍ مُّبِينٍ ۝

He is a special favor of Allah: "Certainly, Allah has shown a special favor to the believers by raising among them a (Prophetic) Messenger from among themselves who recites to them His verses (of the Quran), and purifies them, and teaches them the Scripture (the Quran) and the Wisdom, although before (he came to them) they were in manifest error."

Quran 8:33

وَمَا كَانَ اللَّهُ لِيُعَذِّبَهُمْ وَأَنتَ فِيهِمْ ۚ وَمَا كَانَ اللَّهُ مُعَذِّبَهُمْ وَهُمْ يَسْتَغْفِرُونَ

Allah does not punish people if Muhammad is in their midst: "And Allah would not punish them while you are in their midst, and Allah will not punish them while they seek (His) forgiveness."

In addition to the above Quranic Aya, Muhammad introduced following actions for Momineen to perform to remind themselves of Muhammad's special status, glory, and reverence.

Send Darud to Muhammad and his progeny in every Salat, five times a day. No Salat is acceptable to Allah unless each worshiper sends 'Durood' to Muhammad and his progeny five times a day without fail.

Send 'Durood' to Muhammad every time his name is uttered in any conversation.

Shahada "There is no God but Allah" is not complete unless you add to it "Muhammad is the Messenger of Allah".

The impact of this mandatory worship, minimum five times a day, practically elevates Muhammad to the status of an **anthropomorphic god.**

Muhammad's own psyche was pro male-domination, his conduct spoke quite loudly that he considered most women as consumer goods for men. The details shown in 'Muhammad's 'Harem', presented later in the book, will showcase this aspect more clearly. Muhammad was not cruel to slaves, but he was not anti-slavery.

Muhammad's God Allah did not ban slavery. One man/woman being owned by another man as an asset, was condoned by Allah.

How he succeeded in uniting the blood thirsty tribes is a long story of struggles, machinations, and manipulations.

The mortal fear of hellfire in perpetuity if revelations were not obeyed, and a promise of infinite rewards in Paradise for those who complied with revelations obediently, worked like a charm every time, exactly as Muhammad intended for execution of his plan (to unite the sworn enemy tribes and raise a unified army to invade, conquer, occupy, and rule the Arabian Peninsula as a king).

Muhammad identified the specific causes of disunity and blood feuds and initiated a holistic transformative plan to reform the character and conduct of warring tribes, and to train them to practice total obedience.

(11) Details of how Muhammad reformed and trained the infighting tribes to become one formidable and united community of Momineen.

The point likely to be missed by the readers is that bringing social reforms to the Jahiliya tribes, through specially composed 'divine' revelations, was not the end objective unto itself. It was a means to an 'end objective' of reforming the infighting tribes and transforming them into one large and united, all-inclusive community of Momineen, for a much deeper purpose. All of this was planned and achieved by Muhammad to raise a large, unified and disciplined army under his command, to conquer, occupy and rule the whole Peninsula as an all-powerful, absolute ruler.

Most tribes in the Arabian Peninsula, especially in the Hejaz region, as mentioned before, were mired in generational blood-feuds. This infighting was triggered by hostile behavior of the tribes towards each other, leading to surprise attacks, loot & plunder, and continual carnage. This was a way of life and a tribal tradition. The biggest hurdle for Muhammad in raising a unified army was the blood feuds and acrimony.

Muhammad identified the causes that kept fueling the aggression, militancy, and blood feuds among the tribes. As a prophet of Allah, he would compose 'divine' revelations and announce them as words from Allah to ensure full compliance. **Each revelation was targeted at eliminating a particular cause of aggression and mutual hostility.** After going through many hoops, he succeeded in uniting the infighting tribes into a homogenous, caring & loving community.

That was the only way for raising a unified army to invade and occupy the entire Arabian Peninsula and make it his dominion.

The secret of Muhammad's success in unifying the combatant tribes was the 'complete obedience' or 'total submission to Allah's commands. After reaching that milestone, raising a formidable army mentally charged and fully committed to kill the fighters of non-believers fearlessly, was smooth and easy. The Muslim fighters (Mujahideen) were promised infinite physical and carnal pleasures in Paradise (Jannah) if they got killed (Martyred) in the battles with non-believers.

Given below are the details of Aya and Ahadith used to reform their civic sense, to be cooperative across the tribal divide, and to be homogenous, loving, and caring.

Ahadith (Plural of Hadith) are Muhammads' sayings and actions called 'Traditions', mined from oral traditions, duly checked and verified for veracity and accuracy by acknowledged Imams, nearly two centuries after Muhammad's death.

Following Ahadith relate to the reformation drive and moral training of converts, for raising a unified army of infighting tribes, with the sole intention of invading and occupying the entire Arabian Peninsula under Muhammad's rule.

It was narrated on the authority of Abu Hurayrah that the Prophet said:

1. Do not envy one another.

2. Do not commit Najash [to overbid against a rival purchaser simply to harm him with no intention of buying the merchandise].

3. Do not hate one another.

4. Do not turn your backs on one another.

5. Do not enter into commercial transactions when others have entered into that [transaction]; rather, be brothers to each other, O slaves of Allah.

6. A Muslim is the brother of a Muslim; he does not do injustice to him, he does not let him down, and he does not disdain him.

7. Piety is here, [and he pointed to his chest three times].

8. It is enough evil for a Muslim to disdain his brother Muslim.

9. All of a Muslim is inviolable for other Muslims: his blood [life], his property and his honor. [Ahadees from an acknowledged and authoritative source called 'Sahih Muslim']

Several Aya from Quran, evidently composed by Muhammad in his native dialect, addressing each cause separately, on how to eradicate that evil, is attached. Readers must remember that the Aya quoted here are not in the original Qureshi dialect, instead, they are in literary Arabic, as the end product of multiple editing over two centuries after its original announcements.

(12) Following are the Aya Muhammad presented as divine revelation to secure compliance (through the concept of total 'submission').

****

"Believers! let not a group of you mock another. Perhaps they are better than you. Let not women mock each other; perhaps one is better than the other. Let not one of you find faults in another nor let any of you defame another or call offensive names. Wretched is the name of disobedience after one's faith. And whoever does not repent then he will be among those who are wrongdoers." (**Quran** 49:11)

Killing & *Saving Lives*: "Take not life, which GOD hath made sacred, except by way of justice and law: thus, does GOD command you, that ye may learn wisdom." (**Quran** 6:151)

"If anyone saved a life, it would be as if he saved the life of the whole people" (**Quran** 5:32)

"Do not take a life except for just cause" (**Quran** 6:151; 17:33 2:84; 4:24)

"Stand for Justice even if it is against a close relative." (**Quran** 4:135; 5:8; 16:90; 42:15)

Divine Guidance: "Get ye down both of you— all together from the Garden, with enmity one to another; but if, as is sure there comes to you a guidance from ME, whosoever follows My guidance, will not lose his way nor fall into misery." (**Quran** 20:123)

Justice: A major mission of all Prophets (peace be upon them) was the "establishment of justice among people" (**Quran** 57:25)

Honesty - "Do not touch an Orphan's (weak Person) property unless you are going to improve it." (**Quran** 6:151; 17:35)

"Do not cheat in business transactions - give the correct measure." (**Quran** 6:151; 17:35)

"Fulfill (Honor) your agreements." (**Quran** 17:35)

"Do not Commit Fraud, Bribery or be Dishonest." (**Quran** 83:1; 2:188, 8:27; 17:26)

"Do not go near Shameful deeds." (**Quran** 6:151; 17:32)

"God commands justice and goodness in everything." (**Quran** 16:90)

Pride: "Turn not your face away from men with pride, nor walk in insolence through the earth. Verily, GOD likes not each arrogant boast" (Quran 31:18)

"Do not strut (show off) though the Earth acting like you are so great." (**Quran** 6:151; 17:37)

The message of the new Deen – Muhammad made sure his new Deen includes the same message that was brought by all the Prophets gone before, to all of mankind in the past. This can be summarized as: "Believe in GOD, do Good Deeds, join with Others to Speak the Truth and Be Patient" (**Quran** 103:3)

Muhammad's Deen also has the Commandments in (**Quran** 6:151):

"Do not take ANY OTHER as GOD'S EQUAL" (Sin Called **SHIRK**) (**Quran** 6:151; 17:32)

Insincere piety for show. "A warning to those who pray but are careless in their prayers, who pray only for show while refusing to share even the smallest (simple needs of life) of life from others." (**Quran 107: 4-7**)

"Be kind to your parents." (**Quran 6:151; 17:32**)

"Do not get involved with things about which you know nothing." (**Quran 17:37**)

"Stand for Justice even if it is against a close relative." (**Quran 4:135; 5:8; 16:90; 42:15**)

Muhammad was able to ensure compliance with Allah's divine words by enforcing the concept of 'Islam' whose real meaning is explained below.

ISLAM – Its real meaning.

The concept of total submission is called 'Islam'. It could be total submission to a teacher, master or to the chief of the tribe, or someone else. 'Islam' was NOT the name of Muhammad's Deen (Religion).

Islam was the 'description' or 'essence' (total submission) of the new Deen.

Two centuries after Muhammad's death, that word 'Islam' began to be used as the name of Muhammad's Deen. Until then, a convert to Muhammad's Deen was called a 'Momin' (plural 'Momineen'). The word 'Islam', in various grammatical forms, appeared several times in Quran, but each time to convey the sense of 'total obedience' or, 'total submission'; and definitely not as the given name of Muhammad's Deen. Ref. (A list of ten Aya in Quran is attached where the word 'Islam' in different grammatical forms has been used)

(2:208:6) l-sil'm	Islam	يَا أَيُّهَا الَّذِينَ آمَنُوا ادْخُلُوا فِي السِّلْمِ كَافَّةً
(3:19:5) l-is'lāmu	(is) Islam	إِنَّ الدِّينَ عِنْدَاللَّهِ الْإِسْلَامُ
(3:85:4) l-is'lāmi	(the) Islam	وَمَنْ يَبْتَغِيَر الْإِسْلَام دِينًافَلَنْ يُقْبَلَ مِنْهُ
(5:3:49) l-is'lāma	(the) Islam	وَأَتْمَمْتُ عَلَيْكُمْنِعْمَتِي وَرَضِيتُلَكُمُ الْإِسْلَام دِينًا
(6:125:8) lil'is'lāmi	to Islam	فَمَنْ يُرِدِ اللَّهُ أَنْيَهْدِيَهُ يَشْرَحْصَدْرَهُ لِلْإِسْلَام
(9:74:11) is'lāmihim	their (pretense of) Islam	وَلَقَدْ قَالُوا كَلِمَةَالْكُفْرِ وَكَفَرُوابَعْدَ إِسْلَامِهِمْ
(39:22:5) lil'is'lāmi	for Islam	أَفَمَنْ شَرَحَ اللَّهُصَدْرَهُ لِلْإِسْلَام فَهُوَعَلَى نُورٍ مِنْ رَبِّهِ
(49:17:4) aslamū	they have accepted Islam	يَمُنُّونَ عَلَيْكَأَنْ أَسْلَمُوا قُلْ لَاتَمُنُّوا عَلَيَّ إِسْلَامَكُمْ
(49:17:9) is'lāmakum	your Islam	يَمُنُّونَ عَلَيْكَ أَنْأَسْلَمُوا قُلْ لَا تَمُنُّواعَلَيَّ إِسْلَامَكُمْ
(61:7:11) l-is'lāmi	Islam	وَمَنْ أَظْلَمُ مِمَّنِافْتَرَى عَلَى اللَّهِالْكَذِبَ وَهُوَ يُدْعَىاإِلَى الْإِسْلَام

Once he built the personal Brand, and united the tribes, he was able to raise an army of highly motivated and committed tribesmen, mounted on Arabian horses, brandishing swords and striking like lightning on any opposing armies which stood in his way. All the means of providing motivation to die fighting for furthering Muhammad's cause, has been detailed earlier.

Scholars are too cautious and discreet to voice that opinion, for fear of fatal backlash from faith-crazed Muslim radicals

What he achieved over 22 years of consistent effort is a unique example of his genius and talent for leadership.

Muhammad succeeded in conquering the entire Arabian Peninsula in his lifetime and saying that he became the king would be an extreme under-statement, because he was 'Rasul Allah' (Almighty Allah's Regent in flesh).

How he conducted his life is a textbook case of a brilliant super-genius mind in addition to many other talents of leadership, outstanding communication skills, and a special knack for fruitful arbitration between blood thirsty sworn enemies.

The diagram shown below summarizes the two topics of this post – the Prophet-Believer relationship and the God-Prophet relationship. The inner circle lists the Names of God, and the outer circle lists each prophetic function in relation to the Believers in which Muḥammad reveals one of the Names of God in his very person:

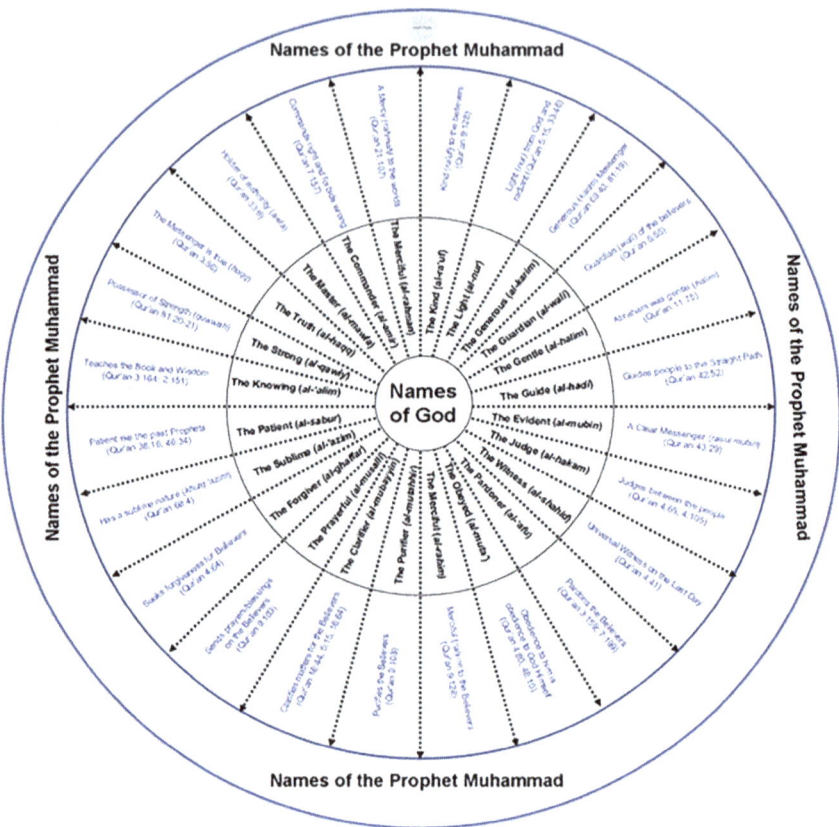

(13) The Prophet-Believer Relationship

"Even as We have sent among you a Messenger from you, reciting to you Our Signs, and purifying you (*yuzakkīkum*), and teaching you (*yuʿallimukum*) the Book (*al-kitāb*) and Wisdom (*al-ḥikmah*), and teaching you that which you do not know."

Qurʾān 2:151 (**see also** 62:2, 3:164)

The above verse shows how the mission of Muḥammad includes much more than revealing the Qurʾān. In fact, only Muḥammad's first duty – "reciting to you our Signs (*ayāt*)" – refers to the collected and compiled Revelations (Qurʾān). The other duties of the Prophet included purification (*tazkiyah*), teaching (*taʿlīm*) of the Book, teaching the inner Wisdom of the Book, and teaching the Believers new knowledge. Thus, the revelation of the Qur'ān comprises only one fourth of the Prophet's overall mission.

The Prophet Muḥammad is the Guide of the Believers

"And verily you [Muḥammmad] surely guide to the Straight Path (*ṣiraṭ al-mustaqīm*)."
Qur'an 42:52

All Muslims pray for God to guide them to the Straight Path in every prayer. But the above verse, revealed to the Prophet, clearly shows that it is actually Muḥammad's duty to "guide to the Straight Path".

"And We have sent down unto you (also) the Reminder; that <u>you may explain clearly (*li-tubayyina*) to mankind</u> what was sent down for them, and that they reflect.
Qur'ān 16:44 (see also 16:64, 14:4)

The above verse demonstrates how the Prophet – in addition to revealing the Qur'ān – must also provide the "explanation" (*bayān*) of the Qur'ān to the believers to foster their own reflections (*fikr*).

The Prophet Muḥammad's Authority over the Believers is unlimited.

"To obey the Prophet Muḥammad is to obey God Himself."
Qur'ān 4:80

"We sent a Messenger only to be obeyed by the permission of God."
Qur'ān 4:64

"Verily, those who give their *bay'ah* to you, they surely give their *bay'ah* to God Himself."

Qur'ān 48:10

The above verses show that **obedience to Muḥammad is equal and tantamount to obedience to God.** It logically follows that all orders in the Qur'ān to "obey God" are only fulfilled by obeying Muḥammad.

"So, whatever the Messenger gives you, take it. And whatever he forbids you, abstain from it."

Qur'ān 59:7

The above verse indicates that it is indeed Muḥammad who determines what is allowed and what is forbidden. Whatever the Prophet gives to the Believers – guidance, prescribed rituals, rules of behavior – must be followed.

Muhammad has more authority and closeness to the Believers than their own souls:

"The Prophet has more authority (*awla*) over the believers than their own souls."

Qur'ān 33:6

The Prophet is the Lord-Guardian of the Believers:

"Verily, your Lord-Guardian (*walī*) is only God, His Messenger, and those who have faith, who establish regular prayers, and give the *zakah* while they bow down."

Qur'ān 5:55

Muḥammad is the final judge and arbiter in all matters:

"But no, by the Lord, they do not have faith, until they make you [Muḥammad] judge in all disputes between them and find in their souls no resistance against your decrees, but they submit (to you) in full submission."

Qur'ān 4:65

"Verily, we have sent down to you the Book with the Truth so that you judge between the people by what God has shown you."

Qur'ān 4:105

"The answer of the Believers, when summoned to God and His Messenger, in order that he may judge between them, is no other than this: they say, "We hear, and we obey": it is such as these that will attain felicity."

Qur'ān 24:51

"It is not fitting for a Believer, man or woman, when a matter has been decided by God and His Messenger to have any option about their decision: if anyone disobeys God and His Messenger, he is indeed on a clearly wrong Path."

Qur'ān 33:36

All of the above verses describe the proper situation of the Believer in relation to Muḥammad. Indeed, the very condition of having "faith" (*īmān*) is to wholeheartedly accept and submit to the judgment, decrees, and orders of Muḥammad without any question.

Muḥammad deserves undue respect, reverence, and honor.

The believers are to honor and respect the Prophet Muhammad:

"In order that you have faith in God and His Messenger, that ye may assist him and honor him, and praise Him morning and evening."

Qur'ān 48:9

"Those who follow the Messenger, the *ummī* Prophet, whom they will find described in the Torah and the Gospel (which are) with them. He will enjoin on them that which is right and forbid them that which is wrong. He will make lawful for them all good things and prohibit for them only the foul; and he will relieve them of their burden and the fetters that they used to wear. Then those who have faith in him, and honor him, and help him, and follow the light which is sent down with him: they are the successful."

Qur'ān 7:157

The Believers must be humble and lower their voices in the presence of Muḥammad:

"O you who have faith! Do not be forward in the presence of God and His Messenger; but fear God: for God is He Who hears and knows all things. O ye who believe! Raise not your voices above the voice of the Prophet, nor speak aloud to him in talk, as you may speak aloud to one another, lest your deeds become vain, and you perceive not. Those that lower their voices in the presence of God's Messenger, - their hearts have Allah tested for piety: for them is Forgiveness and a great Reward."

Qur'ān 49:1-3

Muhammad embodies 'Divine Mercy' and 'Forgiveness'.

God loves and forgives the believers on the condition of obeying the Prophet Muhammad:

"Say (O Muḥammad): "If ye do love God follow me: God will love you and forgive you your sins: For God is Oft-Forgiving, Most Merciful."

Qur'ān 3:31

God's love and forgiveness reach the Believers only through their obedience to Muḥammad. This shows how Muḥammad, in fact, serves as the "gate" and "channel" of God's love and forgiveness.

Obedience to the Muhammad brings the Mercy of God to the Believers: "And obey God and the Messenger; that ye may obtain mercy."

Qur'ān 3:132

Muhammad himself is God's mercy to all worlds: "And we have only sent you [Muḥammad] as a <u>Mercy to the worlds</u>."

Qur'ān 21:107

Muḥammad is gentle out of God's Mercy: "It is by the Mercy from God that you (O Muhammad) were gentle with them, for if you had been stern, they would have dispersed from around you."

Qur'ān 3:159

This verse establishes how qualities of Muhammad, gentle towards the Believers, are actually expressions of the Mercy of God. This suggests that the Prophet's mercy is the manifestation of God's mercy.

Muḥammad is kind and merciful to the Believers: "There has certainly come to you a Messenger from among yourselves. Grievous to him is what you suffer; [he is] concerned over you and to the believers is kind (*ra'ūf*) and merciful (*raḥīm*)."

Qur'ān 9:128

The presence of Muhammad wards off God's punishment: "But Allah would not punish them while you, [O Muhammad], are among them, and God would not punish them while they seek forgiveness."

Qur'ān 8:33

Muḥammad seeks God's forgiveness on behalf of the Believers: "And if, when they wronged their souls, they had come to you, [O Muḥammad], and asked forgiveness of God and the Messenger had asked forgiveness for them, they would have found God Forgiving and Merciful."

Qur'ān 4:64

The above verse shows that a) when the Believers seek the forgiveness of God, they must go into the physical presence of Muḥammad; b) Muḥammad must pray to God and seek God's forgiveness for the Believers; and c) only after Muḥammad's prayer for God's forgiveness will the Believers have "found God Forgiving and Merciful". **This shows how Muḥammad serves as the intercessor and mediator between God and the Believers with respect to God's forgiveness and mercy.**

Some people are too arrogant to accept Muḥammad's prayers for God's forgiveness: "And when it is said to them, "Come, the

Messenger of Allah will ask forgiveness for you," they turn their heads aside and you see them evading while they are arrogant."

Qur'ān 63:5

Despite the Quranic promise of Muḥammad's intercession and prayers, some people – even some Muslims today – are too arrogant to accept the reality and need for the Prophet's special intercessory prayers.

Muḥammad himself pardons and forgives the Believers for their sins and errors: "It is by the Mercy from God that you (O Muhammad) were gentle with them, for, had you been stern in your heart they would have dispersed from around you. So, pardon (*'afu 'anhum*) them and ask forgiveness (*astaghfir lahum*) for them and consult with them upon the conduct of affairs. And when you are resolved, then put your trust in God. Lo! God loveth those who put their trust (*in Him*)."

Qur'ān 3:159

"Hold to forgiveness (*al-'afū*); command what is right; But turn away from the ignorant."

Qur'ān 7:199

The above verses also confirm how Muḥammad has been commanded to pray to God on behalf of the Believers who are seeking God's forgiveness. also command the Prophet to perform another act of forgiveness or pardoning However, these verses (indicated by the Arabic word *'afwa*). Therefore, Muḥammad a) seeks God's forgiveness for the Believers as an intercessor and b) pardons the Believers by his own act of forgiveness (see also 5:13). Both forms of prophetic forgiveness are necessary.

(14) How Muhammad used revelations to shape the perception of followers that Muhammad was the "Earthly embodiment" of Almighty Allah.

- The Prophet Muḥammad is inspired by the Holy Spirit (42:52, 26:192-194)

- The Prophet Muḥammad is a mercy (*raḥmah*) to the worlds (21:107)

- The Prophet Muḥammad is merciful (*raḥīm*) to the Believers (9:128)

- The Prophet Muḥammad is kind (*ra'ūf*) to the Believers (9:128)

- The Prophet Muḥammad is an honorable Messenger (*rasūl karīm*) (69:40; 81:19-21)

- The Prophet Muḥammad is light (*nūr*) from God (5:15) and a radiant lamp (*sirāj munīr*) (33:46)

- The Prophet Muḥammad (like Prophet Abraham) is gentle (*ḥalīm*) to the Believers (11:75)

- The Prophet Muḥammad is the possessor of power (*dhū al-quwwah*) (81:20-21)

- The Prophet Muḥammad is the teacher (*mu'allim*) of the Book and Wisdom and new knowledge (62:2; 3:164; 2:151)

- The Prophet Muḥammad, like his predecessors, is patient (ṣabūr) (38:16, 46:34)

- The Prophet is the witness (*shahīd*) of humankind on the Day of Judgment (2:143, 33:46; 4:41)

- The Prophet Muḥammad is the guardian (*walī*) of the Believers (5:55)

- The Prophet Muḥammad prays to God for the Believer's forgiveness (4:64, 63:5, 3:159, 60:12, 24:62)

- The Prophet Muḥammad forgives the Believers (5:13; 3:159; 7:199)
- The Prophet Muḥammad guides the Believers to the Straight Path (45:25)
- The Prophet Muḥammad's nature or character is sublime (*'azīm*) (68:4)
- The Prophet Muḥammad is the judge of the believers (4:65; 4:105; 24:51; 33:36)
- The Prophet Muḥammad makes things clear to the Believers (5:15; 5:19; 16:44; 16:64; 14:4)
- The Prophet Muḥammad purifies and sanctifies the believers (9:103)
- The Prophet Muḥammad holds authority (*awlā*) over the Believers (33:6)
- The Prophet Muḥammad summons the Believers to that which gives them life (8:24).
- The Prophet Muḥammad recites the Signs of God (2:151).
- The Prophet Muḥammad sends *ṣalawāt* (blessings, prayers) upon the Believers (9:103)
- The Prophet Muḥammad receives offerings (*ṣadaqa*) from the Believers (9:103; 58:12)
- The Prophet Muḥammad brings the people from darkness to Light (14:1; 14:5 65:11)
- The Prophet Muḥammad is a beautiful pattern for the Believers (33:21)
- The Prophet Muḥammad is the object of great respect and veneration (48:9, 49:1-3)
- The Prophet Muḥammad commands the lawful and forbids the wrong (7:157)

- He who gives their allegiance (*bay'ah*) to the Prophet Muḥammad has given it to God (48:10)

- He who obeys the Prophet Muḥammad, obeys God (4:80; 4:64)

Muḥammad is a Light from God which clarifies all things.

"O People of the Book! Now hath Our Messenger come unto you, clarifying for you much of what you used to hide of the Book, and forgiving much. Now there has come unto you a Light (*nūr*) from God and a manifest Book."
Qur'ān 5:15 (see also 5:19, 16:44, 16:64)

"O Prophet! Lo! We have sent thee as a witness and a bringer of good tidings and a warner and a summoner unto God by His permission and as a lamp that gives light (*sirāj munīran*)."
Qur'ān 33:45-46

"Those who disbelieve among the People of the Book and among the Polytheists, were not going to depart (from their ways) until there should come to them the Clear Proof (*al-bayyinah*) – a Messenger from God reciting purified pages."
Qur'ān 98:1-2

Muḥammad's inner character is Sublime.

"You [Muḥammad] are not, by the Favour of your Lord, possessed (majnūn). Verily, for you is an unfailing reward. And you are surely upon exalted character (*khulq 'aẓīm*)."
Qur'ān 68:4

This verse refers to Muhammad's character or inner constitution (khulq) as "sublime" ('azīm). This is significant because the Qur'ān also refers to itself as "sublime" ('azīm) and often mentions God as "the Sublime One" (al-'azīm).

Muḥammad is the Universal Witness of God over Humankind

"So how [will it be] when We bring from every people (ummah) a witness (shahīd) and We bring you [O' Muḥammad] against these [people] as a witness?"

Qur'ān 4:41

This verse is one of the most mysterious in the entire Qur'ān. It indicates that on the Day of Judgment, Muḥammad will be a witness over all of the witnesses of each nation or people. The Prophet's role as universal witness suggests that he must remain spiritually present in the world at all times – in order to actually serve as a witness over the deeds of all human beings.

Muḥammad receives grace, mercy, and knowledge from God

"And if it was not for the Grace of God upon you [O Muḥammad], and His Mercy, a group of them would have been determined to mislead you. But they do not mislead except themselves, and they will not harm you at all. And God has revealed to you the Book and Wisdom and has taught you that which you did not know. And ever has the Grace of God upon you been great."

Qur'ān 4:113

Muḥammad is inspired by God through the Holy Spirit and Light

"Your companion/master (*ṣāḥib*) is not astray or deceived. He does not speak out of caprice/desire (*al-hawā*). It is no less than inspired inspiration (*waḥyun yūḥa*)."

Qur'ān 53:1-4

"The Trustworthy Spirit (*rūḥ<span al-amīn*) descended with it [the revelation] upon your heart (*qalbiqa*) so that you would be among the warners in clear Arabic language."

Qur'ān 26:192-194

"And that We have inspired you [Muhammad] with a Spirit (*rūḥ*) from Our Command. You did not know what was the Book (*kitāb*) and what was the Faith. But We have made it a Light (*nūr*) by which We guide those of our Servants as We will. And verily, you guide me to a Straight Path."

Qur'ān 42:52

Here is how Muslims insist their belief is:

These verses illustrate the nature of the divine inspiration (*waḥy*; *ta'yīd*) which God has granted to the Prophet Muḥammad. Firstly, this inspiration is spiritual in nature and flows through the Holy Spirit that comes from God's Command. Secondly, the inspiration comes upon the Prophet through his heart – the spiritual faculty of the human soul – and not in the form of sounds, words, or letters. Thus, divine inspiration is *not* a form of verbal dictation – such an idea is a complete insult to the spiritual depth of the Prophet Muḥammad. Thirdly, the verses show how whatever Prophet Muḥammad says, does, or thinks is divinely-inspired – not only the revealed Qur'ān – but all of Muḥammad's speech and guidance is guided by God and not from human whims or desires. This prophetic inspiration is continuous and not discrete – it does not cease or stop at one moment and resume at another – but continues like a stream. Finally, it is this inspiration or divine assistance granted to the Prophet Muḥammad that allows him to perform all of the above prophetic functions. The very soul of the Prophet Muḥammad is continuously inspired and guided through the Holy Spirit – this is what makes him more than an ordinary human being. From this we could even conclude that the Qur'ān and the very personality of the Prophet Muḥammad are manifestations of the same Holy Spirit that flows from the Command of God.

Below is a summary of the above Quranic verses about the Prophet Muḥammad:

Today, one can get away by not being too respectful to Allah, but one tiny gesture of not showing enough respect for Muhammad, and that person is history.

List of earliest converts to Muhammad's Deen of '*Wahdaniyet*'. It is significantly different from the traditional historic accounts shown in Muslims' books of doctored history.

Contradictions in Muslims' history books.

Muslim historians record the following persons, including children, to be the earliest converts to Muhammad's Deen. But, some of them are contradicted by Ahadith.

- Yasir ibn Amir - One of the early converts, also the second martyr of Muhammad's Ummah

- Ammar ibn Yasir - One of the early converts

- Abu Dhar al-Ghifari- One of the early converts

- Sumayyah bint Khabbab - Seventh person to convert was the first martyr of Muhammad's Ummah
- Sa'd ibn Abi-Waqqas - One of the first converts
- Lubaba bint al-Harith - Second woman to convert
- Bilal ibn Ribah - One of the early converts
- Abd-Allah ibn Mas'ud - One of the early converts
- Jafar ibn Abi Talib - One of the early converts
- Abd al-Rahman ibn Awf - Among the first converts
- Zubayr ibn al-Awwam - One of the early converts
- Talha ibn Ubayd-Allah - One of the early converts
- Khalid ibn Sa`id - One of the early converts
- Abu Ubaidah ibn al-Jarrah - One of the early converts
- Khabbab ibn al-Aratt - One of the early converts
- Said ibn Zayd - Converted before Umar
- Fatimah bint al-Khattab - Converted before Umar
- Abu-Hudhayfah ibn Utbah - One of the early converts
- Musab ibn `Umair - One of the early converts
- Hamza ibn 'Abd al-Muttalib - Converted in 616 A.D.
- Asma bint Abu Bakr - About the eighteenth person to convert
- Umar - around the fiftieth or sixtieth or so person to convert, and he did so during 4 BH (617–618 CE)
- Umm Salama Hind bint Abi Umayya - Among the first people to convert
- Abd-Allah ibn Abd-al-Asad - Among the first people to convert
- Sawda bint Zama - One of the early converts

Tabari. Tarikh e Tabari. I (Muhammad ibn Sa'ad ibn Abi Waqqas) asked my father whether Abu Bakr was the first of the Muslims. He said, "**No, more than fifty people embraced Islam before Abu Bakr**; but he was superior to us as a Muslim." He also writes that Umar Bin Khattab embraced Islam after forty-five men and twenty-one women.

According to the above quoted Hadith Umar **accepted Muhammad's Deen long before Abu Bakr**. Muslim historians never highlight this fact.

'The Naked Truth' presents critical analyses offered by renowned scholars and researchers. The new technologies of GPS tracking, Satellite imaging, calculating the age of the old manuscripts and numismatic material with modern technology, and other such advancements have unearthed many facts relating to the events of the period spread over those two centuries following the death of Muhammad. Those findings were unknown until recently. In historiographic terms, it was a *'blackout'* period. There are strong indications that the news gap was *'reverently and wishfully filled with devotional concoction'* two centuries after his death. That fabrication was then ignited brighter and loaded with more fantasies, with awe and reverence, for over 12 centuries by Muslim hagiographers and clergy.

The modern-day history detectives have enviable credentials in the world of academia. They are quite impressive and impactful in revealing their findings through audio-video lectures delivered to eager audiences and students in prestigious centers of higher learning. The commentary accompanying the on-site exploration and recording of discoveries, aided with power-point slides showing actual hard evidence, is far more impactful than printed books because the lectures provide the audience with the on-sight audio-visuals of the history investigator. The researchers have overwhelmed the truth seekers with phenomenal discoveries. Watching their audio-visual lectures, commonly available on the electronic medium of 'Youtube' is considered the 'New in-depth study' of research documents and documentaries.

Some of those outstanding professors and analysts of Arabian history are Prof Roy Casagranda of Texas USA, history investigator Dan Gibson, on-site history excavators Tom Holland and Fred Donner, and history detectives Dan Taylor and Jay Smith etc. Their individual research documentaries can be watched on 'Youtube'. I highly recommend my readers to watch them.

In the print medium too, we find priceless information researched and presented by Ibn Warraq, Henry B. Wright, Ryan Mauro, Steve Ray, Robert Spencer, Rev. Sell, Miroslav, and numerous others.

Those giant scholars, in the audio-visual lectures and in the print medium, are found to be walking on the egg shells and tiptoeing around the facts to escape reprisals from die-hard radicals. I am a mere pygmy compared to them, but I have been fool-hardy and bold, and not daunted by concerns of emotional sensitivity and accommodating the feelings of die-hard Muslims --- my preference has been to avoid gray areas! Just plain black & white, Period!

Several investigators of history like Tom Holland, Dan Gibson, Matt Davies, Pr. Maurice, Prof Freedman, Patricia Croner, Jay Smith and several others indicate that Kaaba, particularly the one which had 'Hajr-e-Aswad' (The black stone) installed in one of its corners, was originally located in Petra in Nabatea, modern day Jordan. The details of this controversy are not directly linked with the falsehoods surrounding Muhammad and the *Deen* he synthesized, which I am trying to peel off for a look at bare facts. The details concerning the controversy of the location of Kaaba and its alleged relocation to Makkah is not in the purview of this disclosure and hence its details are not included in 'The Naked Truth'.

Muslim clergy unfortunately, although some of them are highly educated and otherwise enlightened, remain steadfastly in denial. They refuse to accept the new findings as it would demolish the *'godly'* edifice of Muhammad and his mission, leading to an end of their own identity and stronghold.

(15) How Muhammad created a Revenue-stream for personal enrichment.

Muḥammad receives devotional offerings (*ṣadaqah*) from the Believers and thereby purifies, sanctifies, and blesses them with his special prayers.

The Believers must submit an offering to Muḥammad before having a private meeting with him: "O ye who have faith! When you privately consult the Messenger, then present an offering (*ṣadaqah*) before your private consultation. That will be best for you, and purer for you. But if you find not (the means), God is Oft-Forgiving, Most Merciful."

Qur'ān 58:12

This verse establishes how the Believers would seek to have private meetings (*najwā*) with Muḥammad. The Qur'ān recommends that every Believer submit an offering (*ṣadaqah*) to Muḥammad when having this special meeting – and that this offering is a means of purity (*tahārah*) for the Believers.

The Believer's submissions of their wealth to Muḥammad are the means to obtaining the Prophet's special blessings and prayers: "And among the Arabs are those who have faith in God and the Last Day and take what they spend as a means of closeness toward God and the prayers/blessings (*ṣalawāt*) of the Messenger. Behold, it is indeed a means of closeness for them. God will make them enter in His Mercy. Indeed, God is Most Forgiving, Most Merciful."

Qur'ān 9:99

The above verse significantly confirms that some of the Arabs would give a portion of their wealth to Muḥammad – as a means of attaining the Prophet's prayers or blessings (ṣalawāt) and closeness to God. The verse encourages this practice of submitting offerings and states that as a result of spending one's wealth, such people will be made to enter into God's Mercy.

"And (there are) others who have acknowledged their faults. They mixed a righteous action with another that was bad. It may be that Allah will relent toward them. Lo! Allah is Forgiving, Merciful. Take offerings (ṣadaqah) from their wealth and purify and sanctify them by means of it. And pray/send blessings over them. Verily, your prayer/blessing is a source of peace (sakan) for them. And God is the Hearing, the Knowing."

Qur'ān 9:102-103

The next few verses continue and describe those Believers who have performed good deeds, but also committed sins while acknowledging their faults. The Qur'ān orders such people – who have committed any kind of wrong-doing – to give an offering (ṣadaqah) from their wealth (amwāl) to Muḥammad. The Prophet is then ordered to accept these offerings (ṣadaqah) and thereby purify and sanctify the Believers. Muḥammad is also told to give his special prayers or blessings upon the Believers – and that the special prayer of the Prophet is a source of peace (sakan) for them. This verse clearly indicates that it was the prophetic practice of Muḥammad to accept material offerings from the Believers and purify, sanctify, and pray/bless those who submitted such offerings.

In fact, the original concept of zakat was not the idea of charity of alms. *Zakah* and *ṣadaqah* were payments that the believers made to Muḥammad to seek forgiveness of their sins and spiritual purification through his prayers and blessings – as shown in the above verses. On this matter, the renowned scholar of early Islam, Fred Donner has written:

"Later Muslim tradition refers to such charity under the term's zakat or sadaqa, usually rendered "almsgiving"; these two terms are closely associated with prayer in numerous Quranic passages, and later Muslim tradition considers them, like prayer, to be one of the "pillars of the faith" that define a Believer. Recent research suggests, however, that the original Quranic meaning of *zakat* and *sadaqa* was not almsgiving, but rather a fine or payment made by someone who was guilty of some kind of sin, in exchange for which Muhammad would pray in order that they might be purified of their sin and that their other affairs might prosper. Indeed, even in the verse just cited (2:177), one notes that payment of *zakat* is mentioned after prayer, suggesting that it was something different than the giving of wealth to the poor (what we usually mean by almsgiving), which is treated in the verse before mention of prayer. This understanding of zakat or sadaqa as a payment for atonement or purification of sins is clearest in the following verses.

"Others have confessed their sins ... Take from their property sadaq to cleanse them, and purify [*tuzakki*] them thereby, and pray for them, indeed your prayer is a consolation to them. God is all-hearing, all-knowing."

Qur'ān 9:102-103

The verb "to purify" is from the same Arabic root as *zakat*. The fact that Believers were sometimes required to make such purification payments, however, underscores how the community was, in principle, focused on maintaining its inner purity, on being as much as possible a community that lived strictly in righteousness, so as to set themselves apart from the sinful world around them and thus to attain salvation in the afterlife."

Muhammad's mistakes leading to his rejection by Jewish and Christian clergy.

Muhammad being totally illiterate had no way of reading the canonized text of the Old and New Testament. To reproduce the contents of Jewish and Christians' scripture in his own 'divine revelations'. Muhammad had to depend on sources that were within his reach. Sources in his reach happened to be the illiterate Jewish and Christians journey men whom he used to mingle with for many years in the trading caravans.

'The Naked Truth' offers an overwhelming proof of rather embarrassing mistakes made by Muhammad due to his total illiteracy and flawed understanding of the Biblical anecdotes, relating to former biblical prophets. Muhammad obtained the folkloric narrative of Talmud of Jews and Apocrypha of Christians by picking the brains of his sources who were familiar only with the non-canonized Talmudic and apocryphal accounts which were routinely narrated as stories told at campfires for children and illiterate folks. *The text of Talmud is a huge corpus of rabbinical folklore and admitted by rabbis to be grossly fabricated for inspiring the semi-literate and simpler Jewish people. Similarly, Apocrypha are various religious writings of uncertain origin regarded by some as inspired but rejected by most authorities.* They too are part of the fictional stories to affirm and shore up the faith of illiterate Christians who could not read the canonized text of the Bible.

Not knowing the difference, and assuming that he was using the details given in the proper (canonical) texts of Torah and *Injeel* (New Testament), Muhammad presented the fabricated version from Talmudic folklore as 'divinely' revealed message from Allah to him. This blunder by Muhammad evidently occurred because of his second hand, and sometimes third-hand source of information, which actually came from the ignorant and illiterate sources. Events narrated in the canonized Torah (Old Testament) of the Jews, or the canonized *Injeel* (New Testament) of Christians, both of which were claimed to be divinely inspired works, are quite different from fictional tales of Talmud and Christian apocrypha which Muhammad inserted in his 'divine revelations'.

This grievous mistake cost Muhammad any credibility he had with Jewish rabbis and Christian priests. The clergy of Christianity and Judaism immediately understood that Muhammad had gathered the non-canonized information from illiterate sources, similar to himself, who did not know any better, and presented them as divine revelation sent to Muhammad from Allah. As a result, the Jews gave him the derogatory nickname *ha-Meshuggah* (Hebrew: עֲגֵשֻׁמ, "the Madman" or "the Possessed"). Almost all Jews considered him a mad man at best, and a cheap fake at worst. (Ref.: A list of differences between Quran and canonized texts of Torah and New Testament is attached).

Upon realizing his deadly mistake, Muhammad felt embarrassed and frustrated. He realized that he had lost all prospects of converting the highly respected Jews and Christian population to his Deen, from that point onward. He retaliated by hitting back at the Jews by forbidding interest on money lent or borrowed, just to hurt the Jews monetarily, who acted as bankers and money lenders to Christians, Pagans and Zoroastrian, for several centuries in the past. In addition to declaring interest charged on loans as 'Haraam', Muhammad changed the Qibla from Jerusalem to Kaaba in Mecca, thereby completely alienating the Jews for good.

Western and Byzantine Christian thinkers considered Muhammad to be a perverted, deplorable man, a false prophet, and even the Antichrist, as he was frequently seen in Christendom as a heretic or possessed by the demons. (Ref.: Several pages detailing the differences in OLD & NEW Testaments on one hand and QURAN on the other are attached).

Here's another view, soon after Muhammad's death, when sentiments and opinions were still fresh.

"In a conversation that apparently took place on July 13, 634, just two years after Muhammad's death, an old man was asked what he made of "the prophet who has appeared among the Saracens?" He replied that Muhammad "is an imposter. Do the prophets come with swords and chariots?" Another person agreed, noting, "There is no truth from the so-called prophet, only bloodshed." Several months later, in a sermon on Christmas Eve in 634, the patriarch of Jerusalem referred to the Muslims as "the slime of the godless Saracens [that] threatens slaughter and destruction." (Ref.: Walter Emil Kaegi, Jr., "Initial Byzantine Reactions to the Arab Conquest," *Church History*, June 1969, pp. 139-49)

Throughout the medieval period, Christians saw Islam not just as a false religion but as a distortion of the Christian message, a perversion of their own faith. St. John the Damascene (d. ca. 749) considered the "superstition of the Ishmaelites" to be a Christian heresy. (Ref.: Robert Spencer, *Did Muhammad Exist? An Inquiry into Islam's Obscure Origins* (Wilmington, Del.: ISI Books, 2012)).

In this spirit, medieval Christians imagined that Muslims worshiped an unholy trinity: Mahon (i.e., Muhammad), Termagant (A deity of Muslims called Allah) and Apollyon (a place of destruction and an archangel of the abyss). They viewed Islam as the epitome of evil, as a fiendishly clever amalgam of doctrines designed to exploit human weaknesses. In a concise formulation, Norman Daniel explains how Islam stood for "a sexually corrupt tyranny based on false teaching." (Ref.: Norman Daniel, *Islam, Europe and Empire* (Edinburgh: Edinburgh University Press, 1966), p. 6)

Accusations about Islamic manipulation of religion, power, and sex became part of the standard European repertoire and showed an "astonishing tenacity," appearing again and again in various forms and endless variety through the Middle Ages. (Ref.: Southern, *Western Views of Islam*, p. 28). As Richard

Chenevix (1774-1830), the Irish author of a two-volume work on national character, explained, Islam fulfilled every evil impulse:

To suit the various characters which belong to Arabia Felix, to Arabia Petrea, and to Arabia Deserta, [the Islamic] religion must be as diversified as those districts. It must be ferocious for the one, and sensual for the other; vain, luxurious, enthusiastic, wild for all. To the robber, it must inculcate the plunder of unbelievers; to the warrior, it must preach conquest and extermination; to the slothful, it must allow the pleasures of the senses; to all its votaries, it must promise an eternity of voluptuous beatitude, **provided they fall in defense of the prophet.** (Ref.: Richard Chenevix, *An Essay upon National Character* (London: James Duncan, 1832), vol. 1, p. 97).

Muhammad's Harem

Muhammad's first wife Khadijah, widely reported by Muslim historians as 40 years old at the time of her marriage to Muhammad, is substantially different from the age reported by independent scholars and history detectives.

"On the day Khadijah married Allah's Messenger, she was 28 years old". Ibn Ishaq, cited in Al-Hakim, Mustadrak vol. 3 p. 182. Ibn Kathir, Al-Bidaya wa'l-Nihaya vol. 5 p. 293.

Widows whom Prophet Muhammad married after Khadijah's death do fall into two distinct age-groups. But to label these two groups as "the middle-aged" and "the elderly" gives atypical definitions to these terms. The "elderly" group would refer to those brides between 28 and 40, while the "middle-aged" group would mean the teenagers. Muhammad reportedly loved Khadijah, who was the same age as himself, and they were both young (*Saheeh Muslim*). Muhammad rejected Sawdah. She was an older woman but 9 years younger, not older, than Muhammad.

All his other wives were young enough to be his daughters and several were young enough to be his granddaughters. He divorced one woman before consummating the marriage (Ref Bewley/ Saad 8:111) and broke off another courtship (Ref. Bewley/Saad 8:113) solely because he decided that these women were "too old" for him, and he continued to pursue teenagers until the day he died. (Ref. Bewley/Saad 8:105) He does not seem to have been embarrassed by his own preference for teen age females.

The inevitable conclusion is that Muhammad preferred younger women, and the widely repeated claim that almost all of his wives were elderly has no basis in historical fact.

1. **Safiyah**
   Safiyah's age: 16 years and 6 months
   Muhammad's age: 57 years and 3 months
   Age difference: 40 years and 9 months.

   Safiyah was yet another bride who was young enough to be Muhammad's granddaughter.

2. **Juwayriyah**
   Juwayriyah's median age: 20 years and 0 months
   Muhammad's age: 56 years and 9 months
   Age difference: 36 years and 9 months.

   So, another one of Muhammad's wives, Juwayriyah, was young enough to be his granddaughter.

3. **Zaynab**
   Zaynab's median age: 37 years and 2 months
   Muhammad's age: 55 years and 11 months
   Age difference: 18 years and 9 months.

4. **Hind**
   Hind's median age: 28 years and 6 months
   Muhammad's age: 55 years and 0 months
   Age difference: 26 years and 6 months.

5. **Zaynab II**
   Zaynab's median age: 28 years and 4 months
   Muhammad's age: 53 years and 10 months

Age difference: 25 years and 6 months.

Zaynab married five times. Her fifth choice, it seems, fell on a high-status and already-married man, old enough to be her father.

6. **Hafsah**
   Hafsah's median age: 19 years and 7 months
   Muhammad's age: 53 years and 9 months
   Age difference: 34 years and 2 months.

7. **Aisha**
   Aisha's median age at consummation: 9 years and 3 months
   Muhammad's age: 52 years and 0 months
   Age difference: 42 years and 9 months.

   The exact age or age difference down to the day or even to the year do not matter. The real points are that (1) Aisha, was a prepubescent child, and (2) Muhammad was old enough to be her grandfather.

8. **Sawdah**
   Sawdah's probable age: about 40 years
   Muhammad's age: 49 years and 1 month
   Age difference: about 9 years

   The age difference between Muhammad and Sawdah was not inappropriate for a middle-aged couple; but she was certainly the younger spouse.

   And we will state here that Sawdah was the oldest bride whom Muhammad ever married.

9. **Ramlah**
   Ramlah's median age at consummation: 34 years and 7 months
   Muhammad's age: 57 years and 3 months
   Age difference: 22 years and 8 months.

   Ramlah was young enough to be Muhammad's daughter.

10. **Maymunah**
    Maymunah's median age: 35 years and 2 months.
    Muhammad's age: 57 years and 10 months
    Age difference: 22 years and 8 months.

11. Mulaykah

Mulaykah's probable age: about 13 years
Muhammad's age at marriage: 58 years and 9 months
Age difference: 45 years and 9 months.

12. Asma

Asma's maximum age: 20 years and 0 months
Muhammad's age at marriage: 59 years and 3 months
Age difference: 39 years and 3 months.

Asma was once again young enough to be Muhammad's granddaughter.

13. Amrah

Amrah's probable age: about 15 years
Muhammad's age at marriage: 60 years and 5 months
Age difference: 45 years and 5 months.

14. Rayhanah bint Zayd ibn Amr

Rayhanah was a Jewish female from the Nadir tribe in Medina. Muhammad captured Rayhanah in spring 627, a date when her youngest possible age would have been 14. She might have been considerably older than this minimum. Although secondary historians have guessed that she was about 15, this is not stated in the early sources. Since her exact age is not known, I have omitted her from the calculation.

15. Mariah bint Shamoon

Mariyah's age is not stated anywhere. The only certain fact is that, since she bore Muhammad a son in 630, she must have been of childbearing age. Various guesses that she was 20 or 17 betray the assumptions of the secondary historians that if she attracted Muhammad, she must have been young. The truth is, they are probably right. But because we don't know Mariyah's age, it is omitted from the calculation.

16. Fatima ("Al-Aliya") bint Al-Dahhak

The only objective clue to Fatima's age is that she lived another 50 years after Muhammad divorced her. Subjectively, her behavior seems immature and suited to a child aged 15 or 16. But because there is no historical evidence of Fatima Al-Aliya's age, it is omitted from the calculation.

"Al-Jariya" and Tukanah – Concubines

These two concubines were presumably selected for their looks and were presumably young. But presumption is not fact. I do not know their ages and so, I have omitted them from calculation.

This is a condensed list of Muhammad's wives. We can now calculate the mean age of 14 of Muhammad's wives at the time he married them.

1. Khadijah's Median Age: 27 years and 10 months
2. Sawdah's Approximate Age: 40 years
3. Aisha's Median Age: 9 years and 3 months
4. Hafsah's Median Age: 19 years and 6 months
5. Zaynab bint Khuzayma's Median Age: 28 years and 4 months
6. Hind's Median Age: 28 years and 6 months
7. Zaynab bint Jahsh's Median Age: 37 years and 2 months
8. Juwayriyah's Median Age: 20 years and 0 months
9. Safiyah's Age: 16 years and 6 months
10. Ramlah's Median Age: 34 years and 7 months
11. .Maymunah's Median Age: 35 years and 2 months
12. Mulaykah's Approximate Age: 13 years
13. Asma's Maximum Age: 20 years
14. Amrah's Approximate Age: 15 years

    Total Years = 343 years and 10 months

    Mean Age of Muhammad's brides = *24.56 years*

The mean age of Muhammad's brides was about *24½ years*. Even by the historical Arabian standards, a woman of 24 was not quite "middle-aged".

Muhammad as Bridegroom

We can also calculate Muhammad's mean age as a bridegroom. Here is his age when he consummated each of these marriages.

1. Khadijah: 24 years and 3 months
2. Sawdah: 49 years and 1 month
3. Aisha: 52 years and 0 months
4. Hafsah: 53 years and 9 months
5. Zaynab bint Khuzayma: 53 years and 10 months
6. Hind: 55 years and 0 months
7. Zaynab bint Jahsh: 55 years and 11 months
8. Juwairiyah: 56 years and 9 months
9. Safiyah: 57 years and 3 months
10. Ramlah: 57 years and 3 months
11. Maymunah: 57 years and 10 months
12. Mulaykah: 58 years and 9 months
13. Asma: 59 years and 3 months (not consummated, but legalities finalized)
14. Amrah: 60 years and 5 months (not consummated, but legalities finalized)

Total Years = 751 years and 4 months.

Mean Age of Muhammad as Bridegroom = *53.66 years*

Muhammad's mean age at marriage was *53 years and 8 months*. The mean age-difference between Muhammad and all his wives was over *29 years*.

Story of Zayd ibn Haritha

Adoption is forbidden in Islam. For approximately 15 years, Muhammad had an adopted son Zayd, known as "the Beloved of the Messenger of God." Zayd was the first adult male to become a Muslim and the only Muslim apart from Muhammad to be mentioned by name in the Quran.

Although Zayd is a little-known and marginal figure in the standard account of the rise of Islam, he was originally a key figure in the Islamic foundation narrative, according to David S. Powers, professor of Near Eastern studies. His new book, "Zayd" (University of Pennsylvania Press, part of the "Divinations: Rereading Late Ancient Religion" series) aims to restore Zayd's place in history.

Much of Zayd's biography comprises after-the-fact literary constructions driven by political and theological imperatives, contends Powers, and the figure of Zayd is modeled on characters in the Hebrew Bible and New Testament.

As a youth Zayd is like Joseph, albeit with a twist: Unlike the biblical figure who welcomed family reunification, Zayd rejected his birth family in favor of his slave master, explains Powers. Just as Dammesek Eliezer, Abraham's trusted servant, became his master's surrogate son and heir, after being freed Zayd became Muhammad's adopted son and heir. Like Ishmael, Zayd was repudiated by his adoptive father. Like Uriah the Hittite, he was sent to certain death on a battlefield in southern Jordan by the man who fell in love with his wife. And like Isaac and Jesus, Zayd became a prototype of the martyr who gains immortality as a consequence of his willingness to lay down his life for the sake of his God, his prophet and his religion.

"Zayd may have been a real historical person," says Powers, "but there is little or no correlation between the historical person and the spectacular figure we read about in the Islamic sources."

Zayd was absolutely devoted to the prophet who had freed him. Muhammad was equally devoted to Zayd, says Powers: When Zayd wanted to marry Zaynab, a woman above his class, Muhammad helped arrange the marriage. Later Muhammad fell in love with Zaynab himself. The ever-loyal Zayd divorced his wife so that his father might marry her. As a reward for this selfless act, and to undo the scandal that followed, Zayd's adoption was nullified by Muhammad as per an opportune and timely revelation from Allah which disallowed adoption in the new Deen.

The real reason for this story, according to Powers, was to create a pretext for Muhammad to undo the act of having adopted Zayd, thereby ensuring that Muhammad would be sonless.

"Had Zayd continued to be Muhammad's son, he would have inherited the mantle of prophecy," explains Powers. "In order to secure the theological doctrine that Muhammad was not just another prophet but the last prophet, it was necessary to 'sacrifice' Zayd – and, along the way, to abolish the institution of adoption."

Powers' research highlights the complex interplay between biblical, post-biblical and Islamic narratives, a subject that is attracting increasing attention from historians of late antiquity. (Ref.: https://www.youtube.com/watch?v=1L23AH6f0tk (Muhammad's 16 privileges given by Allah))

(16) Notes on Apostasy (A momin renouncing Muhammad's Deen) and its punishment

Muslim clerics have been teaching Muslim students that the religious Punishment for Apostasy (renunciation of Islam, by a Muslim), is death by decapitation. That punishment is meted out in the theocratic states like Afghanistan, Iran, Indonesia, Malaysia, Brunei, Mauritania, Qatar, **Saudi Arabia**, Sudan, the United Arab Emirates, and Yemen. In Pakistan, this punishment is meted out to poor victims through street justice by 'holier than thou' public. However, the Quran is not clear on a ruling.

"Make ye no excuses: ye have rejected Faith after they had accepted it. If We pardon some of you, we will punish others amongst you, for that they are in sin". (Quran 9:66)

"He who disbelieves in Allah after his having believed, not he who is compelled while his heart is at rest on account of faith, but he who opens (his) breast to disbelief-- on these is the wrath of Allah, and they shall have a grievous chastisement." (Quran 16:106)

"But those who reject Faith after they accept it, and then go on adding to their defiance of Faith, – never will their repentance be accepted; for they are those who have (of set purpose) gone astray." (Quran 3:90)

The Tradition (Ahadeeth) however, is quite explicit and clearly approves Capital punishment for Apostates.

Allah's Apostle said, "The blood of a Muslim who confesses that none has the right to be worshiped but Allah and that I am His Apostle, cannot be shed except in three cases: In Qisas for murder, a married person who commits illegal sexual intercourse and the one who reverts from Islam (apostate) and leaves the Muslims." (Sahih al-Bukhari, 9:83:17)

Allah's Apostle said: "The blood of a Muslim man who testifies that there is no god but Allah and that Muhammad is Allah's Apostle should not lawfully be shed except only for one of three reasons: a man who committed fornication after marriage, in which case he should be stoned; one who goes forth to fight Allah and His Apostle, in which case he should be killed or crucified or exiled from the land; or one who commits murder for which he is killed." (Sunan Abu Dawood, 38:4339)

List of murders ordered by or approved by Muhammad.

https://wikiislam.net/wiki/List_of_Killings_Ordered_or_
Supported_by_Muhammad.

The following list of killings is roughly in chronological order.

Ordered by Muhammad	Reasons including writing or reciting poetry
Supported but not ordered by Muhammad	Reasons including "causing offense"
Women and/or children	Reasons including monetary gain
Apostates	Reasons including preventing idolatry or rival prophets

Names in **bold** indicate that the *only* reason why the sources indicate Muhammad wanted them to be killed or threatened with death was because they had mocked, insulted, or cast doubt on him, or to extort economic gain, or to destroy idolatry or rival prophets. All others may have been killed for additional reasons such as posing or inciting a physical threat, or deserved punishment for murder or harming people, as indicated in the Reasons column.

No.	Name	Date
1	'Asma' bint Marwan	January 624
2	Abu 'Afak	February 624
3	Al Nadr ibn al-Harith	After Battle of Badr March 624

Reason(s) for Ordering or Supporting Killing	Result	Notable Primary Sources
Kill 'Asma' bint Marwan for opposing Muhammad with poetry and for provoking others to attack him	Asma' bint Marwan assassinated	Ibn Hisham & Ibn Ishaq, Sirat Rasul Allah Ibn Sa'd, Kitab al-tabaqat al-kabir, Volume 2
Kill the Jewish poet Abu Afak for opposing Muhammad through poetry, and according to ibn Sa'd, instigating the people against Muhammad	Abu Afak assassinated	Ibn Hisham & Ibn Ishaq, Sirat Rasul Allah Ibn Sa'd, Kitab al-tabaqat al-kabir, Volume 2
According to Mubarakpuri, Al Nadir was captured during the Battle of Badr. A Quran verse was revealed about Nadr bin Harith for mocking the Quran as "tales of the ancients". He was one of two prisoners who were executed and not allowed to be ransomed by their clans because he mocked and harassed Muhammad and wrote poems and stories criticizing him. According to Waqidi, he also tortured companions of Muhammad	Nadr bin Harith beheaded by Ali	Quran 83:13 Ibn Hisham & Ibn Ishaq, Sirat Rasul Allah

N0.	Name	Date
4.	Uqba bin Abu Muayt	After Battle of Badr March 624
5.	Ka'b ibn al-Ashraf	September 624

Reason(s) for Ordering or Supporting Killing	Result	Notable Primary Sources
Uqba bin Abu Muayt was captured in the Battle of Badr and was killed instead of being ransomed, because he threw dead animal entrails on Muhammad, and wrapped his garment around Muhammad's neck while he was praying	Uqba bin Abu Muayt beheaded by Asim ibn Thabbit or Ali	Sahih Bukhari 1:9:499, Sahih Bukhari 6:60:339 Ibn Hisham & Ibn Ishaq, Sirat Rasul Allah Tabari, Volume 9, The last years of the Prophet
According to Ibn Ishaq, Muhammad ordered his followers to kill Ka'b because he "had gone to Mecca after Badr and "inveighed" against Muhammad and composed verses in which he bewailed the victims of Quraysh who had been killed at Badr. Shortly afterwards he returned to Medina and composed amatory verses of an insulting nature about the Muslim women". Ibn Kathir adds that he incited the people to fight Muhammad.	Ka'b ibn al-Ashraf assassinated.	Sahih Bukhari 5:59:369, Sahih Muslim 19:4436 Ibn Hisham & Ibn Ishaq, Sirat Rasul Allah

N0.	Name	Date
6	Abu Rafi' ibn Abi Al-Huqaiq	December 624
7	Khalid ibn Sufyan	625
8	Abu 'Azzah 'Amr bin 'Abd Allah al-Jumahi	March 625

Reason(s) for Ordering or Supporting Killing	Result	Notable Primary Sources
Kill Abu Rafi' ibn Abi Al-Huqaiq for mocking Muhammad with his poetry and for helping the troops of the Confederates by providing them with money and supplies.	Abu Rafi assassinated.	Sahih Bukhari 4:52:264, Sahih Bukhari 5:59:370, Sahih Bukhari 5:59:371, Sahih Bukhari 5:59:372 and more Ibn Hisham & Ibn Ishaq, Sirat Rasul Allah Tabari, Volume 7, The foundation of the community
Kill Khalid bin Sufyan, because there were reports he considered an attack on Medina and that he was inciting the people on Nakhla or Uranah to fight Muslims.	Khalid ibn Sufyan assassinated.	Musnad Ahmad 3:496 Sunan Abu Dawud 1244 (Ahmad Hasan Ref) Ibn Hisham, Sirat Rasul Allah Tabari, Volume 9, The last years of the Prophet
Behead Abu 'Azza 'Amr bin 'Abd Allah al-Jumahi because he was a prisoner of War captured during the Invasion of Hamra al-Asad, that Muhammad released once, but he took up arms against him again.	Abu 'Azzah beheaded by Ali	Tabari, Volume 7, The foundation of the community

N O.	Name	Date
9	Muawiyah bin Al Mugheerah	March 625
10	Al-Harith bin Suwayd al-Ansari	March 625

Reason(s) for Ordering or Supporting Killing	Result	Notable Primary Sources
Kill Muawiyah bin Al Mugheerah, because he was accused by Muhammad of being a spy. He went to Uthman (his cousin) for shelter, and Uthman arranged for his return to Mecca, but he stayed too long in Medina. After Muhammad heard he was still in Medina, he ordered his death.	Muawiyah bin Al Mugheerah captured and executed.	Ibn Hisham & Ibn Ishaq, Sirat Rasul Allah
Kill Al-Harith bin Suwayd because according to some Islamic traditions, Allah revealed Quran 3:86-8, which indicated that those who reject Islam after accepting it should be punished. Al-Harith bin Suwayd was a Muslim who fought in the Battle of Uhud and killed some Muslims, he then joined the Quraysh and left Islam. After being threatened with those verses, Al-Harith sent his brother to Muhammad to ask for his forgiveness.	Conflicting Reports 1. Muhammad allowed his return but then decided to kill. Al-Harith was beheaded by Uthman. 2. Allah revealed Quran 3:89 and Al-Harith repented and "became a good Muslim"	Quran 3:86-88 Ibn Hisham & Ibn Ishaq, Sirat Rasul Allah

N O.	Name	Date
11	Abu Sufyan	627
12	Banu Qurayza tribe	February–March 627
13	Abdullah ibn Ubayy	December 627 (during Invasion of Banu Mustaliq)

Reason(s) for Ordering or Supporting Killing	Result	Notable Primary Sources
Amr bin Umayyah al-Damri sent to assassinate Abu Sufyan (Quraysh leader)	3 polytheists killed by Muslims.	Tabari, Volume 7, The foundation of the community
Attack Banu Qurayza because according to Muslim tradition he had been ordered to do so by the angel Gabriel. One of Muhammad's companions decided that "the men should be killed, the property divided, and the women and children taken as captives". Muhammad approved of the ruling, calling it similar to God's judgment, after which all male members of the tribe who had reached puberty were beheaded.	Muslims: 2 killed Non-Muslims: 1. 600-900 beheaded (Tabari, Ibn Hisham) 2. All Males and 1 woman beheaded (Hadith)	Quran 33:26, Quran 33:09 & 33:10 Sunan Abu Dawud 38:4390 Sahih Bukhari 4:52:68, Sahih Bukhari 4:57:66 and more Tabari, Volume 8, Victory of Islam
Kill Abdullah ibn Ubayy, to whom verse 63:8 refers, and who was accused by Muhammad of slandering his family by spreading false rumors about Aisha (his wife). His son offered to behead him	Muhammad calls off assassination and says to Umar "if I had had him (Abdullah bin Ubai) killed, a large number of dignitaries would have furiously hastened to fight for him" Later he reveals a Quran verse forbidding Muslims from attending the funeral of disbelievers and "hypocrites"	Quran 63:7-8 Sahih Bukhari 6:60:424 Sahih Bukhari 5:59:462 Ibn Hisham, Sirat Rasul Allah

NO.	Name	Date
14	Al-Yusayr ibn Rizam	February 628
15	Eight men from 'Ukil	February 628
16	Rifa'ah bin Qays	629

Reason(s) for Ordering or Supporting Killing	Result	Notable Primary Sources
Kill Al-Yusayr ibn Rizam because Muhammad heard that his group was preparing to attack him.	30 killed by Muslims.	Tirmidhi no. 3923 Ibn Hisham & Ibn Ishaq, Sirat Rasul Allah
Kill 8 men who came to him and converted to Islam, but then apostatized, killed one Muslim and drove off with Muhammad's camels.	Muslims: 1 killed Non-Muslims: 8 tortured to death	Quran 5:33-39 Sahih Bukhari 1:4:234, Sahih Bukhari 5:59:505, Sahih Bukhari 7:71:623 and more
To kill Rifa'ah bin Qays, because Muhammad heard they were allegedly enticing the people of Qais to fight him.	1 beheaded, 4 women captured by Muslims.	Ibn Hisham & Ibn Ishaq, Sirat Rasul Allah Tabari, Volume 8, History of Islam

N O.	Name	Date
17	Abdullah bin Khatal	During/after Conquest of Mecca (Jan 630)
18	Fartana	During/after Conquest of Mecca (Jan 630)

Reason(s) for Ordering or Supporting Killing	Result	Notable Primary Sources
Kill Abdullah bin Khatal for killing a slave and fleeing, as well and for reciting poems insulting Muhammad.	2 Muslims execute him, after finding him hiding under the curtains of the Kaaba.	Sahih Bukhari 5:59:582, Sahih Bukhari 3:29:72 Ibn Hisham & Ibn Ishaq, Sirat Rasul Allah Ibn Sa'd, Kitab al-tabaqat al-kabir, Volume 2
Kill Fartana (a slave girl of Abdullah ibn Khatal), because she used to sing satirical songs about Muhammad.	Fartana is killed.	Sunan Abu Dawud 14:2677 Sunan Abu Dawud 14:2678 Sunan an-Nasa'i 5:37:4072 Ibn Hisham & Ibn Ishaq, Sirat Rasul Allah Ibn Sa'd, Kitab al-tabaqat al-kabir, Volume 2 Al-Waqidi, Kitab al-Maghazi

N O.	Name	Date
19	**Quraybah**	During/after Conquest of Mecca (Jan 630)
20	Huwayrith ibn Nafidh	During/after Conquest of Mecca (Jan 630)

Reason(s) for Ordering or Supporting Killing	Result	Notable Primary Sources
Kill Qutaybah (a slave girl of Abdullah ibn Khatal), because she used to sing satirical songs about Muhammad.	Quraybah converts to Islam and is pardoned.	Sunan Abu Dawud 14:2677 Sunan Abu Dawud 14:2678 Sunan an-Nasa'i 5:37:4072 Ibn Hisham & Ibn Ishaq, Sirat Rasul Allah Ibn Sa'd, Kitab al-tabaqat al-kabir, Volume 2 Al-Waqidi, Kitab al-Maghazi
When Muhammad's daughters were fleeing Medina, he stabbed their camels, causing injuries. He was a poet who "disgraced and abused" Islam.	Huwayrith ibn Nafidh killed by Ali.	Ibn Hisham & Ibn Ishaq, Sirat Rasul Allah

NO.	Name	Date
21	Miqyas ibn Subabah	During/after Conquest of Mecca (Jan 630)
22	**Sara**	During/after Conquest of Mecca (Jan 630)
23	Harith ibn Hisham	During/after Conquest of Mecca (Jan 630)
24	Zubayr ibn Abi Umayyah	During/after Conquest of Mecca (Jan 630)

Reason(s) for Ordering or Supporting Killing	Result	Notable Primary Sources
Migyas killed a Muslim who accidentally killed his brother, and escaped to Mecca and became an apostate by embracing polytheism	Migyas Killed	Ibn Hisham & Ibn Ishaq, Sirat Rasul Allah
Ibn Ishaq says Muhammad ordered Sara be killed because she "had insulted him in Mecca"	Conflicting Reports: 1. Ibn Ishaq reports that she embraced Islam but was killed later, during the time of Umar Tabari reports she was killed	Ibn Hisahm & Ibn Ishaq, Sirat Rasul Allah Tabari, Volume 8, History of Islam.
Kill Harith Ibn Hisham, reason unknown, though he was among those who fought against the Muslims in the battle of Uhud.	According to Ibn Sa'd, Zubayr ibn Abi Umayyah and Harith ibn Hisham both sought refuge in a Muslim relative's house, the relative pleaded with Muhammad for mercy, so he pardoned them on the condition they embrace Islam.	Ibn Hisham & Ibn Ishaq, Sirat Rasul Allah Ibn Sa'd, Kitab al-tabaqat al-kabir, Volume 2
Kill Zubayr ibn Abi Umayyah, reason unknown	See Above Results	Ibn Hisham & Ibn Ishaq, Sirat Rasul Allah

N0.	Name	Date
25	**al-Aswad al-Ansi**	During/after Conquest of Mecca (Jan 630)
26	Ikrimah ibn Abu Jahl	During/after Conquest of Mecca (Jan 630)
27	During/after Conquest of Mecca (Jan 630)	Kill Wahshi ibn Harb, for killing Muhammad's uncle during the Battle of Uhud

Reason(s) for Ordering or Supporting Killing	Result	Notable Primary Sources
Muhammad sent a messenger to Yemen instructing that al-Aswad al-Ansi (not to be confused with Habbar al-Aswad) should be killed because he was a "false prophet" and a "liar". Al-Baladhuri reports that al-Aswad was a false prophet and refused Muhammad's invitation to accept Islam	Tabari reports that al-Aswad al-Ansi was killed the day before Muhammad's own death after he sent a messenger to persuade the local al-Abna' people to kill him Al Baladhuri adds further detail that Muhammad chose this plan because the al-Abna' already had grievance against al-Aswad	Sahih Bukhari 5:59:662, Sahih Bukhari 4:56:817 Tabari, Volume 9, The last years of the Prophet
Kill Ikrimah Ibn Abu Jahl, because he was hostile to Muhammad like his father Abu Jahl	Conflicting Reports: 1. Ibn Ishaq says, his wife "became a Muslim and asked for immunity for him and the apostle gave it. 2. Tabari says he was "eliminated"	Ibn Hisham & Ibn Ishaq, Sirat Rasul Allah Tabari, Volume 8, History of Islam
Wahshi Ibn Harb pardoned by Muhammad after he asks for forgiveness and offers to convert to Islam	Ibn Sa'd, Kitab al-tabaqat al-kabir, Volume 2	

N O.	Name	Date
28	Ka'b ibn **Zuhayr ibn Abi Sulama**	After Conquest of Mecca (Jan 630)
29	**Al-Harith bin al-Talatil**	During/after Conquest of Mecca (Jan 630)
30	**Abdullah ibn Ziba'ra**	During/after Conquest of Mecca (Jan 630)

Reason(s) for Ordering or Supporting Killing	Result	Notable Primary Sources
Assassinate ka'b ibn Zuhayr ibn Abi Sulama for writing satirical poems about Muhammad. One of his poems recorded by Ibn Ishaq includes the line, "I was told that the Messenger of Allah threatened me (with death), but with the Messenger of Allah I have hope of finding pardon"	Ibn Ishaq wrote that when one of the Ansar asked permission to behead Ka'b, "The Apostle told him to let him alone because he had come repentant breaking from his past", so he was pardoned.	Ibn Hisham & Ibn Ishaq, Sirat Rasul Allah
For mocking Muhammad through poetry	Al-Harith bin al-Talatil is killed by Ali	Ibn Kathir's Sira al-Nabawiyya
Kill Abdullah Ibn Ziba'ra, for writing insulting poems about Muhammad	Ibn Hisham reports that Abdullah ibn Ziba'ra repented and converted to Islam, so Muhammad pardoned him and that he had fled because "the apostle had killed some of the men in Mecca who had satirized and insulted him"	Al-Waqidi's Kitab al-Maghazi Ibn Sa'd, Kitab al-tabaqat al-kabir Ibn Hisham & Ibn Ishaq, Sirat Rasul Allah

N O.	Name	Date
31	**Hurayrah**	During/after Conquest of Mecca (Jan 630)
32	Hind bint Utbah	During/after Conquest of Mecca (Jan 630)
33	Amr ibn Jihash (convert to Islam)	During the Invasion of Banu Nadir (Aug 625)

Reason(s) for Ordering or Supporting Killing	Result	Notable Primary Sources
Kill Hurayrah (cousin of al Zubara), for mocking Muhammad through poetry.	Tabari Volume 39 states, Hubayrah "ran away when Mecca was conquered, and died in Najran as an infidel". Ibn Ishaq reports that he fled because "the apostle had killed some of the men in Mecca who had satirized and insulted him".	Tabari, Volume 39, Biographies of the Prophet's companions and their successors Al-Waqidi's Kitab al-Maghazi Ibn Hisham & Ibn Ishaq, Sirat Rasul Allah
Kill Hind bint Utbah (wife of Abu Sufyan) for cutting out the heart of Muhammad's uncle Hamza after he died, during the Battle of Uhud	Tabari said, Hind "swore allegiance and became a Muslim.", she was pardoned by Muhammad.	Sunan Abu Dawud 33:4153 Tabari, Volume 8, History of Islam
According to Ibn Kathir and Ibn Ishaq, Muhammad said to Yamin bin Umayr, about Amr ibn Jahsh "Have you seen the way your cousin has treated me and what he proposed to do?" Muhammad accused him of trying to assassinate him.	Amr ibn Jihash is assassinated after a Muslim offers a reward for his killing.	Ibn Hisham & Ibn Ishaq, Sirat Rasul Allah

N O.	Name	Date
34	**King or Prince of Dumatul Jandal**	October 630
35	Umaiya bin Khalaf Abi Safwan	Unknown
36	**Blind man's wife/concubine**	Unknown

Reason(s) for Ordering or Supporting Killing	Result	Notable Primary Sources
Attack the chief of Duma for Jizyah and booty.	1 killed, 2 taken captive. The Chief of Duma was released unharmed.	Sunan Abu Dawud 19:3031 Ibn Sa'd, Kitab al-tabaqat al-kabir, Volume 2 Tabari, Volume 9, The last years of the Prophet
Kill Umaiya bin Khalaf, Muhammad's reason is unknown. But Bilal wanted to kill him for torturing him	Umaiya bin Khalaf killed by Bilal.	Sahih Bukhari 4:56:826
Killed by a Muslim on his own initiative because the woman insulted Muhammad. When Muhammad learned what had happened, he said no retaliation is payable for her blood.	Blind Muslim kills his wife/concubine.	Sunan Abu Dawud 38:4348 Sunan an-Nasa'i 5:37:4075

N0.	Name	Date
37	Ibn Sunayna	Unknown
38	**Abdallah ibn Sa'd ibn Abi Sarh**	During/after Conquest of Mecca (Jan 630)

Reason(s) for Ordering or Supporting Killing	Result	Notable Primary Sources
Muhammad reportedly ordered his followers to "kill any Jew that falls into your power", Muhayissa heard this and went out to kill Ibn Sunayna (a Jew)	Ibn Sunayna killed by Muhayissa	Sunan Abu Dawud 19:2996 Ibn Hisham & Ibn Ishaq, Sirat Rasul Allah
Kill Abdallah ibn Sa'ad, because he became an apostate (left Islam) and fled to Mecca. He also claimed that he was the one who wrote certain verses of the Quran and started to mock Muhammad, which made him angry.	On the day of the Conquest of Mecca, Abdallah ibn Sa'd ibn Abi Sarh accepted Islam again. Misunderstanding leads to his pardoning. He was brought in front of Muhammad and offered his loyalty, Muhammad upheld his hand to indicate that his followers should kill him, but the Muslims thought he pardoned him. He said, "Was not there a wise man among you who would stand up to him when he saw that I had withheld my hand from accepting his allegiance, and killed him?"	Sunan Abu Dawud 38:4346, Sunan Abu Dawud 14:2677 Ibn Hisham & Ibn Ishaq, Sirat Rasul Allah Al-Tabari, History Vol.9

N 0.	Name	Date
39	**Ibn al-Nawwahah**	Unknown
40	Nameless spy	Unknown
41	Man from Aslam tribe	Unknown
42	**Kinana ibn al-Rabi ibn Abu al-Huqayq**	July 628

Reason(s) for Ordering or Supporting Killing	Result	Notable Primary Sources
Ibn Kathir and Sunan Abu Dawud record that Muhammad once said about Ibn an-Nawwahah "I would have cut off your head, if it was not that emissaries are not killed" because he claimed Musaylimah was a Prophet, so Abdullah ibn Masud killed Ibn an-Nawwahah when he was no longer an emissary.	Abdullah ibn Masud beheads Ibn an-Nawwahah	Sunan Abu Dawud 14:2756 Tabari, Volume 10, Conquest of Arabia
Kill a man Muhammad suspected of being a spy.	Salama bin Al-Akwa chases and kills the suspected spy.	Sahih Bukhari 4:52:286
Kill a man from the Aslam tribe for Adultery.	Man from Aslam tribe stoned to death.	Sunan Abu Dawud 38:4414
Torture Kinana ibn al-Rabi to find location of allegedly hidden treasure of Banu Nadir	Kinana ibn al-Rabi ibn Abu al-Huqayq beheaded after being tortured with fire	Sunan Abu Dawud 19:3000 Ibn Hisham & Ibn Ishaq, Sirat Rasul Allah

No.	Name	Date
43	Bahilah and Banu Khath'am tribes	632

Reason(s) for Ordering or Supporting Killing	Result	Notable Primary Sources
Muhammad sends Jarir ibn-'Abdullah to destroy the Kaaba of Yemen, Dhu-l-Khalasah, which was the subject of idolatry. Jarir reports back to Muhammad of the destruction and killings, which Muhammad approves.	100 men of the Bahilah, and 200 of banu-Khath'am were killed in order to destroy the idol of Dhul-Khalasa	Sahih Bukhari 5:59:641, Sahih Bukhari 4:52:262, Sahih Bukhari 4:52:310 Hisham ibn al Kalbi, The Book of Idols

CHAPTER 8
The Quran

All monotheistic religions such as Zoroastrianism, Judaism and Christianity, boast of a holy book of Divine commandments and directions from the 'One & Only' God of monotheists, who they believed, created the Universe, and governs it. The holy scripture of Judaism was the Old Testament (canonized text of TORAH comprising 5 books), Talmud and a few other books. Zoroastrians' scripture is called 'Avesta'. Christians' sacred scripture is the Bible (Canonized New Testament).

Muhammad being totally illiterate, could not read or write. The local lingo at that time was a collection of nearly two dozen dialects, together as a group of dialects called Arabic. Arabic was not a proper language with a literary corpus. It was an oral lingo still evolving as a dialect-continuum comprising almost two dozen different dialects. Some of those dialects were mutually unintelligible. Muhammad claimed that the Deen preached by him was the latest and final Deen of Allah; that all religions sent before by Allah, had lost their validity with the arrival of the new set of 'Divine' commandments comprising the Holy and oral Scripture of Muhammad's Deen in the old fashioned tradition of an ode. Muhammad being illiterate, could not communicate with people in any language except in the native dialect of his tribe al-Quresh. Likewise, he announced the 'divine' revelations verbatim, word by word, in the same oral-dialectal lingo. The passages of revelations were announced by Muhammad piecemeal over 22 years. The ups and downs of Muhammad's secret mission prompted Muhammad to compose the context of revelations. He composed revelations to keep solving the problems that hindered the daily progress of his Deen. The process of learning more and more about the contents of older monotheist religions and using that info to outperform those in his revelations was a continuous process. Put together, Muhammad's revelations were meant to be a long oral ode, in the traditional Arab tribal fashion, as the divine scripture of his Deen.

The idea of an oral ode was not novel to Muhammad, or to people of the Arabian Peninsula. Being a pre-literate oral society, they prided on having some remarkable odes, composed by famous Arab poets; odes being the only means of preserving past events, which could be recounted occasionally in a sing-song manner, for staying aware of their past.

According to the rules of linguistic parsing, the word in the pre-literate era for 'reciting an ode' was 'Quran'. Muhammad's holy scripture, because of his linguistic limitation, had to be an ode. That collection, a few decades after Muhammad's death, was converted into a written text in the nascent script of Arabic, which was still evolving. The script for writing in Arabic language at that time, was a work in progress. It kept evolving for two more centuries, beyond Muhammad's death. The revelations converted to written text had to be brought up to date by paraphrasing and rephrasing many times to convert dialectal version to literary version, time and time again, to keep up with evolutionary changes occurring in the script, for standardization, during those two centuries after Muhammad passed away.

Even though the word 'Quran' meant the act of reciting the ode, followers of Muhammad named the book as 'Quran'.

In the Quran there are 114 surahs, each divided into ayahs (verses). ... The chapters are arranged roughly in **order** of descending size; therefore, the arrangement of the **Quran** is not **chronological**, also not **thematic**. The *haphazard compilation occurred as no record had been maintained for chronological sequence of the revelations*. Surahs (chapters) are recited during the standing portions (Qiyam) of Muslim prayers.

Here is the disclosure of facts about the Quran. ***The Quran was composed by Muhammad, using ALLAH as his pen name***. The purpose of the Quran is to make its believers serve Muhammad's intent and purpose to achieve his goals. Denying this assessment would amount to insulting human intelligence.

Quran's contents were impacted by the ongoing evolution in the script of Arabic language, till it became a completely developed literary language. The whole process of evolution spanned four centuries: two centuries before revelation of the ode, and two more centuries, following the completion of Muhammad's ode. None of the complete copies of hand-written Quran, from the time of 4th Rashidun Caliph Ali ibne Abi Taleb, or the the third Caliph Uthman bin Affan are available now. Most surviving leaves represent a Quran that is preserved in various fragments, the largest part of which are kept in the Bibliothèque nationale de **France**, as BNF Arabe 328(ab). 46 leaves are held at the **National Library of Russia** and one each in the **Vatican Library** and in the Khalili Collections.

Before excavating the facts about the Quran that we see today, let's go over what Muslim scholars have been claiming to be the history of the Quran.

Quote

Orthodox Muslims believe that this medieval Islamic text is the unchanging Word of God. One scholar is daring to question it.

A German academic *Abul Taher* fears a violent backlash from orthodox Muslims because of his "blasphemous" theory that the Koran has been changed and revised. Such a backlash is not to be taken lightly; the Salman Rushdie affair is a solemn reminder of the power of an angry Muslim community. After the author wrote his novel Satanic Verses, which was considered by Muslims to be blasphemous, a fatwa, or religious decree, was pronounced against him in 1989 that left him fearing for his life. Rushdie has only recently reappeared in public after nearly 10 years in hiding. After another attempt recently on his life in Buffalo NY, in which he lost one eye and suffered multiple injuries, he went back into hiding.

According to the Muslim belief, the Koran is the eternal, unaltered Word of God, which has remained the same for 14 centuries.

But Dr Gerd R Puin, a renowned Islamicist at Saarland University, Germany, says it is not one single work that has survived unchanged through the centuries. It may include stories that were written before the prophet Mohammed began his ministry and which have subsequently been rewritten.

Puin's conclusions have sparked angry reactions from orthodox Muslims. "They've said I'm not really the scholar to make any remarks on these manuscripts," he said.

The semitic philologist, who specializes in Arabic calligraphy and Koranic palaeography, has been studying Sa'na manuscripts, ancient versions of the Koran discovered in Sa'na, the capital of Yemen.

So controversial are his findings that the Yemeni authorities have denied him further access to the manuscripts.

He says they shed new light on the early development of the Koran as a book with a "textual history", which contradicts the fundamental Muslim belief that it is the unchanging Word of God.

Any questioning of the authenticity of the Quranic text as the Word of God can expect a hostile reaction. The fatwa, or death sentence, was issued against Rushdie for hinting in Satanic Verses that the Koran may include verses from other sources - chiefly Satan.

Academics offering radical interpretations of the Koran put their lives at risk. In 1990, Dr Nasr Abu Zaid, formerly a lecturer in

Koranic Studies at Cairo University, provoked a national outcry in Egypt over his book The Concept of the Text. There were death threats from Muslim extremists, general public harassment, and in 1995 he was branded an apostate by Egypt's highest court. The court forced him to divorce his wife because under Islamic law, marriage between an apostate and a Muslim is forbidden.

Zaid's proposal was arguably less radical than Puin's. Zaid's book argued that "the Koran is a literary text, and the only way to understand, explain, and analyze it is through a literary approach". A Muslim, Zaid remained in Egypt for a time to refute the apostasy charges but fled with his wife to Holland in the face of increasing death threats.

Puin believes that he will not receive the same reaction, because unlike Zaid or Rushdie he does not have a Muslim name.

His claim that the Koran has changed since its supposed transformation into literary Al-Fus'ha version, and some pre-Islamic texts have crept in, would nonetheless be regarded as highly blasphemous by Muslims. He has not yet written a book on his radical findings, but says it is "a goal to achieve" in the near future.

Dr Tarif Khalidi, lecturer in Islamic Studies at Cambridge University, warns that the book may generate a controversy similar to Satanic Verses. "If Dr Puin's views are taken up and trumpeted in the media, and if you don't have many Muslims being rational about it, then all hell may break loose."

Khalidi fears Muslims will not accept Puin's work on the Sa'na manuscripts as having been done with academic objectivity but see it as a deliberate "attack on the integrity of the Quranic text".

The manuscripts, thought to be the oldest surviving copies of the Koran, were discovered in the ancient Great Mosque of Sa'na in 1972, when the building was being restored after heavy rainfall, hidden in the loft, in a bundle of old parchment and paper documents. They were nearly thrown away by the builders, but were spotted by Qadhi Isma'il al-Akwa, then president of the Yemeni Antiquities Authority, who saw their importance and sought international assistance to preserve and examine them.

Al-Akwa managed to interest Puin, who was visiting Yemen for research purposes in 1979. Puin in turn persuaded the German government to organize and fund a restoration project. The restoration revealed that some of the parchment pages dated from the seventh and eighth centuries, the crucial first two centuries of Islam, from which very few manuscripts have survived.

Until now, there were three ancient copies of the Quran. One copy in the Library of Tashkent in Uzbekistan, and another in the Topkapi Museum in Istanbul, Turkey, date from the eighth century. A copy preserved in the British Library in London, known as the Ma'il manuscript, dates from the late seventh century. But the Sa'na manuscripts are even older. Moreover, the Sa'na manuscripts are written in a script that originates from the Hijaz - the region of Arabia where the prophet Mohammed lived, which makes them not only the oldest to have survived, but one of the earliest copies of the Koran ever.

Puin noticed minor textual variations, unconventional ordering of the chapters (surahs), as well as rare styles of orthography. Then he noticed that the sheets were palimpsests - manuscripts with versions written even earlier that had been washed off or erased.

These findings led Dr Puin to assert that the Quran had undergone a textual evolution. In other words, the copy of the Quran that we have is not the one believed to have been revealed to the prophet.

This is something that Muslims would find offensive. The idea that the Quran is the literal Word of God, unchanging and permanent, is crucial to Islam. The traditional Muslim view holds that the Quran was revealed to Mohammed by God in fragments between 610 and 632 AD. The revealed verses were "recorded on palm leaves and flat stones and in the hearts of men [meaning memorized]," and remained in this state during the prophet's lifetime.

About 29 years after Mohammed's death during the rule of the third Muslim caliph, Uthman, a standard copy of the Quran in a book form, was made, because already divergent readings and copies were circulating in the growing Islamic empire. This Uthmanic recension, according to the Muslim view, was produced with meticulous care, based on earlier copies of the Koran made according to the instructions of the prophet.

Orthodox Muslims insist that no changes have occurred to the Quran since the Uthmanic recension. But this view is challenged by the Sa'na manuscripts, which date from shortly after the Uthmanic recension.

"There are dialectal and phonetic variations that don't make any sense in the text", says Puin. "The Arabic script is very defective - even more so in the early stages of its literature."

Like other early Arabic literature, the Sa'na Quran was written without any diacritical marks, vowel symbols or any guidance on how it should be read, says Puin. "The text was written so defectively that it can be read in a perfect way only if you have a strong oral tradition." The Sa'na text, just like other early Korans, was a guide to those who knew it already by memory, he says. Those that were unfamiliar with the Quran would read it differently because there were no diacritical and vowel symbols.

As years went by, the correct reading of the Quran became less clear, he says. People made changes to make sense of the text. Puin gives as example Hajjaj bin Yusuf, governor of Iraq from 694-714 AD, who "was proud of inserting more than 1,000 alifs [first letter of the Arabic alphabet] in the Quranic text".

Professor Allen Jones, lecturer in Quranic Studies at Oxford University, agrees.

"Hajjaj is also responsible for putting the diacritical marks in the Quran. His changes are a defining moment in the history of the Koran".

After Hajjaj's changes in around the 700s, "the Quranic text became pretty stable", he says.

Puin accepts this up to a point but says that certain words and pronunciations were standardized in the ninth century. He says the ***Uthmanic text was the skeleton upon which "many layers of interpretation were added" - causing the text to change.***

This is blasphemy, according to orthodox Muslims, and is not entirely accepted by other academics.

Jones admits there have been "trifling" changes made to the Uthmanic recension. Khalidi says the traditional Muslim account of the Quan's development is still more or less true. "I haven't yet seen anything to radically alter my view," he says.

He believes that the Sa'na Quran could just be a bad copy that was being used by people to whom the Uthmanic text had not reached yet. "It's not inconceivable that after the promulgation of the Uthmanic text, it took a long time to filter down."

Puin's other radical theory is that pre-Islamic sources have entered the Quran. He argues that two tribes it mentions, As-Sahab-ar-Rass (Companions of the Well) and the As- Sahab-al-Aiqa (Companions of the Thorny Bushes) are not part of the Arab tradition, and the people of Mohammed's time certainly did not know about them.

"These are very unspecific names, whereas other tribes are specifically mentioned," said Dr Puin.

His researches have shown that the ar-Rass lived in pre-Islamic Lebanon and the al-Aiqa in the Aswan region of Egypt around 150AD, according to the Atlas of Ptolemy. He argues that pre-Islamic sources entered the Quran, presumably when the growing Islamic empire came into contact with those regions and sources.

Khalidi says finding pre-Islamic registers in the Quran does not discredit the Muslim belief in any way, because it does not threaten the integrity of the Quran. "The Quran was revealed at a particular time in the vocabulary of the age", he says.

Puin also questions another sacred belief that Muslims hold about the Quran, that it was written in the purest Arabic. He has found many words of foreign origin in the text, including the word "Quran" itself. Muslim scholars explain the "Quran" to mean recitation, but Puin argues that it is actually derived from an Aramaic word, 'Qariyun', meaning a lectionary of scripture portions appointed to be read at divine service. He says the Quran contains most of the biblical stories but in a shorter form and is "a summary of the Bible to be read in service".

Orthodox Muslims have always held that the Quran is a scripture in its own right, and never a shortened version of the Bible, even if both texts contain the same prophetic tradition.

Khalidi says he is weary of constant attempts by western Islamicists to analyze the Quran in a parallel way to the Bible. Puin, however, sees the need for a "scientific text" of the Quran, and this is what he intends to achieve. He says that Muslims believe that "the Quran has been worked on a thousand years ago" and "is not a topic anymore".

Not all Muslim reaction to him has been hostile. Salim Abdullah, director of the German Islamic Archives, affiliated to the powerful pan-Islamic Muslim World League, has given him a positive response.

"He asked me if I could give him the permission to publish one of my articles on the Sa'na manuscripts", said Puin. Warned of the possible controversy it could raise, he replied: "I am longing for this kind of discussion on this topic."

Unquote.

Many other scholars have done critical analysis of the Quran in the 19th and 20th century after exhaustive research of historical data.

The most serious reservations about traditional accounts of the book's origin come from the question of context --- The Quran includes four overlapping kinds of materials: **Oracular** utterances, specially of judgment, **polemical** passages, **narrative** passages, and **religious** law. But with the possible exception of the first, little fits in the seventh CCE Arabian context. The narrative passages largely draw on the Biblical literature about the stories of Adam, Noah, Moses, Solomon, and Jesus as recognizable variants of the original. A number of narratives in the Quran closely resemble the narratives in the Talmud and Midrashic accounts. The accounts of Jesus appear to have drawn on non-canonical Christian sources.

If we place the Quran in the seventh CCE Arabia, the obvious inference would be that significant Jewish and Christian influences were imported into the Hijaz, for which there is little evidence. It may even be plausible to suggest that Arabia was not the birthplace of the Quran, and Islamic scriptures came from the Near East-Syria and Palestine during the 150 years after the Arab conquest. The Quran polemicized against Christian, Jews and idolaters, who are usually identified as pagan Arabs, but Hawting (1999) contends in a convincing fashion that the polemics meant Jews and Christians. They make sense as far as the Jews are concerned as there were substantial Jewish communities in the peninsula and they had conspired with the Quraysh against Muhammad. It seems that God was highly distressed by the errors of Christians. One of the most quoted suras of the Quran is manifestly anti-Trinitarian: In the name of God…say : "He is God, One God, the Everlasting Refuge, who has not begotten, and has not been begotten and equal to Him is not any one (surah 112).

When mentioning Jesus, the Qur'an keeps on reminding us that he was not the son of God…never claimed to be…Christians blaspheme…saying so. The natural inference would be that the Quran emerged in an environment dominated by Christianity, but there were only few Christians in Mecca and Medina.

Jesus in the Quran: Christology in the Quran is thorough. (Parinder 1976; Robinson 1991). Jesus is the dominant prophetic figure in the Quran. The book narrates his birth from a virgin mother, his miracles as a child and his disciples. The Last Supper is described, and Crucifixion is denied, as his being the Son of God. (Dr. Asarul Islam, a famous Psychiatrist and self-claimed scholar of Quran and Tafseer, claims that crucifixion is not denied in Islam. He has a formidable following in the USA and the Indo-Pak subcontinent). Jesus is only a messenger. His titles-Ruh Allah (the Spirit of Allah), and Kalam Allah (a Word of Allah) are described.

The themes of the Quran are akin to non-orthodox Christianity. Also, Mani had offered the same idea that Jesus was only a prophet and did not die on the cross.

There is a more direct resemblance to a form of Jewish Christianity. All the above indicates that the environment of Manichaeism and Jewish Christianity was very similar to the environment in which the Quran was formed. If so, Christianity must have penetrated the peninsula much more than anyone has found evidence of and Muslims must have covered up the level of penetration. It further supports the concept that the Quran owes its formation not to Arabia, but to the region in the north and the time frame after the conquest.

The above leads to an apparent contradiction, the language of the Quran is archaic and based in an Arab environment, but its theme belongs to the milieu of the Near East. The situation would be unacceptable if we stick to the idea of the formation of the Quran in the five decades of the seventh CCE. But a much longer period of formation would allow the editors (redactors is a better term; they after all do this kind of thing) to preserve the older traditions, many of which they could not understand, in a way that was relevant to their own milieu.

John Wansbrough in his *Quranic Studies* (1977) and *The Sectarian Milieu* (1978) applied the methodology of The Higher Criticism of the Bible to the Quran. He hypothesized that the Quran was standardized 200 hundred years later than what Muslim traditions report, and has not been effectively refuted yet (Wansbrough 1977: 52). But it cannot be firmly proven either, as the critics have promptly pointed out.

The Quran is the Word of God ---- The idea-logos has a long history in Greek philosophy and entered both Jewish and Christian theology. It came to mean for both not just God's communications but a pre-existent emanation from God (Gospel of John 1:1-13).

The idea of a pre-existing book is alluded to in the Quran: "No! I swear by the falling of the stars; that is a mighty oath and you know it, it is surely a noble Quran…none but the purified shall touch…down from the Lord…" Quran 56:78 cf. 85:22). Once Muslims began to think along the lines, they 'inherited' a whole set of theological problems which had been a problem for long for Christians. Was the Quran created or pre-existent, how the one in heaven was related to the copies on the earth and if pre-existent, how was it related to the divine essence?

The problem came to a head during the reign of the Abbasid Caliph Ma'mun in 833 CE. He and his successor Mu'tasim patronized the religious group which sought to enforce as official doctrine that the Qur'an was eternal and uncreated. He was flogged mercilessly and jailed as were like minded scholars in a systematic inquisition called Minha, a rare instance in Islamic history, but would not retract.

The Minha eventually failed, and the next Caliph Mutwakkil had to reverse the policy. The orthodox doctrine resembled the orthodox Christian doctrine. The divine word was uncreated, eternally co-existent with God and sent down to earth in the form of a book. Christians called the Word *incarnate*--- the Word made flesh --- Muslims called it *calibrate* - the Word made Book ((Wolfson 1976: 244-63).

Extreme creeds insist that the Quran is God's uncreated Word in whatever form it is found (Wensink 1932: 127). So, the words of the Quran are a theophany, the closest that a believer can come into direct contact with God. So, the Muslim concern to protect the book from defilement is no more superstitious than the Roman Catholic reverence for the Eucharist. Both are concerned with the earthly manifestation of the *Divine Logos*.

The Quran is uncreated and so is inimitable. The Quran itself makes the assertion: (10:38-40; 17:88). On the one hand, though, it was eternal and perfect, yet it had been revealed piecemeal over 22 years, in a historical context, and collected in a not very perfect manner after the prophet passed on.

How could the Quran have existed from eternity and still reflect the context of the life of the Prophet? The Quran was dictated to the prophet and Muhammad was only the faithful (infallible) transmitter. Muslim scholars insist that the Quran must be interpreted in the light of the events of the prophet's life.

Here are the findings about the 'Revelations' in 'The Naked Truth'.

Whenever Muhammad declared that Arch angel Gabriel had brought him a 'divine revelation,' his companions present around him at that moment, attentively listened to Muhammad when he announced it, and some of them tried to commit that revealed passage to memory. Another method was for some companions to inscribe it in phonetic signs (Phonemes) indicating the dialectal sound produced in voicing the revelation verbatim. The symbols used were phonetic, indicating the sound of the word being converted from 'vocalized' state to 'inscribed' state. However, phonemes had an inherent defect. Different phonemes indicating different sounding words looked very similar in shape. A reader could misread the phoneme representing a particular sound for another similar looking phoneme representing another sound, thus reading it as a different and unintended word. Those phonemes were the early form of ABJAD letters borrowed from Nabateans to provide a common script for the many dialects of spoken Arabic in different parts of the peninsula. Cuneiform was the ancestor of phonemes, also called Kufic by linguists. This led to variance in text depending upon who read the inscription made in phonemes. As evolution of Arabic language and its script proceeded, the 14 phonemes progressed to become 28 proper alphabets with the concept of spelling, stringing different alphabets together to form a written word, over a period of 2 centuries after Muhammad had died.

Phonemes are technically based on principles similar to short-hand signs used in stenography. Those phoneme signs were sketched like artwork by companions of Muhammad, on whatever material was at hand, such as hides, papyrus sheets, wooden planks or engravings on freshly made wet plates of clay dough before they dried.

The complete process of developing the multi-dialectal lingo into one literary language through a common script, from start to finish, went on from the 4th until the beginning of the 9th century A.D.

The project of locating all still **available** inscribed passages, as well as memorized passages was concluded in the 29th year after Muhammad's death. There is no way to confirm that every passage inscribed in Muhammad's lifetime, and every passage memorized by some companion of Muhammad, was located and collected, because a good number of custodians and memorizers of various passages had already died.

Following is a sample of the earliest manuscript of the Quran from the late 7th century.

Birmingham Quran manuscript

This is a close up of part of folio 2 recto of Birmingham Quran manuscript.

BnF Arabe 328(c), formerly bound with BnF Arabe 328(ab), has 16 leaves, with two additional leaves discovered in Birmingham in 2015 (Mingana 1572a, bound with an unrelated Quranic manuscript).

This manuscript may date to the mid-7th century: The parchment of the Birmingham fragment has been carbon-dated to between 568 and 645 with a confidence of 97.2%, indicating the animal from which the parchment was made lived during that time.

BnF Arabe 328(c) was part of the lot of pages from the store of Quranic manuscripts at the mosque of Amr bin al-Aas in Fustat bought by French Orientalist Jean-Louis Asselin de

Cherville (1772–1822) when he served as vice-consul in Cairo during 1806–1816.

The 16 folia in Paris contain the text of chapter 10:35 to 11:95 and of 20:99 to 23:11. The Birmingham folia cover part of the lacuna in the Paris portion, with parts of the text of surahs 18, 19 and 20. The text is laid out in the format that was to become standard for complete Quran texts, with chapter divisions indicated by linear decoration, and verse endings by intertextual clustered dots.

Even after improving the Arabic script as used in 1924 for the very first standardized version of printed Quran, **the Arabic language still remains deficient in certain sound indicators among the alphabets**. The closest script in the same technical style, as Arabic, is the script of Persian, Urdu and Sindhi languages. All three of these languages have the following letters and sounds, which are not found in Arabic script.

پ = pay	ٹ = tay	چ = chay
ڈ = daal	ڑ = rhay	ژ = zhay
گ = gaaf		

The claim that the Arabic language has been created by Allah is a fabrication. Facts also prove that Quran's preservation by Allah as a miracle is also a false claim, because the Quran Muslims read today is not identical to what Muhammad narrated to his companions in the dialect of his own tribe.

Years later, when those passages preserved in phoneme signs or Kufic letters, or committed to memory, had to be retrieved from Prophet's surviving companions who were scattered all over the Islamic dominion, a number of significant problems surfaced in completing the project.

1. Once the compilation of 'searched and found' revelations in one volume was initiated, it took over fifteen years, and got completed 28 years after Muhammad's death, during the reign of third caliph Othman bin Affan. **The retrieved parts of Allah's 'divine' message, however, could not be arranged in chronological order as the dates of revelation of each passage had not been recorded anywhere by anyone, including Muhammad himself.**

2. When the collection was completed, another huge problem came to light. Due to variance in the texts caused by faulty phonemes, a total of forty different versions were presented to the third caliph Uthman. The team of volunteers who acted under the appointed team-leader Zaid bin Thabit, was ordered by Caliph Uthman to examine the 40 versions very minutely and identify one version which seemed very close to accurate, in their collective expert opinion. When the team went back to Caliph after a few days with their selected version, the Caliph called it '*Mashaf-e-Awwal*', and ordered the remaining 39 to be destroyed, to preserve uniformity of divine revelations. However, several copies are reported to have escaped destruction.

3. Since there was no record anywhere of the sequential order of revelations, the collected revelations were arranged, by common consent, in the order of longest passages first, going down to the shortest ones in the end. **This is why contents of Quran appear disjointed, erratic, and devoid of seamless flow in its narrative; in sharp contrast to the orderly narrative of Old and New Testament and Zend Avesta of Zoroastrians, in the Greek, Hebrew, Aramaic and Avestan language (predecessor of primitive Farsee language).**

4. **There was no certainty whether the passages retrieved represented 100 percent of the original whole, or, an unknown number of passages remained untraced, uncollected, and hence lost for good.**

5. Collection of dialectal passages led to another problem i.e., oral messages from Allah, *'revealed'* to Muhammad in Qureshi dialect, had to be converted into **script-worthy** passages which, only then, could be written down in proper literary fashion (Al-fusha form) like the holy scripture of other monotheistic religions i.e., Judaism and Christianity in Aramaic, Hebrew, and Greek scripts.

6. The process of converting the original dialectal contents into proper writing, while the script itself was in the early developmental phase, had its own significant implications and effects. Their mention until now, has been avoided by Muslim scholars like plague. Here are the details of ramifications in converting the oral and dialectal contents into a literary text.

Languages and dialects share similar traits but evolve through different mediums. While both are spoken, language evolves through written/literary form, with each evolving element accurately captured through the alphabet, and accents inherently present within that language. In this way language subscribes to a "what you read is what you get" concept.

Dialects, on the other hand, are rooted in the sound, tone, and pronunciation of the word uttered, but they evolve orally through the spoken word. In the evolution of speech, dialects develop their own unique nuances of decibel variation in voice, pronunciation, and most important, tonality. As a result, often these nuances develop outside of the already prescribed format of letters and accents present in language. Because these nuances have their own non-script character which cannot be completely captured when reducing them to language form, dialect captured in literary form (written language) becomes akin to a transliteration (which is when one language is used as a written form to express something in a foreign tongue). Quran, Muhammad claimed, was received by him in Qureshi dialect, the one and only means of oral communication Muhammad knew, and was accustomed to, since childhood. **The oral passages of 'divine' revelations had to be paraphrased and transliterated, to be converted into written literary Arabic.**

What was lost, in the essence and intent of the message, during the process of converting the non-literary dialectal contents into a completely literary language, by transliterating, paraphrasing, and rephrasing the passages, is not known, and cannot be precisely quantified today.

So much for the claim that the contents of the Quran are protected by Allah against any change, however trivial and insignificant.

One cannot help wondering why Allah, in His infinite wisdom, chose an illiterate person like Muhammed, who only knew one particular tribal dialect, which had to be altered by human effort to make it script worthy in literary Arabic. This casts doubt on the existence of Allah, an Almighty God proffered by Muhammad, for reasons already explained in the relevant section of this book.

The Quran printed today is not in the original oral words of Allah, regardless of whether Muhammad's declaration of receiving it through Arch Angel Gabriel is true or false.

Muhammad's intention for the Quran, himself being illiterate, seemed to leave behind an orally recited epic, in the tradition of other orally recounted great odes of the pre-literate era in Arabia. Other examples for non-Arab readers are the epic of Gilgamesh, Odyssey, Iliad, Mahabharata, or Dante's la Divina Commedia etc.

The word 'Quran' does not mean 'read a script'; it means 'recite orally', which in itself is strongly indicative of Muhammad's intention. Whenever Muhammad said the word 'Quran' he meant recitation of his revelations. During Muhammad's lifetime there was no book form of his revelations anyway. **'Quran' as such, means an oral ode meant to be recited; it is not a name**

supposedly given by Allah or Muhammad for all revelations compiled in a book.

The first complete Quran printed with movable type was produced in Venice in 1537/1538 for the Ottoman market by Paganino Paganini and Alessandro Paganini. Two more editions in Latin translation were published during this time.

Paganino & Alessandro Paganini Issue, the First Printed Edition of the Quran in Arabic, of which one copy survived (August 9, 1537)

However, printing of the Quran during this period met with strong opposition *from Muslim religious scholars*. Printing anything in Arabic was prohibited by the Ottoman Empire between 1483 and 1726. Printing was banned by Islamic authorities because they **believed the Quran would be dishonored by appearing out of a machine**. As a result, Arabs did not acquire printing presses until the 18th century. Similarly, Islamic clerics banned the introduction of printing presses in the Safavid Empire of Iran (ruled from 1501 to 1736) and Moghul Empire of India (early 16th century to middle of 18th century A.D.).

King Fawad of Egypt, in the early 20th century A.D. ordered a team of scholars in Al-Azhar university of Cairo to standardize the Quran and print it for the first time, on paper in book form, on a large scale. That order of King Fawad had full support of his religious advisors.

One of the most famous Hafiz (Memorizer) of the Quran whose recitation style is one of the most popular ones, is known as Aasim ibn Abi al-Najud, a.k.a Hafs, 706 A.D to 796 A.D. in Baghdad. The **edited** texts put in the Quran, recited by Huffaz following Hafs' style, from beginning to end, was adopted by Al-Azhar team as the standard version, and printed on paper in 1924. During the previous thirteen centuries only a number of manuscripts, inscribed in hand, having many variants, were in existence.

The details of Hafs version are as follows:

Total Number of:

Juzz	30
Sajda	14
Manzil	7
Suras	114
Makki	86
Madni	28
Ruku	540
Aya	6,666
Haraf	323,760
Zabar	53,243
Zer	39,582
Pesh	8,804
Mudd	1,771
Shud	1,243
Nukta	105,681

It's an interesting fact that the standardized version of the Quran, now followed by the entire Muslim world, was *first printed on regular paper in 1924, less than a hundred years ago. Prior to 1924, for more than thirteen centuries, there were very few copies of the Quran printed on paper – a bigger number of hand-written manuscripts commonly existed, which had numerous differences in their texts.*

Prior to 1924 A.D. many different versions of the Quran existed. The manuscripts in the Topkapi Museum of Turkey, the famous Sana'a manuscript, and manuscripts in Baghdad, Cairo and Greek museums all have differences in texts.

One well known reason for variance in text is the inherent problems of Phoneme described earlier. The total number of variants exceeded two thousand. Some manuscripts had 116 chapters, others 110 and most had 114 chapters. Following video lecture throws interesting light on the story and controversy of how *divine revelations existed in more than 100 versions* according to the famous *'Huffaz'* (Memorizer- cum-reciters of Quran). What is now shown to Muslims in the shape of the standardized Quran appeared only in 1924.

(Ref.: https://www.youtube.com/watch?v=rMo21KF69KY)

However, scholars of Sunni and Shia Sect agree that there has not been a slightest difference in the contents of standardized and printed Quran **since 1924.**

The *Quran that Muslims recite today managed to reach this form, after removing differences arising from misleading phonemes, through common consensus, and many episodes of editing and updating to keep up with the ongoing evolution in the script, in the late 7th, 8th, early 9th century A.D., which was more than two centuries after the death of Muhammad.*

Muhammad's 'divine' revelations make complete sense when viewed in the light of its context. However, Muslim scholars choose to quote verses of the Quran on any occasion regardless, even when the original context of the quoted text was entirely different and was concerned with completely different issues.

Muslims pick the verses of the Quran they find most attractive, and they use these verses to sanitize the rest of the Quran. But is this the correct way to interpret the Quran? Unfortunately, the answer is no. The Quran presents its own method of interpretation—the **Doctrine of Abrogation.**

Quran 2:106—Whatever verse we shall abrogate, or cause [thee] to forget, we will bring a better than it, or one like unto it. Dost thou not know that God is almighty.

Quran 16:101—When We substitute one revelation for another—and God knows best what He reveals (in stages)—they say, "Thou art but a forger": but most of them understand not.

According to the Quran, when Muslims are faced with conflicting commands, they aren't supposed to pick the one they like best. Rather, they are to go to history and see which verse was revealed last. Whichever verse came last is said to abrogate (or cancel) earlier revelations.

What happens when we apply this methodology to Quranic verses on peace and violence? Let's explore!

THE CALL TO JIHAD: THREE STAGES (Commentary on KITAB [Quran] continues....)

When we turn to Islam's theological sources and historical writings (Quran, Hadith, Sira, and Tafsir), we find that there are three stages in the call to Jihad, depending on the status of Muslims in a society.

STAGE ONE—When Muslims are completely outnumbered and can't possibly win a physical confrontation with unbelievers, they are to live in peace with non-Muslims and preach a message of tolerance. We see an example of this stage when Muhammad and his followers were a persecuted minority in Mecca. Since the Muslims were entirely outnumbered, the revelations Muhammad received during this stage (e.g., "You shall have your religion and I shall have my religion") called for religious tolerance and proclaimed a future punishment (rather than a worldly punishment) for unbelievers.

STAGE TWO—When there are enough Muslims and resources to defend the Islamic community, Muslims are called to engage in defensive Jihad. Thus, when Muhammad had formed alliances with various groups outside Mecca and the Muslim community had become large enough to begin fighting, Muhammad received Quran 22:39-40:

Permission (to fight) is given to those upon whom war is made because they are oppressed, and most surely Allah is well able to assist them; Those who have been expelled from their homes without a just cause except that they say: our Lord is Allah.

Although Muslims in the West often pretend that Islam only allows defensive fighting, later revelations show otherwise.

STAGE THREE—When Muslims establish a majority and achieve political power in an area, they are commanded to engage in offensive Jihad. Hence, once Mecca and Arabia were under Muhammad's control, he received the call to fight all unbelievers. In Surah 9:29, we read: *"Fight those who believe not in Allah nor the Last Day, nor hold that forbidden which hath been forbidden by Allah and His Messenger, nor acknowledge the Religion of Truth, from among the People of the Book, until they pay the Jizya with willing submission, and feel themselves subdued".*

Notice that this verse doesn't order Muslims to fight oppressors, but to fight those who don't believe in 'total submission' (including the "People of the Book"—Jews and Christians).

Not surprisingly, we find similar commands in Muhammad's Deen's most trusted collections of Ahadith (traditions containing Muhammad's teachings).

Sahih al-Bukhari 6924—Muhammad said: "I have been ordered to fight the people till they say: La ilaha illallah (none has the right to be worshiped but Allah), and whoever said La ilaha illahllah, Allah will save his property and his life from me."

Sahih Muslim 30—Muhammad said: "I have been commanded to fight against people so long as they do not declare that there is no god but Allah."

Here again, the criterion for fighting people is that the people believe something other than Islam. It's clear, then, that when Muslims rose to power, peaceful verses of the Quran were abrogated by verses commanding Muslims to fight people based on their beliefs. Islam's greatest scholars acknowledge this. For instance, Ibn Kathir (Islam's greatest commentator on the Quran) sums up Stage Three as follows: "Therefore all people of the world should be called to Islam. If any of them refuses to do so, or refuses to pay the Jizya, they should be fought till they are killed."

STAGE FOUR—Abrogation also accounts for shifting attitudes regarding Jews and Christians in the Quran. While Muslims are to be friendly to Jews and Christians when the former are outnumbered, the Islamic position changes when Muslims reach Stage Three, at which point Christians and Jews are to recognize their inferior status and pay the Jizya (a payment made to Muslims in exchange for not being killed by them).

Here are some verses of Quran:

"Against them make ready your strength to the utmost of your power, including steeds of war, to strike **terror** into the hearts of the enemies of Allah and your enemies…" (8:60)

"When your Lord was revealed to the angels, 'I am with you; so, confirm the believers. I shall **cast terror** into the hearts of the unbelievers; so, strike the necks, and strike every finger of them!' (Quran 8:12)

"We will cast **terror** into the hearts of those who disbelieve for what they have associated with Allah of which He had not sent down authority. And their refuge will be the Fire, and wretched is the residence of the wrongdoers." (Quran 3:151)

"And **kill them** wherever you find them and drive them out from where they drove you out; persecution is worse than slaughter. But fight them not by the Holy Mosque until they should fight you there; then, if they fight you, **kill them** — such is the recompense of unbelievers, but if they give over, surely Allah is all-forgiving, all-compassionate. Fight them until there is no persecution and the religion is Allah's; then if they give over, there shall be no enmity save for evildoers." (Quran 2:191-193)

"They wish that you should disbelieve as they disbelieve, and then you would be equal; therefore, do not take friends from among them, until they emigrate in the way of Allah; then, if they turn their backs, seize them and **kill them** wherever you find them; do not take for yourselves any one of them as friend or helper." (Quran 4:89)

"This is the recompense of those who fight against Allah and His Messenger and hasten about the earth to do corruption there: **they shall be killed, or crucified, or their hands and feet shall be struck off on opposite sides**; or they shall be exiled from the land. That is a degradation for them in this world; and in the world to come awaits them a mighty chastisement." (Quran 5:33)

"**Fight them**, till there is no persecution, and religion is all for Allah; then if they give over, surely Allah sees the things they do." (Quran 8:39)

"Then, when the sacred months are over, **kill the idolaters** wherever you find them, and take them, and confine them, and lie in wait for them at every place of ambush. But if they repent, and perform the prayer, and pay the alms, then let them go their way; Allah is All-forgiving, All-compassionate." (Quran 9:5)

"**Fight those who believe not in Allah** and the Last Day and do not forbid what Allah and His Messenger have forbidden, and do not practice the religion of truth, even if they are of the People of the Book — until they pay the jizya with willing submission and feel themselves subdued." (Quran 9:29)

Lo! Allah hath bought from the believers their lives and their wealth because the Garden will be theirs: they **shall** fight in the way of Allah **and shall slay and be slain**. It is a promise which is binding on Him in the Torah and the Gospel and the Qur'an. Who fulfills His covenant better than Allah? Rejoice then in your bargain that ye have made, for that is the supreme triumph. (Quran 9:111)

"O believers, **fight the unbelievers** who are near to you; and **let them find in you a harshness**; and know that Allah is with the god-fearing." (Quran 9:123)

"When you meet the unbelievers, **strike off their necks**, then, when you have made wide slaughter among them, tie fast the bonds; then set them free, either by grace or ransom, till the war lays down its loads. So, it shall be and if Allah had willed, He would have avenged Himself upon them; but that He may try some of you by means of others. And those who are slain in the way of Allah, He will not send their works astray." (Quran 47:4)

And a couple of hadiths for good measure. Both of these statements are attributed to Muhammad:

"Fight against those who disbelieve in Allah. Make a holy war… When you meet your enemies who are polytheists, invite them to three courses of action. If they respond to any one of these, you also accept it and withhold yourself from doing them any harm. Invite them to (accept) Islam; if they respond to you, accept it from them and desist from fighting against them…. If they refuse to accept Islam, demand from them the Jizya. If they agree to pay, accept it from them and hold off your hands. If they refuse to pay the tax, seek Allah's help and fight them. (Sahih Muslim 4294)

"The last hour would not come unless the Muslims will fight against the Jews and the Muslims would kill them until the Jews would hide themselves behind a stone or a tree and a stone or a tree would say: Muslim, or the servant of Allah, there is a Jew behind me; come and kill him; but the tree Gharqad would not say, for it is the tree of the Jews." (Sahih Muslim 6985)

Consider some of Muhammad's later teachings about Christians and Jews:

Quran 5:51—O you who believe! do not take the Jews and the Christians for friends; they are friends of each other; and whoever amongst you takes them for a friend, then for sure he is one of them; surely Allah does not guide the unjust people.

Quran 9:30—And the Jews say: Uzair is the son of Allah; and the Christians say: The Messiah is the son of Allah; these are the words of their mouths; they imitate the saying of those who disbelieved before; may Allah destroy them; how they are turned away!

Quran 98:6—Those who reject (Truth), among the People of the Book and among the Polytheists, will be in Hellfire, to dwell therein. They are the worst of creatures.

Sahih Muslim 4366—Muhammad said: "I will expel the Jews and Christians from the Arabian Peninsula and will not leave any but Muslim."

Al-Bukhari, Al-Adab al-Mufrad 1103—Muhammad said: "Do not give the People of the Book the greeting first. Force them to the narrowest part of the road."

Needless to say, these teachings can hardly be considered peaceful or tolerant.

MUSLIMS IN THE WEST

Since Muhammad obviously commanded his followers to fight unbelievers (simply for being unbelievers), why do Muslims in the West deny this? Here we must turn to Surah 3:28, which reads:

"Let not the believers take disbelievers for their friends in preference to believers. Whoso doeth that hath no connection with Allah unless (it be) that ye but guard yourselves against them, taking (as it were) security."

According to this verse (which uses a variation of the word Taqiyya, meaning "concealment"), Muslims are not allowed to be friends with non-Muslims. However, if Muslims feel threatened by a stronger adversary, they are allowed to pretend to be friendly. Ibn Kathir comments: "In this case, such believers are allowed to show friendship outwardly but never inwardly." Abu Darda, one of Muhammad's companions, put it this way: "We smile in the face of some people although our hearts curse them."

Is Islam a religion of peace? No. Islam is a religion that pretends to be peaceful when Muslims are too weak to win a war. Of course, there are many Muslims who aren't violent. Many Muslims in the West love peace and tolerance. But they didn't get these values from Islam. They got them from the West, and now they're reinterpreting Islam based on their Western values. For dedicated Muslims, however, there are only two possible situations to be in: (1) fighting unbelievers, and (2) pretending to be peaceful while preparing to fight unbelievers. Either way, fighting non-Muslims and conquering the world in the name of Allah is always the goal.

It is quite enlightening to learn what non-Muslim scholars and investigators of history pronounce about the Quran and its authenticity, or otherwise, in their books.

In his Islam and the West: A Historical Survey, Philip K. Hitti says: The sources of the Quran are unmistakable: Christian, Jewish, and Arab heathen.

He supports this assertion by pointing out that during the Prophet's time, paintings of Jesus and Mary were on the inner wall of the Kaaba. That the Quranic material is second hand from hearsay is demonstrated by the Quranic statement that Jesus spoke unto mankind in the cradle and fashioned out of clay a living bird. These statements have a parallel in the apocryphal **Gospel of Infancy**. Mary, the mother of Jesus, is confused with Mary, sister of Aaron. Haman, the favorite of Ahasuerus (Esth. 3:2) is mistakenly made minister of the Pharaoh (Sura 40:38). And the Quranic story of the "two-horned" Alexander the Great. (*Sikander Dhul Qarnayn*) ...must have originated in the Romance of Alexander then current among the Syrian Christians.

However, according to Richard Bell: ...in spite of traditions to the effect that the picture of Jesus was found on one of the pillars of Kaaba, there is no good evidence of any seats of Christianity in the Hijaz or in the near neighborhood of Mecca or even of Medina.

Hitti's argument is that although certain Quranic passages bear resemblance to Biblical passages, they do not warrant the conclusion of borrowing or quoting. They may be explained on grounds other than direct dependence. His explanation is that: ...far from being a slavish imitator, Muhammad Islamized, Arabicized and nationalized the material.

On the sources of the Quran, J Christy Wilson writes in Introducing Islam: Scholars hold that a number of [Quranic stories] may be traced to Jewish Talmudic sources and apocryphal gospels rather than to the Old and New Testaments.

Wilson also mentions the apparent confusion over Haman and Mary. Richard Bell argues in his book, The Origin of Islam in its Christian Environment: ...much of the Quran is directly dependent on the Bible, and stories associated with the Bible.

Allegedly, Muhammad's knowledge of the Bible was acquired gradually: The key to a great deal both in the Quran and in the career of Muhammad lies ... just in his gradual acquisition of knowledge of what the Bible contained and what the Jews and

Christians believed ... we shall see him... consciously borrowing - he is quite frank about it.

Quranic references to the People of the Cave, Moses and al-Khidr and 'Alexander the Great' which were never associated with the Bible are associated by Bell as proof that Muhammad(P) was not working on any real knowledge of the Bible itself but, was dependent on third hand oral sources.

Kenneth Cragg says in the Call of The Minaret: The Biblical narratives reproduced in the Quran differ considerably and suggest oral, not direct acquaintance. There is almost a complete absence of what could be claimed as direct quotation from the Bible.

Cragg is convinced that the alleged Quranic misconceptions of the Trinity and Jesus(P) indicate that the range and quality of Muhammad's(P) oral contacts was insufficient to enable him to have a firm grasp of Christianity.

H A R Gibb in Muhammadanism: A Historical Survey, puts forward another possibility concerning the sources of the Quran: In view of the close commercial relation between Mecca and Yemen it would be natural to assume that some religious ideas were carried to Mecca with the caravans of spices and woven stuffs, and there are details of vocabulary in the Quran which give color to this assumption.

Linden P. Harries writes in his book Islam in East Africa: Muhammad himself borrowed from the Bible, and Muslims today consciously or not, borrow much from the Christian ideology even in matters which the Quran does not support.

According to R. A. Nicholson, the Quran can be traced to the Haneefs and Judeo-Christian sources: We hear much of Christian hermits and also a few persons known as Haneefs, who had rejected idolatry for a religion of their own, ascetic and monotheistic; Muhammad appears to have been in touch with some of them before his call... his journey with the trading caravans of Mecca afforded opportunities for conversation with Jews and Christians of which the Quran preserves the result.

But Nicholson could not explain how much a person would learn from occasional chats with these people as well as on his journeys. He went on to say: Muhammad picked up all his knowledge of this kind by hearsay and he makes a brave show with such borrowed trappings- largely consisting of legends from the Haggadah and Apocrypha.

Concerning the Jewish and Christian influence on the Quran, the New Catholic Encyclopedia writes: non-Moslem scholarship has taken a different view of the matter. It has nearly always held that the major influences on Mohammed must have been principally, but not exclusively, Jewish and Christian, and that those influences were colored by Mohammed's own character and made over to conform to aspects and needs of the pre-Islamic Arabian mind.

It goes on to say: Very probably Muhammad had improvised translations.